PUBLICATIONS OF THE COMMITTEE ON
TAXATION, RESOURCES AND ECONOMIC DEVELOPMENT

6

Proceedings of a Symposium Sponsored by the
Committee on Taxation, Resources and
Economic Development (TRED)
At the University of Wisconsin—Madison, 1971

Other TRED Publications

GOVERNMENT SPENDING & LAND VALUES

Public Money & Private Gain

Edited by

C. LOWELL HARRISS

*Published for the Committee on
Taxation, Resources and
Economic Development by*
THE UNIVERSITY OF WISCONSIN PRESS

Published 1973
THE UNIVERSITY OF WISCONSIN PRESS
Box 1379, Madison, Wisconsin 53701

The University of Wisconsin Press, Ltd.
70 Great Russell Street, London

Printed in the United States of America

For LC CIP information see the colophon

ISBN 0-299-06320-8

CONTRIBUTORS

WILLIAM D. ANDERSON
General Attorney, Natural Resource Economics Division, United States Department of Agriculture

ROBERT U. AYRES
Vice President, International Research and Technology Corporation

ROY W. BAHL
Professor of Economics, Syracuse University

ROY A. BALLINGER
Agricultural Economist, United States Department of Agriculture

ARTHUR P. BECKER
Professor of Economics, University of Wisconsin—Milwaukee

ROBERT F. BOXLEY
Agricultural Economist, Natural Resource Economics Division, United States Department of Agriculture

STEPHEN P. COELEN
Graduate Student in Economics, Syracuse University

ROBERT E. COUGHLIN
Vice President, Regional Science Research Institute

DARWIN W. DAICOFF
Professor of Economics, University of Kansas

THOMAS R. HAMMER
Research Associate, Regional Science Research Institute

JERRY J. JASINOWSKI
Research Economist, The Joint Economic Committee

RICHARD F. MUTH
Professor of Economics, Stanford University

RAYMOND L. RICHMAN
  Professor of Economics, Graduate School of Public and International
  Affairs, University of Pittsburgh

HENRY B. SCHECHTER
  Senior Specialist in Housing, The Library of Congress

MARTIN O. STERN
  Senior Staff Member, International Research and Technology Corporation

JEREMY J. WARFORD
  Economist, International Bank for Reconstruction and Development

CONTENTS

C. Lowell Harriss

___

INTRODUCTION

Government spending rises from year to year—at rates higher than the growth of population, plus full allowance for inflation. Not only money amounts but also types of undertakings multiply. And all of us know from experience that taxes go up.

Scores of new federal undertakings appear almost every year. Some are major. Most, individually, may not seem "large." Nevertheless, the cumulative effects of dozens of "modest" new programs, plus elaborations of those estabilshed, must combine into something not only bigger but also different from what the sponsors of each could take into account.

Moreover, many of the innovations of the 1950s and 1960s involved federal inducements to the creation and expansion of state and local activities. Grant-in-aid programs provided strong, or virtually compelling, pressure on state-local governments to expand activities.

Growth of Spending

Counting the growth of number of "programs" has baffled everyone who has tried. The dividing lines are not clear. Dollar amounts, however, are available.

In dollars of constant (1972) purchasing power for *all* levels of governemnt combined (after adjustment to eliminate double counting of intergovernmental grants and other payments), per capita spending was about $814 in 1950; $1,199 in 1960; around $1,770 in 1970; $1,979 in 1972; and perhaps $2,045 in 1973 (est.).

Another, and for present purposes perhaps more meaningful, measure involves only nondefense spending. The per capita figure for 1950 (in 1972 dollars) was $674. Ten years later the total had risen to $872. As of 1973 all governments combined were spending about $1,672 per person (est).

Such comparisons suffer from statistical and conceptual defects. But the limitations do not need to be discussed here because the major point stands out clearly: nondefense government spending has been, and is, going up faster than population and prices. Defense spending, of course, adds its large amounts: but they have recently stabilized as others have risen.

Another way of looking at the data, also admittedly less than perfect in concept and measurement, may be more satisfactory for some purposes. Expenditures of all levels of government combined ("netted" to eliminate double counting), including defense, were around 27.8 percent of Net National Product in 1950 and around 40.2 percent in 1973 (est.). Government has grown as a sector of an expanding economy—local, state, federal.

These figures largely ignore some important *lending* programs: government insurance and guarantee of loans, and other forms of participation in lending, affect resource allocation—and in large amounts.

Need for Examining Results

What are the results of the rise in dollar amounts of spending— and of the increase, relative to other magnitudes of the economy? In what respects, and to what extent, are we better off because of the growing amounts we channel through government? These amounts are determined by decisions made through *political processes*. What are the characteristics of the various elements of political processes and the significance for decision-making and program execution? How closely do results approximate initial hopes? How do the processes as they *actually* operate compare with those of continual, self-adjusting markets ("business")?

Questions having such broad sweep cannot be "answered" in a meaningful sense. But we can examine units and parts of the whole. Literally hundreds of different programs now operate. They have widely varied effects—for the general public and for individuals and groups. We can try to deal with specific elements. Recent years have seen efforts, by no means the first in American fiscal history, (1) to improve the process of governmental decision-making, and (2) to examine more effectively the results achieved and actual accomplishments as they relate to hopes.

The attempts at better control and evaluation are made at all levels of government. They take many forms. Some are massively ambitious—the Planning, Programming, and Budgeting System undertakings in the federal government and in some states and localities. Some efforts to improve are simple, others sophisticated. Some are as continuing as statutory action can make them. Some, however, have been as fleeting as the enthusiasm of a voluntary group, perhaps fired by good intentions but having little in staff, authority, or knowledge.

The results of the attempts to evaluate the many aspects of government spending include: intuitive judgments; casual observation, penetrating in some cases, superficial in others; elaborate formulation of increasingly complex economic theory; findings from the use of econometric methods; and others. Constant change complicates the problems of effective analyses of government spending.

If any one generalization can be valid, it would be: Americans need to know more about results—*direct and indirect*—the "fruits" of hundreds of different kinds of spending. The same applies to government participation, direct and indirect, in lending and the allocation of credit. Few of us have any conception of how governmental lending programs have expanded in directions, and in amounts. As activity has grown, more of the flow of available capital funds responds to decisions made through political processes.

Results to be studied will include more than those directly observable (and presumably intended). Indirect effects may be more than negligible. Some will seem welcome—the effects of better education in enhancing productivity and thus real income. Others are undesirable, for example, pollution from the city dump. "Spillovers" and "neighborhood effects" and "third-party results" can be significant. The more or less automatic processes of the market cannot, we assume, be expected to take them into account adequately.

One reason cited for the expansion of government activity is the inability of people functioning through normal market mechanisms to make reasonably complete adjustment for all the effects of what is done. Working through government, it is argued, we ought to perform more wisely and efficiently because we can look beyond the limits of considerations which prevail in the marketplace. What are the facts?

Tax Differentials

Another aspect of government "disposal" of resources receives increasing attention—tax differentials. Some activities or groups or regions are taxed less heavily than others. When the general level of taxes is high, the differences in tax rates—and in other features of the structure of a tax or the whole structure—can be of great importance. Where favorable treatments are involved, we now find the term "tax expenditure." Whether it adequately conveys the significance of exemptions, exclusions, lower rates, favorable definitions, and other "special" features of taxation may be debated. There will be no debate, however, over the conclusion that differences in tax treatments can exert significant influence. Obvious and elementary. But how much? With what results on the distribution of real income and resource allocation?

So, greater government spending on more things and heavier and more complicated taxes combine to press for more study of results.

Spending on Farms

The results of government spending are not always those intended. An almost "classic" textbook example has for years been evident to those willing to look a little below the surface. Without appearing to "scoop" two of the papers in this volume, brief comment will help to show the reason for some of our interest.

Some of the federal farm programs provide illustrations of economic processes leading to results generally predictable—but not those presumably intended. Large-scale federal aid to agriculture is entering its fifth decade. The programs continue to receive billions a year (1) from taxpayers and (2) from consumers because output is reduced and prices raised as a result of the use of federal authority, somewhat in lieu of the taxing-expenditure power.

One result of these programs has been a *capitalization* (described later) of expected annual benefits into higher land prices. After land prices have gone up to reflect these benefits, the annual payments to farmers in effect support the higher land prices. As land is sold or new leases made and the identity of operators changes, the land price increase becomes a higher cost. Government benefit payments, therefore, are no longer converted into benefits for the operator, whether owner or renter. The person who owned the land at the time the effects of government programs were capitalized into higher prices will get the fruits of the subsidy into perpetuity.

Deductive economic analysis would lead one to predict certain results. Benefits tied to land get reflected in land price. Predictions based on theory have been confirmed. Society had the knowledge to prevent many of the results which now seem so frustrating. But the knowledge was wasted. Not enough people in power were alerted and moved to action to prevent costly failure.

Taxpayer-consumers are to some extent trapped. To reduce, or eliminate, costly annual benefits which, perhaps, in many cases provide no significant advantage to present farm operators would perhaps impose capital losses on many landowners who did not get the original capital gain.

How many sponsors of linking agricultural aid to specific farms and parts of farms saw that future benefit payments, to the extent that they could be foreseen, would get capitalized into land prices? How many landowners were aware of the one-time nature of the benefit as capitalization took effect? The possibilities were not widely discussed. We moved into apparently permanent programs somewhat by stages. Whatever the explanation of past events, one conclusion seems clear: lessons so strikingly clear will not go unnoticed.

New proposals for government spending ought to be viewed in the light of "capitalizable" results. Taxpayer beware! There are smart people who as potential beneficiaries will try to press programs. However, one can hope that enough of the general public will recognize the probable results to permit adequate allowance for them in the decision-making. But knowledge is needed to forestall avoidable error. With government spending and taxes so large, and with the pressures for expansion so numerous and in some cases so enticing, alertness must be supported by the best analysis and fullest evidence possible.

To what extent are other spending programs likely to get capitalized in land prices? Or in such other forms as broadcasting franchises? Where results of this sort appear, programs will yield fewer—eventually perhaps none—of the benefits presumably intended from annual subsidies, even though the public pays year after year.

Are urban difficulties worse, and government expenditure policies adopted to relieve them, disappointing in part because the fruits take the form of higher land prices? Do some proposals for government spending have more risk than others for such frustrations?

Capitalization

Some readers may welcome a simple illustration of the principle of capitalization. Some of the papers in this volume discuss the process more fully.

Of Tax

Think of a plot of land (location) which, so far as anyone can see, will exist in perpetuity. What will be its price or capital value now? Cost of production does not determine as it does to a large extent for shoes or houses or typewriters.[1] The amount which a potential buyer will pay for the land, that is, giving a capital sum now, will depend upon what he expects it to bring in net benefits (perpetually). The present value of the flow of net benefits, compared with those obtainable from other assets, will set the upper limit to what a potential purchaser will pay. And the present owner will not rationally sell for less:

$$\text{Price} = \frac{\text{Net annual benefits}}{\text{Rate of interest}}.$$

We can, as a very simple beginning, assume that someone considering purchase expects $1,000 in net annual receipts (benefits conceived most broadly) after paying operating costs and present taxes. The returns which are available from other properties of essentially equal "quality" as regards risk and security are 5 percent a year. Under such conditions one can wisely pay as much as $20,000 for this property. The owner would be foolish to sell it for less.

But if yields in general from properties of this type are 10 percent, the price would be half as large. For $10,000 is the capital sum which invested at the prevailing rate of 10 percent yields the $1,000 which this piece of land is expected to bring.

Now assume that taxes rise $100 a year to reduce the net yield to $900. We assume that the spending of the added $100 does not make occupancy of the land more attractive—from better government services. The capital value drops to $18,000 if the interest rate is 5 percent and to $9,000 if the interest rate is 10 percent. In the first case the owner has suffered a capital loss of $2,000—$\frac{\$100}{5/100}$—in the second case, $1,000. The person buying, however, will be no worse off because of the recent tax increase. He has "bought himself free" of tax. He paid $2,000 (or $1,000) less in a capital sum. The $100 a year additional tax passes through the new owner's hands each year. But he took the tax increase into account before buying. The former owner, much as he might have desired to keep the price unaffected by the

---

1. Each parcel of land is to some extent unique. The supply of land—the quantity of space on the earth's surface—is fixed. It does not respond to the price obtainable from use. Cost of production does not affect the aspects of land we are considering here. The quantity, and hence the price, of other things in the long run depends upon cost of production. Land, however, is different. It is here.

tax increase, had no power to alter demand or supply to prevent the land price from falling.

This tax aspect of capitalization has been widely illustrated and recognized. Any standard discussion of the economics of property taxation includes this principle.

Of Expenditure

Less attention has been paid to comparable results of government spending. In most cases (certain farm programs excepted) the ties between change in government spending and desirability of plots of land have not been so closely and directly identified with specific parcels of land. Assume that land which has produced a net income of $1,000 will now receive $100 a year permanently as a government subsidy. The net income rises to $1,100 a year. The land will now be worth $22,000 if the relevant interest rate is 5 percent and $11,000 if it is 10 percent. The land price rises by one-tenth. The principle is clear.

Many factors, of course, affect the actual processes of capitalization. Certainty will not be absolute, and either the tax or the spending may not continue as generally expected. Other conditions in the economy will change, some perhaps as indirect results of the process being analyzed.

The 1971 TRED Program: This Volume

Questions and concerns such as those raised above led the members of TRED to plan the 1971 conference around certain effects of government spending. Obviously, we could deal with only a few subjects. Selection presented many problems.

Our long-standing interest in "land and location" offered some focus. Obviously, capitalization falls in the dead center of our body of special concerns. Nevertheless, we eschewed setting limits which would confine the papers to subjects more or less specifically related to land. Other aspects of the results of government expenditure command attention.

Yet the restrictions of the time set by a two-day conference inevitably limited what we could attempt to cover. Some topics and aspects of topics which we believed to be both relevant and important could not be included because potential authors were unable to participate. Little explicit attention could be given to the results of state or local government expenditure.

This volume includes a variety of topics and represents a sampling of approaches. Some are exploratory in areas where exploration is needed. Methodology is tested. At the conference itself, even more perhaps than here, we came to recognize the vastness of the subject areas which deserve deeper study.[2]

Discussions followed each paper, but they are not summarized here. In revising manuscripts for publication, however, authors were able to draw upon the give-and-take of comments during the conference.

The Papers: A Brief Introduction

Some of the papers or the work reported upon has been done as separate projects with no prior association. They represent work of varied nature as regards to subject matter and methods. No closely knit unity was attempted. Where more than a dozen authors participate, overlapping and duplication may seem better than the further editing to modify individual papers. This is not a set of integrated studies building on each other into a unified synthesis. But the diverse subjects and approaches cast light upon several aspects of a general subject of broad range. It is a topic of great human significance. Among the valuable contributions are suggestions about how and where to proceed.

Two opening papers deal with aspects of theory, and more. Jasinowski draws upon extensive work he and others have done as members of the staff of the Joint Economic Committee. Impressive and pioneering efforts have explored the concepts—yes, plural—of "subsidy." Identification of several forms of subsidy and examination of their significance extend the discussion beyond classification alone. We are shown in systematic fashion some of the various kinds of effects on prices and output, capital values and income—along with problems of judging the effectiveness of results.

Going beyond to the evaluation of subsidy programs Jasinowski classifies and examines problems and indicates areas of research needed. He notes, among other things, some of the issues involved in proposals to redistribute income.

Richman's paper deals with certain aspects of capitalization—of taxes and expenditures. Landowners, he suggests, will get more of

2. One can scarcely envisage the size of a series of volumes which would be needed to contain some discussion of all the topics more or less on a par with those here. Nor can one be sure about the extent of needs for data—except that gaps remain far wider than we ought to tolerate where the amounts at issue are as large as in many government programs today.

the benefits of more programs than intended or recognized. While some landowners benefit in the form of capitalization of a stream of future benefits, others may suffer as a policy reduces the demand for their land. One among his conclusions aroused special interest at the conference—the results to be expected from tax reduction on structures. He believes that more of the tax on capital (buildings) than usually assumed actually falls on land values. A subsidy to encourage new construction, he concludes, would bring rather little net additional result relative to cost (revenue sacrificed).

Richman believes that under conditions which may exist in cities —extensive limits set by zoning and building codes and people's preferences—the amount of capital to be invested is relatively inflexible. If so, most of any tax change, such as reductions for new building, will be capitalized in land prices and bring almost no appreciable change in the form of more and better buildings, compared with what would result otherwise. The reasoning which leads to this conclusion rests, of course, upon starting assumptions, especially that the supply of capital in an area is highly inelastic.

Assuming that land is assessed for its worth at the highest and best use, Richman also questions the generally accepted conclusion that making taxes on vacant land heavier would discourage speculation and "leapfrogging." In reaching this conclusion, as well as others involving farm subsidies, tenant subsidies, intergovernmental finances, and penalties and aids to curb pollution, he utilizes the analysis of capitalization.

Housing comes in for contrasting actions of government. For decades, of course, it has been the base for a considerable portion of the main tax of local government. (Critics point out that if the tax rests on the occupant, it burdens housing more heavily than any other form of consumption except liquor, cigarettes, and motor fuels.) Heavy taxation of housing, however, is not the only evidence of government "involvement" in housing. More recently, programs to encourage housing have become increasingly numerous.

Schechter's paper, the first of two papers on housing, surveys major programs. The author gives more than a "standard" overview. He examines subsidy as a concept and the problems of measuring various forms. He describes the main features of many programs. His paper also summarizes information available on costs and the results of implementation as operations have actually proceeded. The experience, to say the least, does not lend itself to any set of simple conclusions. Interpreting the results is not always clear. One thing, however, *is* clear. The programs are not only complex but much more expensive than shown by outlays to date. We certainly need continuing study of the many aspects. Especially great are the needs for studies on which we must rely for indications of benefits relative to costs. Benefit-cost measures are desirable, not merely in total for the public as a whole, if such is really a meaningful concept, but for those who benefit more specifically, and at whose expense.

Muth analyzes a body of data to measure the substitution of capital for current inputs in housing. Subsidies, for the most part, have concentrated on the capital inputs. They are only a portion of the total involved in meeting the demand for housing. An economist would expect such policies to lead to some change in the allocation of resources used for housing. Muth finds it. Measuring elasticities as well as possible, he concludes that the concentration of special assistance on capital cannot pass muster as the best way to achieve the objectives.

Two papers deal with farm programs. Boxley and Anderson examine tobacco programs. The methods used to get and keep prices above those which would prevail in a free market have included planting restrictions—allotments—which are associated with *specific* farms. The results include striking examples of capitalization. Other effects of the tobacco programs over the years are examined in this impressively documented paper.

Sugar restrictions are discussed by Ballinger out of long and direct contact with the programs. The international aspects of this cartel arrangement are unique. Foreign economies are affected directly by United States quotas. The consumer here, of course, pays more for sugar products. The author refers to the capitalization of land prices; it has occurred as economic theory would lead one to expect. Measured results of various aspects are not available, partly because other forces operate in ways and amounts that change from time to time.

A sophisticated study of transportation costs and benefits ranges widely over an important body of material. Stern and Ayres open with a survey of nationwide transportation expenditure by type and source. They also explore possible magnitudes of costs in terms of time and the significance of stress. This impressive methodological undertaking seeks to measure costs and benefits with special reference to the central business district. Benefits can be large in relation to the cost of some transportation programs. The discussion of measuring effects on land values—and possible use of increments to help cover the outlays—deserves special attention. The authors conclude with eight important points—plausible if not definitively proved.

Some findings have policy implications which are clear in general direction even if not in amount.

Coughlin and Hammer report upon pioneering efforts to determine individuals' responses to the conditions of rivers and streams—fresh or foul or in between. The observers reporting showed a significant source of awareness and ability to differentiate according to actual conditions. The authors also describe a study designed to measure the effects of a city park on land values. Assessments are used to estimate land values at different distances from the park. Being near the park has value. The apparent influence of proximity follows a rather smooth curve. The authors also estimate the total worth of the park in alternative uses—the probable value of the land as residential sites (with no park), with adjustments to avoid possible objections for overstatement. This adjusted total exceeds by a considerable amount the authors' estimates of the positive effects of the existence of the park on neighboring land.

Economists in seeking to measure the benefits of government projects relative to costs have given considerable attention to water resource projects, including flood control. Daicoff concentrates upon the capitalization of benefits in land prices, near selected projects. Two independently made sets of estimates are compared. The figures leave no doubt that there has been such capitalization.

To what extent are the benefits of urban water supply likely to be capitalized in land values? Bahl, Coelen, and Warford examine the possibilities of measuring such results, with special reference to developing economies. The problems of empirical research are studied and found to be not insuperable. Various conditions, of course, will influence the results. The conclusions of other studies are contrasted. The authors conclude that revenues derived from the sale of water will underestimate the true benefits of water supply. Land values, however, will reflect such benefits and can be used to help cover the project costs. The methodology developed, the authors hope, can be used for evaluating and financing other types of investment.

One paper presented at the conference, Mason Gaffney's discussion of the benefits of military spending, could not be completed and revised in time for inclusion here. But an informal seminar on urban renewal led by Arthur Becker has been developed into the paper which closes this volume. From his own direct experience, plus extensive reading and comments made at the conference, Professor Becker has written an enlightening, but scarcely heartening, discussion of the development of urban renewal.

Part I. Introduction and Theory

1 *Jerry J. Jasinowski*

THE ECONOMICS OF
FEDERAL SUBSIDY PROGRAMS

There is probably less known about subsidies than any other major public finance instrument. At the federal level we have no comprehensive understanding of what sudsidy programs exist and, correspondingly, what objectives subsidies serve, what good or bad effects subsidies have on the private market, and what cost burdens subsidies impose upon the treasury and society. Yet new subsidies are constantly being proposed, often enacted, and the total subsidy system grows in size and cost to the general public. The system of federal subsidies seems to be somewhat out of control in that it continues to grow despite the fact that we know so little about it.

The Joint Economic Committee has undertaken a two-part study designed to bring more facts about and analysis of federal subsidy programs into the public record. One part of this study consists of a series of study papers dealing with the conceptual aspects of the subsidy instrument and evaluating particular federal subsidy programs. The other part of the JEC effort consists of a staff analysis, which will precede the study papers mentioned above, and is designed to spell out what we tentatively regard as some of the basic economic principles applicable to subsidies and to provide an accounting of the gross budgetary cost of as many federal subsidy programs as possible. This study is to set the stage, so to speak, for the subsequent case studies the Committee will receive and the public hearings it will hold. It aims at the audience of noneconomists who generally formulate, legislate, and occasionally evaluate federal subsidy programs.

This paper is a sampling of the basic economic theory that is embodied in that staff study, which was produced jointly by Carl Shoup and myself.[1]

The views expressed herein are those of the author and are not necessarily shared by the staff or members of the Joint Economic Committe.

1. See *The Economics of Federal Subsidy Programs: A Staff Study,* prepared for the Joint Economic Committee of Congress (Washington, D.C.: Government Printing Office, January 1972).

Defining a Subsidy

Perhaps the major problem in any comprehensive study of subsidies involves a determination of the frame of reference by defining the term *subsidy*. Resolution of this question is important in setting the scope of what government activity one is to consider, as well as in developing principles that explain how a subsidy works. It is also a question that is extremely complex, controversial, and about which there is no unique answer. Somewhat different definitions of a subsidy can be framed for different purposes. Definitions are meant to facilitate analysis, not to determine it, and must be so framed.

For the purposes of our study *subsidy* is defined as the provision of federal economic assistance, at the expense of others in the economy, to the private sector producers or consumers of a particular good, service, or factor of production. The government receives no equivalent compensation in return, but provides the assistance on the condition of a particular performance by the recipient—a quid pro quo —that has the effect of altering the price or cost of the particular good, service, or factor to the subsidy recipient, with the intent of encouraging or discouraging the output, supply, or use of these items in the related activity. The assistance may take the form of: (a) explicit cash payments; (b) implicit payments through a reduction of a specific tax liability; (c) implicit payments by means of loans at interest rates below the government borrowing rate, and from loan guarantees; (d) implicit payments through provision or goods and services at prices of fees below market value; (e) implicit payments through government purchases of goods and services above market price; or (f) implicit payments through certain government regulatory actions.

Simply put, we have said that a subsidy is any one-way governmentally induced income transfer to private sector decision-making units that is designed to encourage or discourage specific private market behavior. We have emphasized that it is government financial assistance that modifies but does not entirely supplant private market activity and market prices. A subsidy is therefore linked with the market price or quantity: the subsidy is so much per unit of the good or service used, or is a certain percentage of the market price. We have also emphasized that a subsidy requires a specific economic quid pro quo or performance from the recipients in the particular market to which the subsidy is tied. In keeping with these two points of emphasis, we have excluded all government goods and services distributed free and all untied cash welfare payments.

The Financial Form of a Subsidy

As the preceding statements have indicated, a subsidy for a particular purpose may take any one of several financial forms. These financial forms are the means by which the income transfers associated with subsidies are accomplished. Moreover, in each instance the income transfer may pass through another level of government before it reaches the private sector firm or household.

Direct Cash Payments

In the simplest and commonest form of cash subsidy the money flows from government to the firm or household that engages in the activity specified in subsidy law, and the amount of money so flowing increases as the firm or household increases its engagement in that activity. This kind of activity is evidently one that the government wants to see expanded. A somewhat more complicated form of cash subsidy is that which is paid for doing less of a certain thing, that is, for reducing the amount of output or input associated with some economic activity. Here, evidently, the output or the input is considered undesirable by the government. Air carrier payments are an example of the first case and wheat payments an example of the second.

Tax Subsidies

The chief noncash subsidy employed by the federal government takes the form of tax reduction. These special provisions of the tax law are distinguished from the rest of the tax system in two ways: (1) they are special provisions of the tax law that are conditioned on the taxpayer's performing a particular action desired by government; (2) they are so designed that the total tax burden is smaller if the taxpayer acts in the desired manner because the flow of income at the margin is from government to the private sector. Two common examples are investment credit and the oil depletion allowance.

Credit Subsidies

Government also grants a subsidy when it provides credit at more favorable terms than the private market. It may do this by making a simple cash grant to the borrower or lender to offset all or part of the interest charges; by government itself loaning money at an interest rate below the rate at which the borrower could otherwise have obtained the loan; by guaranteeing a loan in order to assure the private-sector lender against default; by establishing insurance funds where premiums do not cover claims; and by making soft or non-recourse loans. This financial form is clearly quite versatile.

Benefit-in-kind

This is a case where government sells to the private sector a good or service at a price below market value, or below cost in those cases where there is no readily discernible private market. It is an implicit cash payment subsidy. The effect of the benefit-in-kind subsidy could be achieved equally well by selling the good at market price or cost and then returning to the purchasers a direct cash payment equivalent to the difference between this market price and the purchase price. The benefit-in-kind subsidy demonstrates that government can subsidize the consumption of milk, for example, either by giving a money grant to the consumers or producers, or by selling milk to consumers at a price below the market price.

Purchase Subsidies

A purchase subsidy results when the government purchases a good or service from the private sector at a higher price than it would have to pay on the market in order to encourage a particular private market activity. An income transfer is thus made in the form of an extra money payment to the private sector seller of the good or service, and the net worth of government declines in the process of exchange. Necessarily, the direct recipient of the subsidy payment is a producer rather than a consumer. Examples of such subsidies are government purchases of agricultural commodities for price support and purchases of stockpile commodities for national defense purposes.

Regulatory Subsidies

The term *regulatory subsidies* is coined here to describe phenomena rarely discussed under the heading of government subsidies, since government does not itself give out money or payments-in-kind. Yet, it is government's power that makes possible the subsidy, which takes the form of an income transfer between two subgroups in the private sector. Government regulatory actions with respect to much of transportation, quotas, and the minimum wage requirements are examples.[2]

Having defined a subsidy, and having explained its various finan-

2. For an interesting treatment of government regulatory powers as a subsidy device, see Richard Posner, "Taxation by Regulation," *Bell Journal of Economics and Management* 2 (Spring 1971) : 22–50.

cial forms, let us now move to substantive issues, asking what it is that subsidies are intended to do, what are their probable effects, and how they may be evaluated.

The Market Economy and Economic Arguments for a Subsidy

The arguments used to justify subsidies often have nothing to do with what a subsidy actually can do economically. The arguments for subsidies are also extraordinarily nebulous. Perhaps the most widely used justification is the vague assertion that the activity to be subsidized is in the "national interest," without any specification of just how it is in the national interest. An important variant of this justification occurs when the national interest is "national defense," a term that has been used to justify everything from the raw material stockpile to the interstate highway system. An argument of roughly the same analytical merit can be found in statements that a certain activity must be subsidized because there is a great "need" for certain goods or services—without spelling out the exact nature and size of this need—and that the need can be met only by government action. Often statements about need are couched in hyperbole, such as, "transportation is the lifeblood of the country," or, "agriculture is what made this country great."

We would like to shift the focus of the discussion of the subsidy objectives away from these vague, emotional appeals to the relatively specific economic objectives that a subsidy might reasonably be expected to achieve. This is appropriate in view of the fact that a subsidy is an economic device designed to alter private economic markets that have in some way been found unsatisfactory.

In the JEC staff study, we indicated that there are certain market failings that are obviously not well suited to correction by subsidies, such as public goods and monopoly problems. We also indicated that there are very few subsidies that are large enough to have a significant effect on aggregate demand and employment. At the same time, we acknowledged that subsidies may be well suited to remedy structural imbalances, as between capital and labor, or for particular unused labor.

We argued that subsidies are best suited to correcting defects of the market that prevent an optimal allocation of resources, that is, where there is too much of a certain kind of output in some cases and not enough of a certain kind of output in another. These market shortcomings are cases where resources are not allocated efficiently because of decreasing cost industries, a lack of information, immobility of resources, and the presence of external benefits. The correction of these shortcomings should be especially prized because they may well increase the total real output of the nation.

In the JEC staff study, we attempted to take a fairly undogmatic view of the suitability of redistributing income via a subsidy. First, we pointed out that such subsidies differ from efficiency subsidies in that they make some persons better off but only by making some others worse off. Second, we presented the traditional argument that income transfers tied to consuming particular goods were less efficient than untied transfers. These two considerations would seem to provide considerable merit for the case that untied income transfers, not subsidies, are the "best" means for achieving the sole objective of redistributing income. But then we acknowledged that tied income transfers might not be considered inefficient if one takes into account the preferences of donors.

It would be naive to leave this subject of redistribution without noting that special interests are prone to trumpet a need for subsidies on grounds of alleged economic efficiency when in fact their only objective, and sometimes the only likely result, is a redistribution of income in their favor. This natural desire to get something for nothing is not monopolized by any one group in the community. It explains, in fact, the existence of many of the economically indefensible subsidies that can be found throughout the federal system in the United States. How such subsidies came to be is more the province of the political scientist and the sociologist. Whether they do in fact benefit the special-interest group they were designed to serve is for the economist to estimate. Sometimes these subsidies benefit certain other groups, indirectly, more than they do those who pushed for them.

The Incidence of a Subsidy—Price Effects

The incidence of a subsidy is its final resting place, as distinguished from its initial impact, which is governed by the law establishing the subsidy. This incidence is determined by the market price effects that follow the subsidy payment. These price effects are a measure of what individuals are made better off as a result of the subsidy.

A subsidy may be paid to those who sell the product or to those who buy it. It makes no difference, as to the price effects on buyers and sellers, which course is followed unless market imperfections arise. If the subsidy is paid to sellers, the market price falls but not by the full amount of the subsidy. The fall in market price is a measure of the benefit to consumers. Because the market price does not fall by the full amount of the subsidy, some subsidy benefit is left over for the seller. Or, we could say that the new price to sellers, including the subsidy, is greater than the old price to sellers. Obviously, the benefits of the subsidy are divided between the buyers and the sellers.

There is, in fact, a general rule that is applicable here. The benefit of a per-unit subsidy will be divided, by market forces, between the *buyer* and the *seller* in the ratio that the elasticity of the *supply* curve bears to the elasticity of the *demand* curve, at the initial point of equilibrium:

$$\frac{\text{buyer benefit}}{\text{seller benefit}} = \frac{Es}{Ed}.$$

If supply is relatively inelastic, this ratio is low, and most of the subsidy benefit goes to the sellers. On the other hand, when the elasticity of supply is great, while demand is inelastic, the above ratio will be large, and most of the subsidy benefit will go to the buyers in the form of a price reduction. This rule holds strictly only for a small subsidy but is a useful point at which to begin analyzing the incidence of most subsidies.

A particular subsidy on a product with a highly inelastic demand may cause the price of that product to fall almost by the full amount of the subsidy per unit. Very little of the subsidy is then left to the producer. Yet the legislator may have intended the subsidy to be one that would benefit chiefly producers, not consumers. And the subsidy, under our assumption above, is being paid directly to producers. There are thus three aspects to be distinguished: legislative intent, impact (the place where the subsidy is paid by government), and incidence (what really happens to market prices). The point to be made here is that the incidence may very well differ from the impact. The impact is set by law. The subsidy law stipulates to whom the subsidy shall be paid—here, to the producer, not the consumer. Yet the incidence may be almost wholly on the consumer. In the world of subsidies, incidence is something to be sought for; it is a good thing in the end. In the world of taxes, on the other hand, nobody wants the incidence to be on him.

There is, of course, nothing in the above scheme that tells us how the benefits to the seller are divided among factor claims for profit, rent, interest, and labor. Nor have we taken into account what will happen to the prices of nonsubsidized goods, or how much benefit will go to foreign consumers, or what happens when the market is not competitive. Finally, we have not taken into account the effect of the taxes necessary to finance the subsidy. All of these would have to be taken into account for a thorough determination of the net incidence of a subsidy. The question of how far down this road it is useful to travel will depend on the particular case.

The question of how far one carries incidence analysis should not obscure the need for some additional effort to estimate these price effects of a subsidy. Such effects are the primary determinant of the degree to which a subsidy redistributes income, which is an explicit or hidden objective of most federal subsidy programs. Yet the legislative debate about these subsidy programs does not usually even distinguish between impact and incidence. From my perspective, then, an analysis of the direct impact of a subsidy payment, by income class, or an analysis of the first-stage incidence between buyers and sellers, would be quite valuable.

Capitalization of a Subsidy

There is of course a special price effect that should be noted. A subsidy that is tied to the use of a particular producer good that is durable, and not readily reproducible, say a certain parcel of agricultural land, will tend to become capitalized in the price of that producers good for possible resale. Anyone buying that parcel of land from the one who owned it when the use-subsidy was announced can, like the original owner, look forward to a stream of benefits from the government in the form of the subsidy. He will therefore offer a price for that parcel of land higher than otherwise. Given competition among would-be buyers, the price of the land will rise by an amount equal to the present value of the future stream of monetary payments that will come with possession and use of it.

If, for example, of two parcels of land, one has been allotted a quota, in the sense that the government promises to pay a subsidy of, say, so much per unit of produce (up to some ceiling, in practice), while the other parcel has not been allotted a quota, the first parcel will normally sell for more than the second. The excess sales price will equal the discounted value of the flow of benefits represented by the government subsidy. This value will be difficult to compute, and since the computation requires forecasting, buyers will accordingly differ in their ideas as to what it should be. Nevertheless, there will be some roughly estimated minimum that most will probably agree on, and this minimum excess will serve as a basis not only for a seller's reservation price but also for a mortgage.

If buyers have bought, and lenders have granted loans on this parcel of land, on the assumption that the government's subsidy program is not going to be changed in the near future, these capitalized expectations become a powerful force opposing any reduction in the subsidy. The government will be accused of injuring innocent vested interests if it proposes to reduce or abolish the subsidy paid on this parcel of land. The case is analogous to that of the tax on land, where a large unexpected increase in the tax is opposed on the grounds of unfairness to those who have purchased or lent on what they consider an implicit promise by the government to make no such radical change.

This problem arises of course only with a subsidy payment that stretches over time and is linked with a virtually nonreproducible durable good that has been sold after the subsidy has been introduced. The problem is, therefore, not applicable to all subsidies, but it is intense where it does occur and is a partial explanation of why some types of subsidy seem virtually unassailable after a certain length of time has passed.

The Effectiveness of a Subsidy—Output Effects

When we speak about the output or quantity effect of a subsidy, we are referring to the increased production and use of the subsidized good, service, or factor as a result of the subsidy. This output effect is measured in unit sales, not in dollar volume of sales. The dollar volume may rise only because the market price of the item rises in response to a subsidy paid to consumers. What is in question here, however, is not price, but the physical units. If, indeed, the subsidy is paid to the seller, then the dollar volume may be a good indicator of the unit sales. But it is fundamentally physical units, or some output measure related to physical units, that are of interest for the output effect.

The output effect is a measure of the effectiveness of a subsidy in reallocating resources in order to increase economic efficiency. The economic efficiency of the economy may be hampered by the market's inability to allocate resources in a way that yields maximum total output. It is then argued that an optimal subsidy should be injected into the market to correct this situation. A large increase in unit sales is both evidence that the hypothesis about the market imperfection was true and a correction of the market defect. A very small increase in unit sales is evidence that, from the point of view of economic efficiency alone, the market imperfection was simply not significant. The chief aspect of the alleged market imperfection was to make the distribution of income different than it would otherwise be; and correspondingly, a subsidy exerts its chief effect in allocating incomes rather than the pattern of resource use.

Output effects may, admittedly, be desired in order to achieve some other economic objective, such as increased exports, or on some more or less arbitrary grounds not connected with the economist's concept of economic efficiency. A special interest group may persuade legislators to grant a subsidy in the hope that consumption of the industry's product, or use of the subsidized factor, will be greatly expanded. Then the output effect must be estimated carefully to ascertain whether the aims of this special interest group can in fact be achieved. Usually, however, a special interest group is more concerned with the price effect; they hope that the rewards of those already in the business will be increased by a subsidy that does not bring with it a fall in market price.

Subsidies for food, medical services, and housing exemplify an assumption that a market imperfection has greatly restricted the quantity of these items consumed by low-income households. Subsidies designed to increase the output and use of such items may conveniently be referred to as consumer-use subsidies. Those who support these subsidies on grounds of a genuine market imperfection will be correspondingly disappointed if the output effect turns out to be small. They will have been proved mistaken in their appraisal of the market. Of course they may still favor the subsidy on redistributive grounds, but that is another matter.

Obviously, a subsidy will *not* be successful in increasing output in a market where supply and demand conditions prevent significant increases. This will occur if either the supply or demand of the item is very inelastic. If demand is almost perfectly inelastic, consumers will not significantly expand their purchase of the item as the price to them is lowered. Similarly, if the supply is almost perfectly inelastic, producers will not significantly expand their production as to price to them (including subsidy) is raised. In either case, output and consumption of the item are not increased significantly.

Let us consider some of the implications of these inelasticities. If demand is inelastic, that is, if the number of units purchased increases less than in proportion to the decline in market price resulting from the subsidy, consumers of the subsidized good will themselves spend less on it than under no subsidy. Some of their income is thereby released for expenditure on other, nonsubsidized goods, or for savings. The subsidy is partly dissipated—using this term to express the point of view of those who expected a large quantity effect—in spending on those other goods and in savings. Indeed, if the demand proves to be very inelastic, consumers' own expenditure on the subsidized good will be reduced by almost the amount of the subsidy the government is paying to the producers of that good. In that case, the government might just as well take the simpler course of paying the consumers a straight cash grant, of the same amount, to be used as they wish.

Costs of Subsidies

The benefits to be obtained from a subsidy, either through its price effects or output effects described above, are obtainable only at a cost. This cost is composed of three elements. First, there is the budgetary cost, the amount of money the government pays out in subsidy, less a certain amount of automatic recoupment that occurs as the existing tax system captures part of the increase in wages, profits, and rents that the subsidy creates. The gross budgetary cost, the amount paid out, is thus reduced to a net budgetary cost through this automatic partial recoupment. We may call this the net income transfer cost.

Second, there is a budgetary administrative cost, the cost of administering the subsidy and administering whatever tax or tax increase is imposed to finance the subsidy. Administrative effort uses up manpower and other resources, unlike the transfer aspect of subsidy costs, which represents simply the transfer of money from one group (taxpayers) to another group (subsidy beneficiaries). In this sense, the administrative costs are real costs to the economy, while the transfer costs are not.

Third, the taxes used to finance the subsidy almost surely impede somewhat the efficient use of resources in the private sector. Persons and firms consume and produce in patterns and by methods that they would prefer not to adopt, but do adopt, just in order to minimize their tax bills. The losses in consumer satisfaction and in productive efficiency that result from being thus induced to act in nonpreferred ways are, in the economist's term, an "excess burden."[3]

3. Ironically enough, taxpayers in the aggregate do not after all succeed in reducing their tax bills, despite recourse to tax-saving methods of consumption or production. The government, requiring a certain amount of money, simply sets the tax rate high enough to bring in the needed revenue, despite the tax-reducing actions taken by taxpayers.

Such a burden is an efficiency loss and represents an unproductive use of the real national income of the economy.

It must of course be noted that subsidy recipients are induced by a subsidy to take actions other than those they would have chosen, just in order to qualify for the subsidy. But such action is desirable as part of the government's overall plan, while tax-reducing actions by households and business firms are certainly not part of what is desired. Therefore the two sets of reactions are not on a par: one is desired, the other is not. The desired reaction, instead of creating an excess burden, increases the real national income if policy-makers have made the correct economic judgments. The undesired reaction, that taken by tax-minimizing households and firms, reduces the real national income by inducing a recourse to relatively inefficient methods of production and less satisfying patterns of consumption. It is possible, of course, for a subsidy to create an excess burden, though in a reverse direction, if it is handed out with insufficient attention to actual correction of a legitimate market imperfection, or if it corrects a market imperfection only by bringing about other economic distortions.[4]

The question now arises, should a congressman or other policy-maker add all three elements of cost, as given above, to get a total cost that is meaningful? Should he add the budget cost of net income transfers to the budgetary administrative cost and the excess burden cost? Or should he keep the net income transfer cost separate, as being not a cost in the sense of using economic resources but a transfer cost between two groups within the economy, and thus obtain the resource cost to the economy by adding only the administrative costs and the excess burden costs?

A good rule to start with is that the two kinds of cost should be kept separate, but, as we shall see, the problem is a bit more complex than this. The basic rule reflects the fact that the net income transfer cost is not in itself a drain on the economy's real resources of manpower, raw materials, and the like. It is, instead, a political cost in the sense that somebody, initially at least, is made worse off—he who pays more in tax than he receives in benefits from the subsidy—while somebody else is being made better off at his expense.

Even this political cost can in principle, though hardly in practice, be wiped out if the subsidy is one that is designed to reallocate resources to make good some market imperfection, and thus increase

4. See, for example, Charles Schultze, *The Distribution of Farm Subsidies* (Washington, D.C.: The Brookings Institution, 1971), Appendix A.

the total real output of the economy by moving manpower and materials and equipment into industries and places where they will be more efficient than they will be if left to the free play of the market place. Those who lose initially by the subsidy and the tax to finance it could in principle be compensated from this extra lump of national income, with some left over, to make some persons real net beneficiaries of the process. In practice, no such compensation is likely to be made, at least not completely, and so a political cost remains.

If the subsidy is used clearly for redistributive purposes, and not to remedy a market imperfection, the political cost of the net income transfer becomes serious. Now there is no increase in the national income, and there can be no question of compensating those who are made worse off by the subsidy-tax combination. To be sure, we might conceive of this redistribution of income as being a real good, if those who have to give up some income under it are found quite willing to do so in order to achieve the ethical and other intangible advantages that they see in a more nearly equal distribution of income. No doubt there is a certain amount of this feeling. But it would be oversimplification to claim that it largely explains why redistributive subsidies are enacted.

Under a redistributive subsidy, therefore, the policy-maker must weigh the costs of discontent aroused in one group against the benefit accruing to the subsidized group and strike some kind of a balance, positive or negative. Alternatively, he can keep these two items separate, and simply add, to the real costs of administration and of excess burden, something to account for the discontent of the taxpayers in order to get a total cost to offset against the satisfactions received by the beneficiaries of the subsidy. Adding the real costs of administration and excess burden that diminish the effectiveness of the economy as a whole, and the income transfer costs, reflected here as political costs, of those who are definitely made worse off by the subsidy with its supporting tax, will be somewhat like adding apples and oranges. But the policymaker obviously cannot ignore the costs of these income transfers in the circumstances outlined here.

Let us now examine the much misunderstood notion of recoupment. As I have indicated, part of a straight cash subsidy may be recouped by the government in the form of an automatic increase in tax revenue, as the subsidy proceeds become taxable, or as the profits or wages or rent they give rise to becomes taxable. Accordingly, the subsidy can then be financed by a somewhat smaller increase in tax rates or by the introduction of fewer new taxes than if there were no automatic recoupment at all. Another way to put it is that the subsidy, in the aggregate and over a period of years, may not be quite as large as it looks, since a portion of it may be recouped by the existing tax system. The amount of the recoupment, of course, depends upon the elasticities of supply and demand.

A correct assessment of the significance of automatic recoupment is that it must be considered in planning the subsidy but should not be used as a justification for a subsidy. Since a subsidy transfers income from one area of the economy to another, the increase in tax receipts from one sector results in decreases in tax receipts from some other sector. Recoupment is therefore a money transfer that has nothing to do with any real economic benefits. Again, subsidies should be justified economically in terms of their direct effects on private market behavior and increases in real social welfare.

Evaluation of Subsidies

Evaluation of a subsidy implies some comparison, however rough, of its costs with its benefits. The comparison must be made both with respect to (1) the total benefit of the subsidy and its total costs and (2) the last increment of the subsidy's benefit and the corresponding costs, or what we may refer to as its marginal costs and benefits. A subsidy may show an overall excess of benefit over cost, yet it may at the same time be partially wasteful in that it has been somewhat excessive and could be cut back with a decrease in cost greater than the decrease in benefit. On the other hand, a subsidy may show an excess of total benefit over total cost, yet still be too small. Perhaps an increase in the subsidy would bring an increment of benefit that would exceed the increment in cost. If this is so, efficiency would dictate that the subsidy be increased to the point where one more unit of subsidy does so little good that the cost of that increment of the subsidy exceeds the increment of benefit obtained. This marginal analysis is essential in evaluating any subsidy.

A second test, partly implied in the first, is that the subsidy be the most efficient way of obtaining the desired end. Although it may show an excess of benefit over cost, some other approach—direct free government distribution of the benefit, for example—may exhibit a still better relationship of benefit to cost. In that event, the subsidy is inefficient.

A subsidy's benefits may come chiefly through its output effects or chiefly through its price effects. Generally, though not always, the output effects are the ones to look at if an increase in economic efficiency through reallocation of the economy's resources is the important goal, while the price effects are the more significant if the proximate goal is income redistribution. This point is important enough to warrant some further discussion, together with some recapitulation of conclusions reached in earlier sections of this analysis.

If the goal of the subsidy is to increase the efficiency of the economic system by reallocating resources, this implies that some persons are to be made so much better off by that reallocation that they could compensate those who would be made worse off by it, and still have a net gain. The money value of this net gain would seem possible of computation, in principle, though perhaps difficult or impossible in practice. In principle, the subsidy rate should be increased until this net money gain, after compensation paid to those made worse off, exceeds the sum of (1) the cost of administering the subsidy and the tax that finances it, and (2) the excess burden caused by that tax. At this point the rate of subsidy becomes too high for efficiency. The proper rate for a subsidy, then, from the viewpoint of efficiency, is found by comparing benefits and costs at the margin of the subsidy.

If redistribution of income is the goal of the subsidy, no such excess of money-computed benefit over money-computed cost is required to justify the subsidy. Here the subsidy admittedly makes some persons worse off, and bars any compensation to them. Evidently such a subsidy can reflect only a majority opinion, or the opinion of a powerful minority, on an issue where there is a natural conflict of interests. Such conflicts, of course, involve competing power groups and can only be resolved by the political process. The economist can assist in the resolution of this conflict by informing the public and the policy-maker how various programs distribute their income benefits, so that the income redistribution effects of subsidy programs may be appraised in full view of the community's sense of fairness. Too often in the past this battle over the distribution of income via subsidy programs has favored the politically powerful because the community at large did not understand what income transfers were occurring.

A number of important problems have been glossed over, partly because of space limitations and partly because we have not come up with solutions. But the chief difficulty is not so much the deficiency of analysis as it is the failure to apply even the crudest economic principles to the questions we have been considering. It is my hope that the framework sketched here will enable decision-makers and their staffs to ask the right economic questions about subsidy programs.

2 *Raymond L. Richman*

THE CAPITALIZATION OF PROPERTY TAXES AND SUBSIDIES

Introduction

The benefits of government subsidies and expenditures are often capitalized and appear as an increase in the value of real estate, whether or not the landowner as such was the intended beneficiary. This should not surprise anyone, since, other things being equal, anything which increases the anticipated yield of a parcel of land will increase its value through the process of capitalization of the anticipated increase in yield.

A problem arises when (1) the landowner is the sole, principal, or important beneficiary of a program intended to benefit the tenant or someone other than the landowner, and (2) when those who are not beneficiaries are saddled with the burden of financing the subsidy to the unintended beneficiary, the landowner. Another problem arises when the benefit accruing to the landowner frustrates the goal of the legislation. A program to benefit farm workers may make it more difficult for them to own farms because of the diversion of the benefits to the landowner in the form of higher land prices.

To complicate things further, there is no permanent benefit to subsequent purchasers of land. That is, the only landowner who benefits is the one at the time that anticipations of increased yields become more favorable. A subsequent purchaser will pay the capitalized value of the anticipated stream of income and will receive a return on capital no greater than if there had been no increase in income. He will pay a higher price for a proportionately higher stream of income. Frequently a government program will benefit an intended beneficiary, not a landowner, and at the same time benefit some landowners. Often some landowners will benefit and others will lose; the program thus results in an increased demand for land in some locations or with certain characteristics, while the demand decreases for other land in different locations or with different characteristics.

Failure to understand the process of capitalization may result in

19

considerable frustration of the legitimate goals of a program. In no case is this clearer than in the case of real estate tax incentives which are intended to benefit the occupier but often benefit only the landowner. The process by which government spending and subsidies, indeed government programs of any kind, will be capitalized into land values may be illustrated by the process by which real estate taxes are capitalized into land values.[1]

The Incidence of Real Estate Taxes

The incidence and economic effects of real estate taxes are unsettled.[2] It is generally believed that taxes on the value of improvements raise contract rents by the amount of such taxes in the long run and are borne by the occupier, or in the case of land are believed to be borne by the landowner. It is also held that the tax on improvements diminishes the demand for capital in real estate uses, lowering rates of return generally, and may affect the incomes of factors associated with the construction industry, at least in the short run. The conclusion that taxes on improvements are shifted forward in their entirety in the long run does not follow from the traditional theory. A more careful consideration compels one to note that the marginal parcel in the absence of the tax becomes submarginal as a result of the tax on improvements. Thus, some of the burden of a tax on improvements must be borne, under the traditional theory, by landowners of supramarginal parcels.

How much of the burden is borne by occupiers and how much by landowners? We are dealing with two factors of production: land, which is in completely inelastic supply, and capital, having varying elasticity of supply, which is combined with land on a given parcel. Capital will be used up to the point at which the marginal net yield equals the appropriate interest rate. The magnitude of the effect on intensive capital use clearly depends on the elasticity of the production function. The greater the elasticity of capital in the potential uses of a given parcel of land, the greater the likelihood of forward shifting.

1. Capitalization refers to the process by which the right to a future stream of income is valued. Anything which adds (subtracts) to the income stream will increase (decrease) the value of the right, that is, its capital value.

2. Much of the theory that follows is derived from the analysis contained in the author's article, "The Incidence of Urban Real Estate Taxes under Conditions of Static and Dynamic Equilibrium," *Land Economics* 43 (May 1967) : 172–80.

In the case of urban real estate, as a result of people's preferences, zoning laws, and building codes, the amount of capital to be invested is relatively inflexible. Even where there are no limits on the height of buildings, the construction of a marginal unit, for example, an apartment or office building, is likely to be prevented by setback and parking requirements and other zoning provisions.

While capital will be economized marginally, the conclusion appears inevitable that the proportion of capital in urban land uses, certainly residential and only to a lesser extent commercial and industrial uses, is highly inelastic. If this is true, the bulk of the burden of a tax on improvements, that is, the tax on capital, must be borne by the landowner and is capitalized. Buyers' bids will discount the capitalized value of nearly all of the entire prospective tax liability. This is nearly opposite to the conclusion which has been drawn generally that the tax is forward shifted.

How much of the tax will be capitalized in the long run depends on the existence of alternative competitive uses for land parcels which require less capital than the optimum use. In the case of urban residential land, the amount of capital "required" for economic use of a particular lot falls within a narrow range. The value of the lot will discount the prospective taxes on the lot as optimally improved.

While there appears to be greater elasticity of capital improvements on zoned commercial parcels than on zoned residential, it is much less than appears at first glance. The improvements can range from parking lots to giant office and hotel complexes. Yet what makes land valuable for use as a parking lot are the surrounding capital intensive uses. Not all of a downtown area can be parking lots! Nor should all of it be giant office buildings.

Moreover, in an urban area there are no marginal parcels, that is, parcels defined as having no value. Land for a considerable radius beyond the city has a speculative value for residential and commercial uses considerably in excess of any agricultural alternative. Thus there is a value to vacant land which permits capitalization of prospective taxes on the improvements. A tax on the superior use will be borne by the landowner as long as there is no competitive valuable use or where the competitive use requires the same proportion of capital. Before considering the implications of this revision of the traditional conclusions, it is worth noting again that if the tax on improvements is capitalized, the value of vacant land capitalizes not only taxes on land but also taxes on potential improvements in its most valuable use.

From Theory to Policy

If one grants that there are qualitative benefits to the community, arising from a given policy of subsidy or exemption, it does not follow that the policy should be implemented unless the benefits are net after calculation of all costs. For example, the theory outlined above does not deny that exempting improvements from property taxation will have some beneficial effects. Marginal improvements which would not have been made in the presence of a tax on the value of improvements will be made in the absence of such a tax.

To state that there is some marginal benefit is insufficient if the marginal benefit is obtained by granting subsidies or exemptions to the total improvement, some or much of which would have taken place anyway. To illustrate, suppose that $11,000 would be invested in an improvement if there were no tax on improvements, and if there were an improvement tax, $10,000 would be invested. For the purposes of our illustration, suppose the tax rate to be 5 percent; thus, to obtain the $1,000 of marginal improvement will cost $500 annually in revenues. The benefit from $1,000 in improvement is unlikely to exceed the average rate of return generally, let us say arbitrarily, 10 percent. In that case $100 of annual benefit will be produced at an annual cost of $500 to the municipal treasury. Further, it is not irrelevant, if $500 is to be raised by other taxes, to ask what the effects of higher rates elsewhere would be and what the resulting distribution of income would be. In any calculation of benefits and costs, total benefits, direct and indirect, private and social, must be weighed against total costs similarly calculated. Finally, even when it is determined that total benefits exceed total costs, one must ask whether there is an alternative policy with a higher benefit-cost ratio.

The proposition can be maintained that the tax system should never be used to reward or subsidize any economic activity, that its sole purpose is to raise the desired level of public revenues equitably, subject to the trade-off with considerations of administrative efficiency, costs, and economic effects. No doubt, if one is pressed hard, he would have to concede that some tax provisions are the most efficient means of achieving one or another social goal. It is probably wise, however, to start from a position of opposing all suggestions for using the tax system as a means of penalizing undesirable activities or of subsidizing desirable ones and to depart from this position only when incontrovertible evidence shows that it would be the best means of achieving desirable goals.

One is frequently tempted to recommend changes in the real estate tax base, or to grant exemptions from it on a temporary or permanent basis to one or another group of taxpayers, or to those engaged in some activity which is to be encouraged. As in the case of any public policy, subsidies or expenditure must meet the tests of effectiveness, cost, economic effects, and equity. It is not enough to demonstrate the existence of beneficial direct and indirect effects. How important are the benefits? How much do they cost? Who pays? Is there a better alternative? All of these questions are important.

Taxes, Subsidies, and Other Government Activities Which Affect Land Values

Certain taxes and subsidies will affect land values directly by capitalization of the tax or subsidy without affecting the demand or supply of housing or other land uses. Others will not be capitalized directly but will have an effect on land values by changing the demand and/or supply of housing and other land uses.

Changes in Rates

Other things being equal, a change in rates of tax will be capitalized. The implication of this is that the landowner, at the time the change is effective or anticipated, will bear the burden or benefit. An increase in rates will lower land values; a decrease will increase land values. Subsequent buyers purchase "free" of the burden or pay the capitalized value of the benefit. This fact has implications for students concerned with the progressivity of either the tax system or the property tax. The burden or benefit will not be transferred forward.

To put it another way, real estate levies in effect make government a partner in the ownership of real estate. The annual levies, subsequent to the imposition of increased rates, are proprietary income. Is the real estate tax progressive, as Professor Mason Gaffney has argued in a recent paper?[3] If so, it is progressive in a historical sense as a capital levy may be said to be progressive, subsequent annual levies being the proceeds of the property interest acquired by the imposition of the tax.[4]

Recent proposals to lower property tax rates would in effect make a capital contribution to landowners. Lower rates would provide

3. Mason Gaffney, "The Property Tax Is a Progressive Tax," in *1971 Proceedings of the National Tax Association,* ed. Stanley J. Bowers (Columbus, Ohio, 1972), pp. 408–26.

4. Raymond L. Richman, "Regressivity and Incidence of Real Estate Taxes Reconsidered," ibid., pp. 431–35.

windfall gains to all who purchased property after the last change in rates. If the original levy of rates were progressive, it would follow that reduction in rates would be regressive!

Changes in Assessment Ratios

Real estate is normally assessed at a fraction of its fair market value. Whether the fraction is 20 percent or 90 percent, any change in the ratio imposes a new burden or grants a benefit. An increase (decrease) in the assessment ratio increases (decreases) the tax liability, assuming tax rates to be unchanged, and the increased (decreased) tax liability will be capitalized.

The implication for policy is that assessment ratios should remain unchanged in order to be neutral. If they are changed to equalize ratios among several jurisdictions, tax rates should be adjusted accordingly to compensate, thus preserving neutrality. Changes in assessment ratios simply change the effective tax rates.

Charitable Exemptions

The case for exempting charitable, religious, and educational institutions is considerably weakened by recognition that the purchase price for a parcel already discounts the future taxes on both land and buildings in an optimum use. Exempt institutions are thus able to buy properties at a much lower price than their "real" value. The exempt institution pays a price lower than the economic value of the land by the capitalized value of the tax. The price it pays for the land is $R / r + t$, but the value of the land is R / r, where $L =$ land value, $R =$ the economic rent in the parcel's optimum use, $r =$ the opportunity cost of capital, and $t =$ the tax rate. For example, if a parcel has an economic rent (in perpetuity) of \$100, its value, discounted at .06, is \$1,667. If the tax rate is .04, the exempt institution will pay \$1,000, plus the value of the improvements, if any.

Housing Subsidies

Subsidies appear to be an obvious "solution" to the problem of housing low-income families. The question is, however, what form the subsidy should take. One proposal is to exempt rehabilitation and renewal expenditures from taxation for a period of years.

The landowner is paying a tax on land (or ought to be) on its value, given its optimum improvement. Since the tax on land is based on the value of land given its optimum improvement, taking into account the total taxes that would be paid if the parcel were optimally improved, the net increase in the property owner's tax liability as a result of rehabilitation expenditure would be less than the tax rate multiplied by the additional capital invested.

Let ΔT = change in tax liability
t = tax rate
C' = rehabilitation expenditure
ΔY = change in income produced by
the new capital expenditure
r = appropriate discount rate.

Then, $\Delta T = tC' - \dfrac{t(\Delta Y - rC')}{r}$. The latter element is already being taxed. For example, let $t = .04$, $\Delta Y = .10C'$, and $r = .06$; then $\Delta T = .04C' - \dfrac{.04(.10C' - .06C')}{.06} = .013C'$.

The impediment of the tax on improvements in the above example is not the tax rate (.04) multiplied by the cost of the improvement ($1,000), but .013 times the cost of the improvement.

Land Taxes as a Deterrent to Speculation

It has been suggested that orderly contiguous development of parcels is disrupted by land speculators who hold their properties off the market in anticipation of future increases in land value. This forces developers to "leapfrog" the withheld parcels, thus imposing social costs in the form of higher expenditures for water, sewage, transportation, and communications. If the taxes on improvements were eliminated and the burden imposed on land, it is alleged that higher taxes borne by vacant land would discourage speculation and, consequently, leapfrogging. It is further alleged that higher land taxes would induce improvements and increase the supply of housing and so on. As a result of the capitalization of land taxes (and taxes on improvements), neither of these claims is valid. Since land for a considerable radius from the city has a value in residential use greater than the agricultural alternative, parcels which are not "ripe" for development compete currently with parcels which are "ripe." Their prices indicate their relative values for current or future improvement. If the owner of "ripe" land holds out for a higher price than justified by anticipated income, the prospective developer will find leapfrogging an equally attractive alternative. The community of course will be the loser. Tax policy is not the answer; town and country planning might be.

Land speculation is not deterred by higher taxes on land, for example, by a shift of taxes on improvements to land. Since taxes on land are capitalized, the speculator substitutes a smaller purchase price and a higher annual tax for a larger purchase price and a smaller annual tax. They are economically equivalent. In any case, properties ripen over time. Not all vacant land can or should be improved at once. Holding land idle for future use is by no means an uneconomic practice. Dynamic equilibrium requires the supply of improvements to increase in proportion to demand. To develop property too soon will result in inadequate returns.

The Capitalization of Excise Taxes and Farm Subsidies

Excise taxes will be backward shifted in the long run when one of the factors of production is inelastic in supply. Among excise taxes which are possibly backward shifted to land, at least in part, are taxes on tobacco. If all the land on which tobacco is grown is clearly superior for growing tobacco as compared with any other use, it would be shifted backward and capitalized. On the other hand, if some tobacco land competes with other equally valuable uses, the tax will not be capitalized and all the shifting will be forward. The likelihood is that much tobacco land has equally valuable uses and that the tax will shift resources to such other uses without being capitalized.

Widespread agricultural subsidies will have effects predicted by the traditional theory. When submarginal land is brought into use, rents will increase on the land worth using without the subsidy. However, many farm price support and subsidy programs are specific to particular parcels. Only those enrolled in the programs at a certain date may participate. As a result, the subsidy benefits the owner of particular parcels and the entire subsidy is capitalized in the form of higher land prices. Subsequent purchasers receive no benefit from the programs.

Subsidies to Tenants

Subsidies to tenants will increase the demand for housing and tend to raise contract rents in the short run, but not in the long run. Their effects are similar to general increases in income, but being restricted to low-income families, they increase demand for moderate income units at the expense of demand for substandard or low-quality housing. The decreased demand for substandard and low-quality housing will tend to lower rents of the latter, thus encouraging their renewal, rehabilitation, or redevelopment.

Subsidies to new housing units, which are rented to low-income families at market rentals minus the subsidy, increase the supply of housing in proportion to the increase in demand and are therefore not capitalized in the short or long run. A subsidy in the form of tax exemption to a certain category of taxpayer, for example, old-age exemptions and veteran's exemptions, will not be capitalized except to the extent that total demand for residential real estate increases by persons in those categories. The subsidy is specific to the recipients and does not attach to the land.

Intergovernmental Competition

To the extent that taxes on land and improvements are capitalized, there is no possibility of intergovernmental competition. Low tax rates in one community, as compared to another for parcels otherwise identical, will create no incentive for the taxpayer to locate in the former. In the former he will pay higher land prices and a lower annual tax payment; in the latter, lower land prices and a higher annual payment. These are economically equivalent. Imperfect capital markets, consumer ignorance, or psychological reactions may bias consumers toward one or another, however.

Penalties and Subsidies Designed to Eliminate Pollution

Taxes or other penalties designed to curb pollution may in some instances be shifted backward to the landowner. This is the case where the economic activity concerned is a clearly superior use of the land. The tax will be capitalized until the price of the land decreases to its value in a nonpolluting competitive use.

Similarly, subsidies designed to clean air and streams will increase values of land in the areas affected. How much of the subsidy will be capitalized depends on the relative costs and benefits. As in the case of any government expenditure which affects a specific area or use, a case can be made for financing some of the expenditure by taxes on the indirect beneficiaries in proportion to their benefit.

Part II.   Housing and Agricultural Subsidies

3 *Henry B. Schechter*

FEDERALLY SUBSIDIZED
HOUSING PROGRAM BENEFITS

In his transmittal to the Congress of the Third Annual Report on National Housing Goals, on June 29, 1971, President Nixon noted that there was a "need to deal with inequities which arise when some families receive subsidies and others do not, the inevitable result of having to allocate scarce resources." The president went on to state that his administration was committed to a search for answers to this and other housing problems.

Within the Congress, too, there has been concern about the aggregate size and distribution of the federal housing subsidy costs and benefits. This subject can be expected to receive a thorough review during the next year or two, and major legislative changes in the federally subsidized housing programs are to be expected. This paper presents an analysis of the distribution of housing subsidy benefits which may prove useful as legislative review of the housing subsidy system gains momentum.

There are various types of benefits to be realized from the federally subsidized housing programs. In the first part of this paper, benefits which may accrue to participants in the program are identified. The second part develops some qualitative judgments as to the nature and recipients of benefits that have evolved in connection with the rapid growth of subsidized housing. The last part of the paper is devoted to an examination of some of the major subsidized housing programs to identify the incidence of net program benefits.

Only those programs which involve a nonrepayable government expenditure are treated as subsidized housing programs. Mortgage insurance and guaranty programs are excluded; they are considered to be self-sustaining, and thus far, in the aggregate, they have been. No attempt is made here to assess auxiliary social benefits of subsidized housing. In addition, the relatively minor expenditures for program administration will be ignored. My focus is housing assistance or subsidy payments intended to benefit low- and moderate-income occupants under the various programs.

In accounting for the benefits engendered by the programs under consideration, however, certain federal tax exemptions that affect required payments for housing under the programs will be analyzed. Certain other tax benefits, which may be defined as a subsidy in the context of inducing a greater overall housing supply,[1] will also be noted, although this is not a benefit that relates specifically to the subsidized programs. Such tax benefits (for example, accelerated depreciation) have been permitted to induce greater rental housing production in general, rather than for greater production under federal subsidy expenditure programs. Therefore, while the auxiliary tax benefits accruing to owners of subsidized rental housing are not benefits from government spending, they should be noted as a benefit accruing to the housing owners.

Concepts of Housing Subsidy

To develop a methodology for comparing costs and benefits of federally assisted housing programs, William Ross, when he was the Deputy Under Secretary of Housing and Urban Development, concluded that the most useful measure of benefits to the occupant of an assisted housing unit is the difference between rent for "private housing of comparable quality" and rent paid by the occupant of the assisted unit.[2] Monthly housing expenses can be substituted for rent, with due differentiation regarding an equity interest accumulation, in considering benefits in subsidized home ownership programs.

In arriving at differences between rent for comparable private market housing and assisted housing, the comparable private market rent data must be used with caution. As a practical matter, in this paper the full unsubsidized rent or monthly housing expenses established by FHA will be used in comparison with the rent or expenses paid by the occupants in a number of subsidized housing programs. It is then necessary to judge whether those full rents or monthly housing costs (or the house prices) exceed the costs for comparable private housing in the unsubsidized market.

1. For a broader definition of subsidy in government programs, see Julius W. Allen, "Subsidy and Subsidy Effect Programs of the U.S. Government," Committee Print, Joint Economic Committee (Washington, D.C.: Government Printing Office, 1965).

2. William B. Ross, "A Proposed Methodology for Comparing Federally Assisted Housing Programs," Papers and Proceedings of the Seventh-Ninth Annual Meeting of the American Economic Association, *American Economic Review* 57 (May 1967) : 91–100.

An obvious case of excessive cost of assisted housing was uncovered by a congressional committee in March 1971 in connection with existing homes sold to eligible buyers under the Section 235 home ownership program. It was found that FHA had been overappraising numerous homes by a few thousand dollars for each, so that real estate speculators had been reaping substantial windfall benefits.[3] In some instances fraud and bribery were involved. The Secretary of HUD, after looking into the matter, temporarily suspended the program for existing housing and took corrective measures before he reinstituted it.

The foregoing illustration is an extreme example of benefits from government spending programs in housing which may go to someone other than the intended beneficiary, the housing occupant. It represents a flow of net benefits which go to a participant in the housing supply process as a result of procedures and mechanisms of program operation. Less apparent net benefits may accrue to housing input suppliers under legal program structures and procedures if the payments for their services, capital, and material are greater than for comparable unsubsidized housing,[4] or if they are greater than they might be under another form of subsidy—for example, direct loans at below market interest rates versus interest rate subsidies. These questions will be explored later in analyzing individual programs.

A broader conceptual question concerns the effect of the growth of the subsidized housing programs upon cost levels for housing production and financing. Have the additional demands for resources needed to support the increased housing production led to higher wages, materials prices, financing charges, and profit margins which absorb part of the subsidy payments? The price levels for the various inputs (land, labor, materials, and financing) are responsive to many demands besides subsidized housing. General economic inflation and price rises will contribute to higher wage demands, for example, at the same time that housing production rises because of federally subsidized housing programs. Nonresidential building activity also influences many of the cost elements affecting housing.

Nevertheless, there is undoubtedly some marginal housing cost and

3. See "Interim Report on HUD Investigation of Low and Moderate Income Housing Programs." Hearings before the Committee on Banking and Currency, House of Representatives, March 31, 1971.

4. Different regional and local distributions of subsidized and nonsubsidized programs cause national program data to reflect different geographic variations in costs, as will be indicated in qualifications of comparisons developed later in this paper.

price effect because of the higher residential construction volume that results from the subsidized housing programs. It is not possible to measure precisely the price changes which have occurred in response to multitudinous nonresidential building and general economic demands or from increased unionization and administered pricing. Higher labor and materials costs will result if a greater proportion of available resources is devoted to housing production, unless there are offsetting decreases in other demands or cost reductions due to technological advances and volume production. Some judgments can be made as to the effects upon materials and labor input costs induced by the subsidized housing program through an examination of cost levels associated with the growth of the program and by examining broader economic influences during the same time period.

Land price increases associated with the growth of subsidized housing programs may be somewhat more measurable from program statistics. Professor Lester C. Thurow of M.I.T. has written that "any plan designed to stimulate housing demand will tend to be self-defeating. . . . The subsidies become capitalized into the value of the land and policies that were designed to increase the supply of housing simply end up increasing the price of land." He also points out that a part of the subsidy, proportional to the land-to-housing cost ratio, simply transfers an existing resource from one owner to another. He raises a question as to whether the benefits from increased land values should be allowed to accrue to the present owner or whether they should be taxed away.[5] The amount of land capital gain is a question of measurement, insofar as data will permit. The point that only transfer of an existing resource is accomplished might also be raised about transfers of available labor and materials resources at their market prices at a given point in time. If a distinction is made on the basis that land value has increased without productive effort by the owner, and land value increments are taxed away, such policies should be applicable to all land holdings, not just to sites for subsidized housing.[6]

The form of interest rate subsidies inherent in the housing programs may cause a flow of net benefits in favor of lenders and savers, when compared with the return possible under alternative methods of program organization and subsidization.

5. Lester C. Thurow, "Goals of a Housing Program," in papers submitted to the Subcommittee on Housing Panels, Committee on Banking and Currency House of Representatives, June 1971, Part 2, p. 447.

6. Also, in order to cushion the impact of a large one-time tax upon current land value, it would probably be desirable to introduce land value taxation gradually over a number of years.

Finally, how much net benefit accrues to the home-builder as a consequence of the subsidized housing program volume? Are the profits greater than they would have been in the absence of such programs? Do they result in such volume and increased profit margin as to constitute a greater return than is commensurate with the effort and risk involved?

Subsidized Housing Production and Prices

The incidence of the foregoing specific types of net benefits can best be estimated for individual programs because of differences in benefit payment formulas. However, the effects upon input price levels which absorb subsidies also have to be considered in terms of changes in the aggregated activity of housing programs involving government spending. In a sense, the several programs constitute a collective government program to provide low- and moderate-income housing, and they have a collective impact upon the demand for input resources required in housing production.

Four major continuing programs have provided the bulk of the subsidized new housing production: the HUD Section 235; the Farmers Home Administration homeownership programs; the low-rent public housing program; and the Section 236 moderate-income private rental housing program.

There are a number of older assisted housing programs which are now inactive or being phased out.[7] They will not be examined individually, but their program activity levels will be considered in the collective impact of the change in assisted new housing program activity upon input cost factors and net benefit distribution.

In the past four fiscal years, the annual volume of new housing units started under the federally assisted housing programs has increased significantly, from 126,000 in fiscal 1968 to an estimated 438,000 in fiscal 1971. Over the same period, of total new housing starts, the federally subsidized program starts rose from 8 percent to 25 percent. The most substantial increases occurred in the last two fiscal years, ending June 30, 1970, and June 30, 1971, when the total subsidized new unit starts were 302,000 and 438,000, respectively, and accounted for 21 and 25 percent of total new housing starts. (See Table 3.1.)

7. These include Section 221(d)(3) below-market interest rate moderate income rental housing program and the Section 202 direct loan rental housing for the elderly program—both financed with 3 percent interest rate loans; and the rent supplement low-income, private rental housing program financed with market rate FHA-insured mortgages.

During the first of those two years, in fiscal 1970, unsubsidized housing starts declined drastically (in response to tight money conditions) and total new housing starts declined by 15 percent. However, nonresidential building volume was 7 percent greater than in the preceding twelve months.[8] General inflationary forces were strong, as reflected in a 6 percent rise in the Consumer Price Index. The Boeckh indexes of construction costs rose about 6 percent for nonresidential buildings, but only 3 percent for residential. The rise in the latter index was limited by a significant decline in lumber prices, following

Table 3.1—Total and Federally Assisted Housing Program Starts, Fiscal Years 1968–1971 (in Thousands of Units)

Fiscal year	Total housing starts	Federally assisted housing program starts	
		Number	Percentage of total starts
1968	1,460	126	8
1969	1,600	163	10
1970	1,359	302	21
1971	1,791	438	25

Sources: 1968–70. Second and Third Annual Reports on National Housing Goals; 1971 estimated on the basis of preliminary data from HUD and Farmers Home Administration.

an upsurge in the preceding twelve months. Prices of materials less sensitive to home-building activity levels and building construction labor wage rates rose significantly, with wage rates rising more than materials prices. On balance, the rise in residential building construction costs in fiscal 1970 would seem to be related primarily to nonresidential building and general economic inflationary influences, rather than to the growth of the subsidized housing programs, although that growth probably had some marginal effect.

In fiscal 1971, the unsubsidized new housing starts rose 28 percent, subsidized housing starts rose 45 percent, for a rise in total starts of about 33.3 percent. In contrast to a gain in the preceding fiscal year, nonresidential building volume (in constant dollars) declined by about 13 percent.[9] The Consumer Price Index rose only 5 percent, compared with 6 percent in the preceding twelve months. Over the fiscal year, however, the Boeckh construction cost indexes rose by

8. U.S. Department of Commerce, Bureau of Domestic Commerce. Based on new construction put in place in constant dollars, *Construction Review*, monthly issues.

9. Department of Commerce. *Construction Review* 17 (July 1971) : 16, Table A–2, fiscal 1971 estimated on the basis of figures for first eleven months.

about 8 percent for residences and about 9 percent for other types of buildings.[10] In contrast with fiscal 1970, there was an upsurge in lumber prices as housing construction rose sharply in the second half of fiscal 1971. There was also a 9 to 10 percent increase in the hourly earnings of all contract construction workers.[11]

Data for fiscal 1971 indicate a stronger influence of the subsidized housing construction than in fiscal 1970 in leading to a rise in residential construction costs. A rough approximation of this influence might be based on the assumption that, without the rise in residential construction occasioned by the increase in subsidized housing, residential construction costs would not have risen more than the general price level, as reflected in the Consumer Price Index, or only about 5 percent instead of 7.5 percent. That would mean that roughly 2.5 percent of the cost would be due to the incidence of the subsidized housing. It would represent incremental compensation to the labor and material input suppliers to reallocate more resources to housing production.

Under the subsidized housing programs, since the occupant's required debt service or rental payments are generally a fixed percentage of his income, the amortization of the increased cost requires an increase in subsidy which represents a transfer inducement payment to the labor and materials suppliers. The higher labor and material costs were necessary for reallocation of resources to produce more housing. The change in cost levels did not represent an added cost for subsidized housing only, but for all housing. Therefore, to the extent that subsidies had to be increased to cover increased production costs for comparable private housing, the dollar benefit to the subsidized housing occupant was being increased. Whether certain component costs of housing increased more for subsidized housing than for other housing can be judged in the context of selected individual program analyses.

Section 235 (i) Home Ownership Assistance Program

The HUD Section 235 homeownership program was enacted in 1968. An estimated 140,000 units started in fiscal 1971 were sold with

10. U.S. Department of Housing and Urban Development, *Housing and Urban Development Trends* (Washington, D.C.: Government Printing Office, 1972), p. 20, Table C–3.

11. Estimated on the basis of data for eleven months from Department of Labor, published in Department of Commerce *Construction Review* 17 (July 1971), Table G–4.

Section 235 financing. To be eligible for the purchase of a home and subsidy benefits under the program, a family's adjusted income generally may not exceed 135 percent of local public housing admission limits. Under an alternative income limit formula, 20 percent of the subsidy funds may be used for somewhat higher income families. The adjusted annual income is the gross income minus 5 percent of income of adults and $300 per minor, exclusive of all incomes of minors.

An eligible buyer purchases a home with a private FHA-insured mortgage bearing the prevailing rate of interest, currently 7 percent. A monthly assistance payment, made on his behalf by HUD, is the lesser of either (a) the difference between 20 percent of monthly adjusted income and the required monthly payment (for principal, interest, mortgage insurance premium, hazard insurance, and property taxes) or (b) the total monthly debt service (excluding hazard insurance and property taxes) and the monthly principal and interest obligation at a 1 percent interest rate.

Although up to 30 percent of the subsidy funds may be used to assist purchasers of existing homes, the Section 235 program has become primarily a new home program. New homes accounted for about 84 and 89 percent, respectively, of homes financed under the program in the last quarter of 1970 and the first quarter of 1971.[12] Furthermore, the annual volume of new homes built under Section 235 has become greater than the volume under any other FHA one- to four-family new home mortgage insurance program, and they accounted for 13 percent of the FHA new home units in 1969, 64 percent in 1970, and 71 percent in the first quarter of 1971.[13] Consequently, certain inferences about effects of the Section 235 program may be drawn from monthly data for all new homes sold with FHA-insured mortgages during 1970–71, as well as from program data.

Most of the available data are national data, so that comparisons of cost components for subsidized versus nonsubsidized housing may be affected by differences in the geographic distribution of units produced under the two programs. There would probably be differences in the cost comparisons were the cost elements for subsidized and nonsubsidized housing available for a smaller geographic area with relatively uniform component costs.

An element of cost for identical areas was compared by looking at

12. Based on information in HUD–FHA quarterly reports on "Characteristics of Home Mortgage Transactions Insured by FHA under Section 235 (i) ."

13. Ibid., and FHA Monthly Reports of Operations (301 reports), December 1969, December 1970, and March 1971.

land costs for new homes under Section 235 and under the regular nonsubsidized FHA Section 203 mortgage insurance program. Sample data on the cost per square foot of the improved site under both programs was obtained for the first quarter of 1970 and the first quarter of 1971 for forty-five Standard Metropolitan Statistical Areas in which there had been new home construction activity over this year of rapid growth in Section 235 activities. Under that program, the price of the site, per square foot, had increased in twenty-nine places, decreased in twelve, and showed no change in four; under the 203 program it had increased in thirty places, decreased in fourteen, and showed no change in one. The direction of change was the same in twenty-seven of the forty areas for which there were changes under both programs. Of the thirteen areas for which the square foot prices moved in opposite directions, prices increased in eight areas under the Section 235 program, and in five under the Section 203 program. In the great majority of places, land used for Section 203 homes was significantly more expensive than for Section 235 homes in the first quarter of 1970 and also in the first quarter of 1971, although the differences were narrowed during the year in many places.

The use of more expensive land for new homes financed under Section 203 than for those financed under Section 235 is also reflected in annual data for 1970. The average cost per square foot was 39 cents for Section 235 homesites and 84 cents for Section 203 homesites.

The average lot size for the subsidized Section 235 homes in 1970 was actually larger than for the 203 homes—9,849 square feet versus 8,851 square feet.[14] Apparently, as phrased in an FHA report summarizing the 1970 Section 235 new and existing home activity, "the new homes were more often in the less urbanized locations."[15] Also, within SMSA's the new Section 235 homes probably were built on cheaper, more outlying land than the Section 203 homes.

From all of the foregoing, it would appear that Section 235 program activity had spurred a greater utilization of cheaper, probably more outlying, land (for the limited price homes that could be built under the program) than has been used for new unsubsidized one-family homes. The statutory mortgage limits, which also establish practical home price limits, have tended to keep prices of land for Section 235 new homes relatively low. The home purchasers receive

14. FHA reports: "Trends of Home Mortgages Insured Section 203 (b) " and "Specific Characteristics by Total Acquisition Cost, New 1-Family Occupant Purchase Homes, 235 (i) , 1970."

15. FHA "Statistical Highlights" of the 235 program in 1970.

a decent sized lot—and probably will benefit from future appreciation in land values. Whether the sellers and developers of the Section 235 lots are benefiting from unduly high land values cannot be ascertained without recent year data on land value for comparable sites in specific localities. However, an average Section 235 new homes site-to-value ratio of 17 percent in 1970, compared with 21 percent for new Section 203 homes, indicates that if land values have increased in response to Section 235 activity, they have risen to a comparatively reasonable level in relation to the value of the house. Although there may be individual area exceptions, the data do not indicate that a significant capitalization of subsidy into higher land values had occurred under Section 235 by 1970.

On the other hand, 1970 data on the sales price per square foot of living area, after land cost is eliminated, would suggest that higher profit margins may be entering into 235 home sales than for comparable Section 203 unsubsidized housing. The average square foot sales data for all 235 and all 203 new homes are not comparable because the former homes had an average of only 1,017 square feet of living area and the latter an average of 1,267 square feet, almost one-fourth more. The square foot cost is partly a function of size, tending to go down with increased size which permits the cost of kitchens and bathrooms, and their equipment, to be spread over a larger area.

The average sales price of a new Section 203 unsubsidized home in 1970 was $23,056, and the living area square foot sales price, exclusive of the cost of land, was $14.15. The comparable average square foot sales price was $15,00 for new homes in the upper-end interval of the Section 235 price distribution, where the average sales price was $23,313. In the next lower Section 235 price interval, with an average sales price of $20,233, the comparable square foot sales price, excluding land, was $14.90.[16] The differences are, no doubt, in part a result of the smaller size of the Section 235 homes, averaging 1,160 and 1,128 square feet in the two price intervals cited, compared with 1,267 square feet for the Section 203 homes. In comparing homes of roughly the same price ranges, however, a 9 to 10 percent smaller living area means a higher price for equivalent housing.

A higher square foot cost under Section 235 than for comparable nonsubsidized housing is also indicated by census data for all new

16. Calculated from data in FHA reports: "Trends of Home Mortgage Characteristics—Mortgages Insured—Section 203 (b) " and "Specific Characteristics by Total Acquisition Costs, New 1-Family Occupant Purchase Homes, 235 (i) , 1970."

homes sold in 1970. About 80 percent of the FHA-insured homes sold in the $15,000 to $20,000 price range were Section 235 homes whose characteristics were reflected in all FHA-insured homes in that price range.[17] The census data on average price per square foot, excluding value of the improved lot, for homes sold in the $15,000 to $20,000 price class in 1970, showed the following by different types of financing: FHA-insured, $12.90; VA-guaranteed, $12.20; and conventional, $12.80.[18] The higher Section 235 square foot costs than for other homes in the same price bracket might be explained by either (1) locations in higher construction cost areas, (2) more amenities, or (3) higher profit margins.

The Section 235 homes did not entail higher construction costs. They are generally located in less-urbanized, lower-rent areas than Section 203 homes,[19] and probably in lower-cost areas than most conventional homes. New homes sold in the $15,000 to $20,000 price class were 71 percent financed with FHA-insured mortgages[20] (primarily under Section 235), and roughly 60 percent of the new homes in that price bracket were in the South,[21] which is a relatively low construction cost region.

As far as amenities are concerned, among Section 235 homes, only 14 percent were centrally air-conditioned, although the ratio was 17 to 21 percent in some of the upper-price brackets, but 30 percent of all Section 203 homes were centrally air-conditioned. Over 77 percent of all the Section 203 homes had more than one bathroom, a ratio matched by 235 homes only in the highest income bracket, but among all Section 235 new homes in 1970, only 39 percent had more than one bathroom. Garages were included with 58 percent of all Section 203 homes, but only 40 percent of all 235 homes, although the comparable ratios were 45 and 49 percent in some of the upper-price brackets. A higher proportion of 235 than 203 homes had basements, 22 percent versus 17 percent. On balance, it would appear that higher square

17. Ibid. About 64 percent of all new homes financed with FHA-insured mortgages in 1970 were under Section 235, and about two-thirds of those were in the $15,000 to $20,000 price class, but only about 30 percent of the nonsubsidized new homes under FHA programs were in that price bracket.

18. Department of Commerce, Bureau of Census—HUD, "Characteristics of New One Family Homes: 1970," Table 39.

19. For Section 235, 30 percent, but only 14 percent of Section 203, FHA new home commitments in 1970 were located in six southern states (South Carolina, Georgia, Florida, Alabama, Louisiana, and Mississippi).

20. HUD, "Characteristics of New One Family Homes," Table 42.

21. Ibid., Table 68.

foot costs do not reflect more amenities in Section 235 than 203 homes; in fact the amenities provided are probably fewer and entail a lower cost for a house of a given size. The data suggest, therefore, that higher square foot living area prices produce a relatively higher profit margin in Section 235 new homes sales than in the sale of comparable nonsubsidized homes.

Based on a comparable sales price per square foot of living area (exclusive of land costs) for roughly comparable price brackets, the producer of Section 235 homes may have a profit that is greater by about 5 percent of the sales price, exclusive of land, or 4 percent of the total sales price.[22] This might be expected, given the greater salability of a substantially subsidized home (which also enhances the profit margin through lower construction financing interest costs) .

The greater salability is confirmed by the reported selling time of new homes, by type of financing. In late 1968 and early 1969, the average time from start to sale for a new home financed with an FHA-insured loan was about one-half month less than one financed with VA-guaranteed loan and about one month less than one financed with a conventional loan. The FHA faster sales advantage has increased over the past two years. By late 1970 and early 1971, the FHA-insured home selling time was averaging about one and one-fourth months less than homes with VA-guaranteed financing and two to two and one-half months less than conventionally financed homes. For homes completed before sale, the time from completion to sale had become less than one month for those with FHA-insured financing, over two months for those with VA-guaranteed loans, and two to three months for conventionally financed homes.[23] The average savings in construction financing interest would probably be about .5 of 1 percent of the total cost, a net benefit of the program which is not reflected in the selling price or subsidy, but is realized by the builder.

The median monthly subsidy for a new home buyer under Section 235 was $77 during 1970 and it had gone up to $81 by the first quarter of 1971.[24] These amounts represented about 47 percent of the regular total monthly payment. The regular total monthly payment was divided about as follows: 78 percent, mortgage principal and interest;

22. Sales prices of $14.90 to $15.00 per square foot exclusive of land for Section 235 homes in the $20,000 to $23,000 price range, versus $14.15 for Section 203 homes with an average price of $23,056, all figures for 1970.

23. Department of Commerce, Bureau of Census and HUD, "Sales of New One-Family Homes," C–25 Construction Reports, March 1970 and June 1971.

24. FHA annual and quarterly reports on characteristics of transactions and profiles of homebuyers.

5 percent, mortgage insurance premium; 3 percent, hazard insurance; and 14 percent, real estate taxes.[25] The mortgage amount to be amortized is essentially the sales price in Section 235 cases. Since mortgage debt service absorbs three-fourths of the subsidy, the higher selling price of about 4 percent than for comparable nonsubsidized housing means that about 3 percent of the subsidy payment represents a net benefit to the builder-seller. The rest (that is, 97 percent) is a net benefit to the homeowner.

However, the entire subsidy may be greater than the cash payment. The Internal Revenue Service now has under consideration the question of whether an owner of a subsidized home may deduct the full mortgage interest on the mortgage and the full real estate taxes from his income for federal income tax purposes, when close to one-half of those expenditures is covered by subsidy. For the median-income, median-family size Section 235 homeowner, the deductions for that part of interest and property taxes paid by subsidy would mean an additional $10 per month. This would be for a family of four, with an annual income of $6,150, who would be in the 16 percent marginal income tax bracket. About 84 percent of Section 235 home-buyers in the first quarter of 1971 had incomes between $3,600 and $7,200.

If that additional subsidy benefit is allowed, and if the interest rate form of subsidy is accepted as a "given," it would appear that 97 to 98 percent of the Section 235 subsidy benefits accrue to the home-owner. That conclusion has to be modified, however, if direct loans are considered as a possible alternative method. Direct loans would be made with funds borrowed by the treasury so that the basic interest cost might be reduced to a 6 percent rate (on treasury obligations) instead of an effective mortgage interest rate of 7.5 to 8 percent. Although the FHA ceiling for mortgage interest rate presently is 7 percent, the payment of discount points brings the effective rate up to about 7.75 percent. Furthermore, between one-fourth and one-half of the discount point payments are being absorbed by the Government National Mortgage Association under its "tandem plan",[26] providing an additional subsidy. In effect, the government presently is subsidizing an interest difference between 7.5 or 7.75 and 1 percent, or providing an interest rate subsidy of about 6.5 percent. Under a direct

25. Based on preliminary data provided by FHA.

26. Under this plan, GNMA issues a commitment to purchase the Section 235 mortgage at 97. At the same time it obtains a commitment from FNMA for the latter to buy its mortgage at its secondary market "free auction" price. The latter prices have been at 94 to 96 for the bulk of the 7 percent mortgages. GNMA absorbs the difference, using authorized special assistance funds.

loan program the difference would be between 6 percent and 1 percent, that is, 5 percent, or about 23 percent less. Since about 84 percent of the mortgage debt service in the first five years of a thirty-year 7 percent loan goes to interest, that proportion, or about 66 percent, of the (78 percent) cash subsidy toward debt service is for interest, and 23 percent of that, or about 15 percent of the subsidy payment could be looked upon as a net benefit accruing to lenders and savers. Under that concept, only about 83 percent of the net benefits would be flowing to the homeowners. (The other 2 percent would accrue to the builders.)

Before leaving the Section 235 program, some differences between new home and existing home buyer benefits and characteristics should be noted. In the first quarter of 1971, the monthly Section 235 subsidy was $81 for a new home purchaser and $75 for an existing home purchaser. There were also noteworthy differences between new and existing home purchasers. There was little difference in median gross annual income—$6,155 for new home purchasers and $6,089 for existing home purchasers. Significant demographic differences were indicated, however, by medians for age and size of family. Among new home buyers, the median age of head of family was twenty-nine and the median number of persons was four, compared with an age of thirty-four and six persons for existing home buyers. Also, only 1 percent of the new home buyers, but 18 percent of the existing home buyers, had welfare assistance as their primary source of income. Finally, the new home median sales prices was about $17,900 (including closing costs), but the existing home sales price was about $16,600. The median mortgagor share of the monthly payment was $91 for new home buyers and $89 for existing home buyers. The figures—particularly as to family size—suggest that new home buyers were receiving greater qualitative benefits than existing home buyers in terms of housing acquired relative to housing needs.

Farmers Home Administration Section 502 Home Loans

The Farmers Home Administration Section 502 program, operating in rural areas (up to 10,000 population), provided financing for between 90,000 and 100,000 home purchases in fiscal 1971, about two-thirds being new homes. Low- and moderate-income families may purchase homes under income limits determined for local areas; subject to an established state-adjusted income limit; the adjustment is the same as under Section 235—$300 per minor, plus 5 percent of income are deducted.

There are two layers of subsidy. A "thin layer" of subsidy is received indirectly by all home purchasers under the program through a below-market interest rate on the mortgage loans. Thus, during fiscal 1971, the interest rate on the Section 502 mortgage loans was 7.25 percent. These loans are insured but made directly by Farmers Home Administration, pending later sale to private investors. In borrowing money in the market for purposes of making the loans, Farmers Home Administration paid about 8.75 percent (issuing notes collateralized by the mortgages). Therefore, there was about a 1.5 percent interest rate subsidy to all home purchasers that was made up from appropriations.[27] In dollar terms, that subsidy amounted to about $195 per year, or $16 per month on a $13,000 loan.

In addition, about 38 percent of the Section 502-financed homes, those of buyers with the lower incomes, also received an "interest credit" to reduce their effective interest rate to 2.5 percent, adding an additional 4.75 percent interest rate subsidy for the lower one-third. The "interest credit" in dollar terms averaged about $608 per year or $51 per month on the average loan amount of $13,000. The "interest credit" is subject to reduction in later years if the income of the borrower rises.[28]

For the one-third of Section 502 home purchasers who received both layers of subsidy, the initial total subsidy amounted to about $800 per year, or $66 per month. Few of the Section 502 home buyers would also be able to receive a tax benefit from an income deduction of interest paid by the government. Their family size is larger than other home buyers, and their median gross income is less than $4,000, and 80 percent had incomes of under $5,000.[29] Their adjusted income after personal exemptions, therefore, would in most cases be below the minimum taxable amount for a joint return filed by a married couple.

There is little unsubsidized housing cost data available for comparison with costs of the Farmers Home Administration housing which is produced in small communities scattered across the country. The land costs probably are a relatively minor part of the total. The median square foot area is between 1,100 and 1,200 square feet, so that the per square foot sales price, including land, is about $11.30. Since square foot costs of all new homes sold in calendar 1970, ex-

27. If the subsidy is measured as the difference between the interest rate that the home-buyer would have had to pay on an insured mortgage loan from a private lender and the 7.25 percent that he paid, it would be a 1.75 to 2 percent interest rate subsidy.
28. Based on data provided by Farmers Home Administration.
29. Ibid.

clusive of land, averaged between $13 and $14,[30] the $11.30 appears to be relatively low. Judging from the available data, a major portion of the subsidy benefit would appear to accrue to the home-buyer. However, the Section 502 homes are often in sparsely populated areas of relatively low market values, and data were not available on what they may have in the way of amenities, so that a judgment cannot be made as to whether any of the subsidy supports a greater sales price than would be prevalent in the absence of subsidy.

Rental Housing—The Section 236 Program

Section 236 is the rental housing counterpart of Section 235. The subsidy formula is similar, although the mechanics of subsidy payment are geared to a rental housing operation. A monthly housing assistance payment is made by HUD to the project owner on behalf of an eligible tenant. The established local income limit for eligibility is generally 135 percent of the local public housing admission income limit. The assistance payment may not exceed the lesser of (a) the difference between the FHA-established "market rent" based on the full mortgage interest rate (currently 7 percent) and rent based on a 1 percent mortgage interest rate; or (b) the difference between the "market rent" and 25 percent of the tenant's income.[31]

There are insufficient data to provide a basis for judgment of whether the subsidy is supporting higher land or construction costs than would be entailed in the production of nonsubsidized, comparable rental housing. A few observations can be developed from the data, and, perhaps more importantly, points in the production process which may lend themselves to sizable gains can be identified.

Land costs per dwelling unit for Section 236 projects were considerably lower in 1970 than for nonsubsidized FHA-Section 207 projects. The 236 median per unit land cost was about 20 percent or $200 lower than Section 207 for walk-ups, and more than 45 percent or $830 lower for elevator apartments. Part of the explanation may be that the 207 units were larger, with a median size of 915 square feet, versus 815 square feet for the 236 units. The Section 207 units also, no doubt, had better locations which would make for higher land prices.

30. Department of Commerce, Bureau of Census—HUD, "Characteristics of New One-Family Homes: 1970," Table 41, p. 89.

31. A 25 percent proportion of income is required as a minimum rental payment, in contrast with 20 percent for the Section 235 homeowners payment toward housing expenses, because the homeowner separately must pay for maintenance, repair, fuel, and utilities which are included in the rent.

That is suggested also by the fact that about 37 percent of the Section 207 units, but only 11 percent of the Section 236 units, were in elevator apartments which usually are built where land is expensive. In addition, the median ratio of land price to project replacement cost was close to 8 percent for Section 207 projects and about 5 percent for 236 projects. All the foregoing evidence indicates that higher per unit land costs were involved in Section 207 than in Section 236 projects in 1970. This may have been due to differences in geographic location within the country, as well as to differences in location within given metropolitan areas. There is no indication whether the land being used for Section 236 projects was priced higher than similar land in comparable locations in the same area. An examination was made of site costs per square foot for Section 236 projects built in the same metropolitan area to see whether the price had increased as the program progressed. Data for some twenty areas failed to indicate a definite pattern of increases.

The foregoing facts do not gainsay the observation that perhaps the greatest potential for gains in the development of multifamily housing—subsidized and nonsubsidized—is through land acquisition and revaluation. The FHA estimate of the fair market value of the land, prior to construction of improvements, is added to development costs to make up the total project replacement cost. The latter amount serves as the basis for a 90 percent mortgage for the limited distribution sponsor,[32] or a 100 percent mortgage for the nonprofit sponsor. The mortgage proceeds, therefore, can be the vehicle for realization of a significant gain in the value of the land above the true acquisition price of the land to the sponsor-builder of a limited distribution project or to the builder or land developer.

For income tax purposes the builder-sponsor of a limited distribution project often has a separate corporation that acquires the land, gets it rezoned, and then sells it to the builder-sponsor organization. Regardless of who handles the rezoning, it is a process by which the value of the land can be greatly enhanced. Suburban land in undeveloped or farm use, not having residential zoning classification, might sell for $500 to $2,500 an acre; if zoned for one-family residential, for $2,500 to $10,000 per acre. When rezoned to multifamily use, however, the land may increase to $25,000 to $30,000 per acre for garden type apartments and $40,000 to $50,000 per acre for high-rise

---

32. A private sponsor whose annual distribution of cash dividends from rental income is limited to a 6 percent return on the equity investment, generally a limited partnership or a corporation.

apartments. It can be seen that, on a five acre site a value gain in
the range of $100,000 to $200,000 is quite possible. Not all the gain
will be pure profit, since there are expenses involved in the rezoning
proceedings, plus property taxes and mortgage interest to be paid
while the land is held prior to development. However, the taxes and
mortgage interest will be based on the land value before rezoning and
will be small in comparison with the gain to be realized. Moreover,
if the prerezoning land-owning corporation holds the land for at least
six months and then sells it to the sponsor-builder, the gain is taxed
at the lower capital gains tax rate, rather than at regular income tax
rates.

Rezoning and a separate land acquisition corporation may not be
necessary to get essentially the same effect if usable land can be picked
up in a marginal location. Once the FHA accepts the land for a multifamily insured mortgage project, the land value is likely to be based
on recent sales of land for comparable uses, with some allowance for
the difference in location. The greatly enhanced land value accrues,
once the site is to be used for multifamily housing. It is necessary to
carry the project through to construction completion and have a high
loan-to-value ratio mortgage, however, in order to realize the gain in a
relatively short time.

A potential for unusual gain during the construction stage also may
be available to the builder-sponsor limited distribution corporation,
and to a lesser extent to a builder acting as a contractor for a nonprofit
sponsor. First, there are tax shelter benefits because various current
expenses, such as construction financing interest and fees and property
taxes, can help to establish losses to offset current income from other
sources in a consolidated income tax return.

The builder-sponsor of a limited distribution project is allowed
certain fees and other expenses which certainly cut down on actual
cash investment requirements. These include: (1) a builder-sponsor
profit and risk allowance equal to 10 percent of total costs exclusive
of land and legal and organization fees; (2) builder's general overhead allowance of 1.5 percent of such costs; and (3) organizational
expense allowance of 1.5 percent of such costs. These fees are probably
reasonable for most projects because of the risk, effort, and know-
how required of the builder-sponsor. There may be economies of
scale which make the remuneration relatively high on large projects.
More significant, however, is the capability to build up the required
10 percent equity largely or wholly from such fees, and the builder
can then recoup his payment by selling equity shares in a limited

partnership to investors in high income tax brackets.[33] For them, tax benefits can be realized through losses that are established by virtue of accelerated depreciation allowances. Since such allowances are available to all new rental housing, however, the tax benefits are primarily a subsidy to rental housing production in general, rather than a subsidy for Section 236 or other subsidized housing programs.

A limited distribution owner of a Section 236 project must have an equity investment equal to at least 10 percent. Irrespective of whether this equity comes in whole or in part from a cash investment, from land owned by the project owner, or from a builder's profit and risk allowance (of 10 percent on construction costs exclusive of land), it represents an equity. A limited return of 6 percent, calculated on the basis of that equity, may be distributed from project income. Such cash distributions are only a small part of the return to investors, however, after taking account of the value of annual tax deductions. These deductions permit book operating losses to be established which can then be offset against other income earned by the owner or owners. Losses can be passed on to limited partnership shareholders in proportion to their percentage of equity ownership. The losses are established primarily through deductions for accelerated depreciation allowances which are quite high in the early years of ownership.

Since depreciation is allowed on the entire value of buildings (equal to roughly 90 percent of total property value) there is a great deal of leverage for deductions created by a 10 percent equity. Thus, assuming a building value equal to 90 percent of total (land and improvements) investment, the deductions during the first year on a forty-year-life project, using double declining balance depreciation, might be 4.5 percent of the total project investment. Furthermore, there are also one-time nonoperating deductions, such as construction financing interest costs and local taxes, which will raise total deductions in the first year or two to over 5 percent of the total project investment. Against a 10 percent equity, such deductions are equal to 50 percent of the equity investment. For an equity investor in the 50 percent income tax bracket the after-tax value of the deduction would be equal to 25 percent of the equity investment.

The value of the depreciation, plus the 6 percent cash distribution that is permitted, can give the equity investor in the 50 percent tax bracket a return of roughly 30 percent in the construction and initial

---

33. There are also architectural design and supervision fees of 4 percent and 1.33 percent, respectively, which might be partly paid for through equity stock shares.

operating year of a Section 236 project. As the depreciation base and the mortgage interest rate deductions are decreased in ensuing years, the annual rate of return to the equity investor will decline, reaching perhaps 20 percent by the fourth year, 15 percent by the eighth year, and 12 to 14 percent in the tenth year. The undiscounted annual rate of return on equity, from cash flow distributions plus depreciation allowances, could average about 20 percent for the first ten years of ownership, as the total of the returns could have a value equal to roughly twice the initial equity investment.

As has been noted, the main factor in producing a high annual rate of return is the accelerated depreciation, which is available to the owners of new nonsubsidized rental housing, as well as for subsidized rental housing. In fact, the nonsubsidized rental project owner might be able to set rents high enough to obtain a higher annual cash flow return than 6 percent. On the other hand, the nonsubsidized project, over a period of years, is much more likely to experience higher vacancy rates which would reduce rental income and the rate of cash flow return. That risk is to a large extent eliminated in a Section 236 project where occupancy is likely to average better than 95 percent, the rate upon which rental income to provide the 6 percent cash flow return was calculated.

The rate of return on equity will not be quite so high on new housing investments with higher equity-to-replacement cost ratios where the leverage effect is less. However, there are nonsubsidized rental housing programs under which FHA-insured mortgages may equal up to 90 percent of value. Also, the value appraisal of conventionally financed rental housing may produce a mortgage which covers 90 percent of the actual replacement cost. If the return on equity resulting from accelerated depreciation were to be considered, in part, a subsidy, it would have to be considered a subsidy for the provision of all new rental housing owners rather than a subsidy for owners of Section 236 housing.

There is another tax benefit available to owners of Section 236 projects, upon disposition after ten years, however, which is not available to owners of nonsubsidized projects. That is the provision for capital gains treatment of sales proceeds representing depreciated book value in excess of straight line depreciation. Such "recapture" of excess depreciation is entirely taxable as income if the Section 236 project is sold during the first twenty months, and thereafter the amount subject to recapture is reduced by 1 percent per month. All proceeds from sale of a Section 236 project are subject to capital gains treatment after ten years of ownership by the original owner. The total of accelerated depreciation over the ten years may equal about 40 percent of the total original property cost.[34] Assuming that the property is sold for an amount equal to the original cost, the capital gains tax would equal 10 percent of the original project cost, reducing the potential average annual return on equity from about 20 percent to about 19 percent. However, the remainder of sales proceeds above the outstanding mortgage balance,[35] available for after-tax distribution, would raise the average annual return by about 0.6 of 1 percent. The net effect of the sales transaction, therefore, would make a potential annual average return of 19.6 percent of equity.

In contrast, if a nonsubsidized property is sold during the first 100 months, all sales proceeds representing depreciation in excess of straight line depreciation are subject to income tax "recapture." Thereafter, the excess depreciation subject to recapture reduces by 1 percent a month. Therefore, if a nonsubsidized rental housing project is sold at original cost after ten years, about 80 percent of the excess depreciation is subject to regular income tax. The income plus capital gains taxes then would equal about 13 percent of the original project cost, in contrast to the 10 percent in the case of the Section 236 project sale.[36] After subtracting taxes and adding the value of mortgage amortization in the sales proceeds, the potential average annual rate of return would be 19.2 percent, in contrast with 19.6 percent for the subsidized project. That difference in return, which represents an additional tax revenue loss to the treasury, represents a further subsidized housing subsidy cost.

There is a potential for further enhancement of the return on equity investment through a higher project rental income than calculated when the project was approved. The project rental income was calculated on the basis of 95 percent occupancy, but there is a good probability that a higher occupancy rate will be achieved for subsidized rental housing. Although such additional income would

34. This is more than would be possible on a forty-year life for the entire property because certain components, such as plumbing, appliances, and others are depreciated on a shorter life basis.

35. That amount, representing amortization of the original mortgage loan amount, would be equal to about 6.6 percent of the original mortgage amount, or 6.0 percent of the total original cost.

36. The 13 percent is derived from a 50 percent income tax on 80 percent of the excess depreciation. The latter is equal to 20 percent of original cost, and 80 percent equals 16 percent, so that income tax accounts for 8 percent. The balance of the tax is capital gains on the balance of depreciated book value (equal to 20 percent of original cost) at a 25 percent rate.

provide a greater net cash income after expenses than required for the permitted 6 percent annual return through cash distribution, the extra cash can be used to make mortgage prepayments. The accelerated reduction of mortgage debt principal can be realized as an additional equity gain upon disposition of the property and would represent a subsidy benefit in proportion to the ratio of subsidy payments to full "market rent" collections during the period of ownership.

There is one other possible tax benefit that the owners of a Section 236 project might be able to realize. If the project is sold at a net profit to the tenants (or a cooperative or other nonprofit organization of the tenants) and the profit is reinvested in another Section 236 project, the capital gains taxes may be indefinitely deferred and the recapture of sales proceeds representing excess depreciation for income taxation can be avoided entirely.[37]

If such sales can be arranged after a few years of ownership, the average annual returns on equity to investors in Section 236 limited distribution projects, from tax savings and cash distributions, could be 25 percent or more. In such instances the 6 to 7 percent greater return than on a nonsubsidized housing project would represent an additional subsidy for low- and moderate-income housing producers who also organize tenant ownership organizations to purchase the property.

Most of the foregoing discussion has been applicable to builder-sponsors who act as limited distribution profit-motivated sponsors. As such, they also are responsible for the provision of adequate project management to "deliver" the subsidized housing service benefits to eligible families. Where there is a nonprofit sponsor, it has to provide management, and only the builder-contractor and/or land supplier makes a profit. In such instances, a failure in management will curtail the value of benefits for tenants and may make the project short-lived, leaving the builder-contractor as the chief beneficiary. Such events have developed where builders have found church groups or other organizations to sponsor a project on land in which the builder has an interest. The number of such cases has been limited, as FHA attempts to screen nonprofit sponsors rigorously.

The maximum contractual assistance payment per unit in Section 236 projects for which FHA mortgage insurance commitments were made from the (fiscal 1969) inception of the program through fiscal

---

37. The excess depreciation represented in the reinvested sales proceeds is subject to recapture upon sale of the new property, although the holding period to avoid recapture is reduced by the period of ownership of the property that has been sold.

year 1971 is about $75 per month.[38] Perspective as to value received for the $75 amount, which is heavily weighted by activity during the calendar 1970 months, can be gained through some comparisons between new Section 207 nonsubsidized unit rents and rents charged to tenants in new Section 236 projects committed in calendar 1970. The median rent for a Section 207 unit was $227 and the median rent to be paid by a Section 236 unit occupant was $139, a difference of $88, or $13 more than the previously mentioned $75 Section 236 per unit subsidy.[39] This would indicate that the Section 236 "market rent," before deduction of subsidy, was also less than Section 207 rent by $13. (The Section 236 "market rent" had not been tabulated.)

Since the mortgage terms are the same and the median per unit mortgage amounts were almost the same—a median of $15,172 for Section 207 and $14,975 for Section 236—there would be (practically) little difference in debt service. About an $800 greater per unit equity investment under 207 would also explain only part of the difference in the establishment of market rents. Most of the difference, therefore, would have to be found in operating and maintenance expenses. The greater incidence of elevator projects under the 207 program and the greater concentration of these projects in large central cities would contribute to higher maintenance and operating costs. In addition, greater market competition to attract renters to nonsubsidized housing might lead to better maintenance, albeit at somewhat increased cost. The $800 greater equity investment, plus $200 greater mortgage amount per unit, adds up to about $1,000 more in per unit capital cost for Section 207 units than for Section 236 units. This is accounted for by somewhat higher land costs and by about 100 additional square feet of living area in the median sized unit in Section 207 projects.[40]

On the whole, the available evidence would suggest that the housing services being obtained through payment of occupant rent plus subsidy is in line with private market rent for equivalent housing. If this observation can be sustained, the low- and moderate-income occupants are the beneficiaries of the housing subsidy payments. Whether the

38. April 30, 1971, HUD table and accompanying text in "HUD–Space-Science Appropriations for 1972," Hearings before a Subcommittee of the Committee on Appropriations, House of Representatives, Ninety-second Congress, First Session, Part 2, Department of Housing and Urban Development, pp. 466–68.

39. These and other unit characteristics are based on data in Tables 57 to 59 and 73 to 75 prepared for the *1970 HUD Statistical Year Book.*

40. We are dealing with added space after the kitchen and plumbing equipment costs are already established, so that the cost per square foot added is lower than total development costs per square foot.

observation can be sustained will depend upon the quality of management during operation, as well as the durability built into the Section 236 projects. Only detailed field investigations or time will tell.

Insofar as the tax benefits arising from accelerated depreciation and capital gains treatment are concerned, they represent a subsidy to the equity investors who are in high income tax brackets. There is no doubt that they have stimulated the production of subsidized multi-family housing. Exclusive of public housing, the production of subsidized new rental housing has increased from 73,000 units in fiscal year 1969 to 162,000 units in fiscal 1970 and was at an estimated level of about 145,000 in fiscal 1971.[41] If the available tax incentives were reduced, it would probably lead to some reduction in production of low- and moderate-income rental housing. However, there are possible alternative means of compensating for such a reduction in tax incentives to high income investors. One alternative would be to fill a higher proportion of the subsidized housing requirements through the homeownership programs where moderate tax benefits would go to the low-income homeowner, rather than to high-income equity investors. Another possibility would be to foster a strengthened, expanded body of nonprofit sponsors. The latter course would entail government expenditures for increased training for and technical assistance to nonprofit sponsors. However, the cost of such activities would probably be less than the tax revenue losses entailed in tax benefits for equity owners of limited distribution projects.

Public Low Rent Housing

There are now several programs to provide low-rent housing under the heading of public housing. The more important of these programs will be treated briefly, to identify variations in the basic subsidy formula and in program mechanisms which affect the net subsidy benefit distribution.

The basic subsidy formula and program mechanism can best be described with regard to the original public housing program, now identified as the "conventional" public housing program. Under this program, a local housing authority acquires the site for a project, has project design plans prepared, and takes competitive bids for construction. There is some hidden subsidy involved in construction financing,

41. Data for 1969 and 1970 are from "Third Annual Report on National Housing Goals," Table A-2, p. 31. The estimate for 1971 is based on preliminary data provided by HUD and FHA.

which is obtained primarily through the sale of short-term, tax-exempt notes by the local housing authorities. The notes are backed by the local housing authority's right to borrow an equal amount from HUD, if necessary. The short-term notes are usually repaid from the proceeds of long-term (forty year), tax-exempt bonds issued by the local authority after the project is completed. Such bonds are, in effect, guaranteed by the United States government through an annual contributions contract between HUD and the local housing authority. It calls for federal annual contributions, up to a maximum amount sufficient to meet the debt service on the bonds. Less than the maximum annual contribution may be required if there are residual receipts from rents charged to the low-income occupants after all operating expenses have been met.

Over the past decade, as project operating costs increased while tenant incomes and rents lagged behind, there were fewer and fewer local authorities with residual receipts, with the result that federal annual contributions approached the contractual maximum for annual contributions. In many local public housing programs operating costs exceeded rental income and local authorities raised rents to avoid insolvency. Initial attempts to cope with the problem consisted of authorizations for an additional subsidy up to $120 per year for units occupied by elderly or handicapped persons, displacees, disaster victims, large families, and very low income families. This proved to be insufficient. Then Congress enacted in 1969, and clarified in 1970, the Brooke Amendment. It stipulates that no public housing tenant should pay more than 25 percent of his income for rent, and it authorizes federal subsidies for operating and maintenance expenses, where needed, to assure the low-rent character of the projects and to achieve and maintain adequate operating and maintenance services.

The federal subsidy thus consists of four parts: (1) annual contributions to pay the debt service on the bonds issued to raise the capital costs; (2) special subsidies for the elderly, handicapped, and so on; (3) additional subsidy for operating expenses and for deferred maintenance, repair, and modernization; and (4) tax-exempt financing benefits. There is also a local contribution of partial tax exemption, as 10 percent of shelter rents collected are paid in lieu of property taxes under cooperation agreements with local governments.

Public housing is the oldest subsidized housing program in the country, established by the United States Housing Act of 1937. By 1971 there were some 965,000 units, and most of them had been built under the conventional public housing program. Federal subsidy payments (excluding the federal cost of tax exempt financing) were estimated at about $675 per unit annually, or $56 monthly for fiscal 1971.[42] This relatively low per unit subsidy reflects the low construction costs of many older projects built over the past thirty-three years and the lower bond interest rates which were prevalent during most of the period. The per unit monthly subsidy payment for public housing units owned by local authorities, for which commitments will be made in fiscal 1972, is estimated at $131, and for leased units at $127.[43]

The latter figures do not take into account the hidden subsidy involved in the tax-exempt financing. Based on an average total per unit development cost of $18,667 in 1970[44] and public housing tax-exempt bond interest rates of about 5.75 percent (in May and July 1971), there is an additional subsidy of $30 per unit per month.[45] Total monthly per unit subsidy cost for current new construction thus would be about $160 per month.

The latter figure is considerably higher than the estimated per unit subsidy of $75 per month under Section 236. However, the public housing occupants have substantially lower incomes and pay substantially lower rent than Section 236 project occupants. Thus, whereas the previously cited median rent in Section 236 projects committed in 1970 was $138, the median gross rent paid by all families moving into public housing in 1969 was $50.[46] The Section 236 median rent, at a 25 percent rent-to-income ratio, reflects an income of $6,624. The median income of the public housing tenants who moved in during 1969 was $2,548. Although the move-ins to public housing were into older as well as new public housing, the incomes would not be measurably different. Nor has the income distribution of public housing occupants changed much from year to year. About two-thirds of those who moved in were receiving assistance or benefits, and the same was true for 95 percent of the elderly and 44 percent of other occupants reexamined for continued occupancy in 1969.[47]

42. Based on HUD data in "Summary of the HUD Budget for Fiscal Year 1972," p. HM-1.

43. Hearing: "HUD–Space-Science Appropriations for 1972," p. 469.

44. HUD table on total development cost per unit for low-rent public housing projects placed under construction in 1970.

45. Total monthly payments over forty years to amortize $18,667 at 5.75 percent would include a total interest cost of $29,073 or $60 per month. Assuming that the holders of tax-exempt bonds are in the 50 percent income tax bracket, the lost revenue is $30 per month.

46. *1969 HUD Statistical Year Book*, LRPH Table 20, p. 208. The actual period is twelve months ending September 30, 1969.

47. Ibid. "Assistance" consists of funds given on the basis of need by organizations, some private, but primarily public. "Benefits" are nonsalary funds, not given on the basis of need by government agencies, and old age, survivor, and disability insurance paid by the Social Security Administration.

Part of the higher subsidy per unit for public housing than for Section 236 housing is, no doubt, due to higher development costs of close to $3,000 per unit. There are probably a number of contributing factors which make for higher average public housing development costs. One of them may be a high concentration of public housing units in high-cost northern localities. A state distribution of public housing units started in 1970 shows New York with the largest percentage, 6.3 percent, Pennsylvania second with 5.8 percent, and Illinois third with 5.5 percent. The comparable state percentages for Section 236 units in projects committed in 1970 were New York 4.2 percent, Pennsylvania 4.3 percent, and Illinois 4.5 percent. About 10 percent of the Section 236 units were in California, which is not a low construction cost state, but well below New York. There may also be somewhat lower economies of scale in public housing which had an average of 96 units per project as compared with 112 units under Section 236.[48]

Per unit land costs are to a large extent a matter of geographic location and require local data to judge their reasonableness. Insofar as national data provide a clue, it is noted that the national average per unit land costs for new public housing in 1970 was $940. Available data on Section 236 average per unit land costs by project show a median of $830. Comparable measures would probably show the figures to be fairly close. As indicated in the discussion of the Section 236 program, the supplier of land can make a substantial capital gain, but there are no data to indicate the degree or frequency of such gains in public housing.

Given the low-income of the public housing occupants and the low rents which they are charged, there can be little question that they are the recipients of a substantial net benefit and represent most of the federal subsidy. The admittedly inadequate land and development cost data which have been scanned do not suggest any significant above-normal market costs for these elements. A substantial amount of local area construction cost and land data for public and comparable private housing would have to be obtained and analyzed to ascertain whether the public housing cost levels account for some of the net subsidy benefits.

There is a question, however, regarding the net benefit incidence of the subsidy involved in the tax-exempt financing which is federally guaranteed through the HUD annual contributions contracts, which assure funds for debt service. The federal subsidy pays virtually the full interest on the bonds (since project residual receipts to reduce

48. HUD tabulations for 1970.

annual contributions below the maximum are negligible), but the federal cost also involves the loss of taxation. The net cost to the federal government would be less if it financed the projects through United States Treasury borrowing. When public housing bonds in 1971 carried about a 5.75 percent interest rate, long-term treasury bonds were yielding about 6.5 percent and could have been sold for about 6.75 percent. The net cost of treasury financing would be reduced to between 3.38 and 4.25 percent, however, assuming that the average marginal income tax rate for the bondholders was between 50 and 33.3 percent. If net federal annual financing-cum-taxation cost is 2 percent greater than necessary, about $20 of the calculated $160 monthly subsidy might be viewed as a result of the financing structure of the program, which channels about one-eighth of the subsidy to the high income holders of tax-exempt bonds.

The matter is complicated by the political aversion to federal capital grants which would greatly raise the total expenditures figure in the annual budget and the federal debt level. As a practical matter, the federal government is just as committed to repayment of the tax-exempt public housing bonds as it would be to repay treasury bonds, and the continuing annual costs are significantly higher. Separate capital budgeting for subsidized housing might help to clarify the matter and make it more acceptable to finance such housing with direct loans from funds borrowed by the treasury.

The tax-exempt financing device is used in the various public housing programs, but other program elements differ. The largest program other than the "conventional" new construction is the "turnkey" method program under which most of the new public housing is now being built. Under this method, local housing authorities invite proposals for the provision of a specified number of public housing units with a given unit size distribution and certain other general characteristics. Any private builder or developer having a site or a structure, or an option to buy, can submit a proposal to the local housing authority to build or rehabilitate in accordance with his prepared plans and specifications. The local authority selects the best proposal and enters into a contract with the builder or developer to purchase the property upon satisfactory completion.

Aside from the avoidance of preparation of plans and issuance of invitations to competitive bidding by the local authority, the chief departure from conventional method is the provision of the site by the builder or developer. Such sites have tended to have a higher per unit cost than conventional public housing sites selected and acquired by local housing authorities. This difference has been more than offset, however, by lower site improvement costs on turnkey project land.[49]

The turnkey developer receives a developer's fee and an overhead allowance, which covers many of the planning and administration costs incurred by the local housing authority under the conventional method. Furthermore, the dwelling construction and equipment costs per square foot of area have been lower under turnkey.[50] It should be noted, however, that there are still significant costs of administration, negotiation, and so on, incurred by the local authority under the turnkey method.

There would appear to be potentials for less time-consuming construction with lower square foot costs under the turnkey method. Whether the savings are reflected in lower subsidy, or whether they result in net subsidy benefits accruing to land suppliers, builders and/ or local housing authorities will depend on (1) turnkey prices negotiated by the local housing authorities and (2) their efficiency in carrying forward such negotiations and other functions in connection with turnkey projects.

A third program or method for provision of low-rent public housing is through leasing. Local housing authorities may lease units in private structures which are made available to low-income families at subsidized rents. The local housing authorities receive annual contributions from HUD which are used to pay the balance of the required rents. The federal subsidy may not exceed the subsidy that would be required for a comparable newly built structure if it were owned by the local housing authority. Leased units are generally in existing structures, but agreements may be made with a builder for new housing to be constructed for lease by the local authority for low-rent public housing. Lease terms, including optional renewals, can be for up to twenty years for new housing and fifteen years for existing housing.

Subsidized rent for privately owned housing focuses attention upon the net subsidy value reflected in equity accumulation. To the extent that value in land and usable structures exceeds unamortized debt on the property, there is an equity accumulation which reflects subsidy payments that have contributed to the capital debt amortization. In public housing owned by a local housing authority, that equity interest accumulates to the benefit of the public body, the local housing author-

49. Based on 1970 average-cost data compiled by the HUD Cost Analysis Section, Low Rent Public Housing Branch.
50. Ibid.

ity. A stock of publicly owned housing to meet low-income rental housing needs is accumulated. In leased private housing, the accumulated equity interest accrues to the property owner in the form of a stock of privately owned housing.

When new private housing is constructed and leased for low-rent public housing, pursuant to a preconstruction agreement with a local housing authority, the property owner can also take advantage of accelerated depreciation tax benefits. The maximum twenty year lease assures rental income on a 100 percent occupancy basis, so that buildings can be held and operated profitably for at least sixteen and two-thirds years, after which all sales proceeds above depreciated book value are taxed at a capital gains rather than at a regular income rate.

The tax benefits are no greater than those available to an owner of nonsubsidized new rental housing. However, the long-term leases remove a great deal of the risk in rental housing investment which creates the need for tax incentives for rental housing production. If the rents nevertheless provide the owner with a return equal to that enjoyed by other rental property owners—and perhaps higher in view of the allowable leases assuring 100 percent occupancy rental income—the rents and supporting subsidy would appear to provide a higher return than warranted by market conditions. To the extent that such higher returns are realized, the property owners are receiving some of the subsidy benefits. A detailed analysis of leased new housing under the public housing program would be required to ascertain whether the property owners are actually obtaining an equal or higher return on their investments than other rental property owners under the negotiated lease agreements.

One other public housing program, which is still small in volume, should be mentioned, that is, the Turnkey III Homeownership program for low-income families. Under this program, an occupant of a dwelling unit owned by a local authority can acquire ownership of the property. He makes monthly payments based on a percentage of his income. His monthly payments are sufficient to cover all operating expenses and reserves, including a budgeted amount for maintenance and repair. The latter amount is credited to a Home Ownership Reserve account set up for him. At the same time, the local housing authority utilizes federal annual contributions to make debt service payments to amortize the capital debt. When the homeowner's income and assets, including the reserve account set up for him, improve so that he can assume ownership with FHA-insured or conventional financing at a price equal to the unamortized capital debt on the structure, he may acquire it at that price. Under this program, therefore, the occupant benefits from the rental housing subsidy while he is a tenant and in addition receives the benefit of the accumulated equity.

The Tandem Plan—Interest Rate Subsidies

The tandem plan originated during the tight money period of 1969 to help provide mortgage financing for the subsidized private housing programs, primarily Sections 235 and 236, which are financed with private FHA-insured mortgages. During this period, lenders required that discount "points" be paid by the builder or developer, or other seller of housing to be financed with FHA-insured loans, in order to increase the yield above the ceiling interest rate on such mortgages. In many instances this would have made it economically infeasible to produce subsidized housing. Under special assistance authority of Section 301 of the National Housing Act, the president could authorize the Government National Mortgage Association (GNMA) to purchase subsidized housing mortgages at par or at modest discounts. However, this would involve very substantial federal outlays—billions of dollars—which would add to budget deficits.

The tandem plan gets around the budgetary problem; GNMA issues a commitment to purchase a Section 235 mortgage, for example at 97, so that the builder would not have to pay more than 3 points (that is, 3 percent of the mortgage amount) when he delivers the mortgage after completion and sale of the house. Simultaneously, GNMA obtains a commitment from the privately owned, federally sponsored Federal National Mortgage Association to purchase the mortgage at its "free market" price. If that price should be less than 97, GNMA would absorb the loss, which might be, for example 2 points, if the free market price were 95. In effect, an additional subsidy is added through this process.

In August 1971, when mortgage discounts were again climbing, the tandem plan was extended to all FHA-insured and VA-guaranteed mortgages up to $22,000 and $24,500, respectively, for homes of four or more bedrooms. Certain FHA-insured multifamily mortgages were also made eligible. Special assistance funds in the amount of $2 billion were made available. In this way, the present FHA and VA 7 percent mortgage interest rate ceiling could be maintained, instead of being raised to a level competitive with other security yields. The financing subsidy was thus made available for "nonsubsidized housing."

The subsidy contributes to the payment of higher effective mortgage interest rates. In one sense, homebuyers and renters are the beneficiaries, since the higher effective interest rates are occasioned by market supply and demand for long-term funds and must be met for the housing to be made available. Viewed in a broader framework, fiscal and monetary policies (and the lack of other credit allocation policies) have permitted the rise in effective interest rates, which in turn causes a redistribution of income in favor of savers and lenders, the creditors. In that framework, the savers and lenders are the beneficiaries of the subsidy distributed via the tandem plan.

Conclusion

Any conclusions about the distribution of housing program subsidy benefits that relate to comparable costs of subsidized and nonsubsidized housing costs are dependent upon the quality of available data. In this paper, therefore, its conclusions related to comparable costs must necessarily be highly qualified.

The greater amount of data available for home ownership than for rental housing programs, though such data are still inadequate, suggests that limited income owners of subsidized new homes receive a high proportion of the subsidy benefits. These include some equity accumulation, as well as part of the current housing expense. A small part of the benefits from a program serving a broad and ready market may go to the housing producers.

Evidence as to comparable costs of unsubsidized and subsidized housing is scarce and tenuous. It provides little basis for judgments as to absorption of housing assistance payments to support greater housing production costs for subsidized housing than for comparable housing that is not subsidized.

Tax benefit incentives in the form of accelerated depreciation are available to producers of all new rental housing, not just for private subsidized rental housing. That tax benefit, therefore, should be viewed as a subsidy for rental housing production in general, rather than specifically for subsidized housing. There is an additional tax benefit for subsidized housing investors, however, in a shorter holding period requirement before all sales proceeds, including those which equal past excess depreciation deductions, are taxed as capital gains, rather than income. Another potential tax benefit can be realized by the owners. If a subsidized private (Section 236) rental project is sold to tenants, even after only a few years of ownership, any sales profits reinvested in a similar project within one year are not subject to regular income taxation.

The availability of many tax benefits to private subsidized rental housing investors suggests that low-income needs can be met at a lower subsidy cost through subsidized home ownership and programs to foster more qualified nonprofit sponsorship of subsidized rental projects.

Low-rent public housing has occupants with a much lower income distribution than other subsidized housing. The rents paid are much lower, making for a much higher monthly subsidy per unit. Per unit development costs in public housing have also been somewhat higher than in other subsidized rental housing, but this may be caused by the differences in geographic distribution of such housing units and by their being somewhat smaller projects (in 1970).

Public housing entails a "hidden" subsidy through financing by tax-exempt local bonds that are virtually federally guaranteed. Direct treasury loans would be less costly to the federal government but would have a greater impact on current budget accounts. The extra interest cost subsidy involved in tax-exempt financing flows to high-income investors in such bonds.

Leased public housing (in private structures) operates so that part of the subsidy which covers capital debt amortization accrues to the private property owner in the form of his housing stock. In publicly owned housing, the stock is retained for public equity ownership. Leased new housing, under the public housing program, gives the private owner the tax benefits available to rental property investors while removing substantially all risk of vacancies for ten to twenty year lease terms.

Financing of private federally subsidized housing through private mortgage lending also entails a higher interest rate than would be entailed through direct federal loans. The latter would have a large impact on current budget accounts, but the impact on the economy would not be significantly different. The differential in interest cost of private over direct loans might be viewed as a subsidy to savers and lenders.

A similar subsidy may be entailed in the "tandem plan" under which the GNMA pays "discount" points above a certain level in the financing of "nonsubsidized" housing with FHA-insured and VA-guaranteed loans. In one sense, the government is helping to pay a higher effective market interest rate than the homebuyer is charged, and this is a subsidy to the homebuyer. In a broader sense, if alternative fiscal and monetary policies or other credit allocation tools could have brought about lower interest rates, then the higher rates in effect might be viewed as causing a subsidy to be paid in favor of savers and lenders.

ACKNOWLEDGMENTS

The author wishes to acknowledge the helpful review and comments of Julius W. Allen and Israel M. Labovitz of the Congressional Research Service.

4 _Richard F. Muth_

CAPITAL AND CURRENT EXPENDITURES IN THE PRODUCTION OF HOUSING

I

When, as a graduate student, I first thought about the matter of housing demand, it seemed quite natural and perhaps even important for some purposes to think of real estate, or land plus structures, and utilities, appliances, and even house furnishings as inputs into the production of housing. In my work to date, however, like almost everyone else, I have treated housing as the output of real estate alone. Recently, though, I came across data described below in Section III relating to the relative costs of real estate services and current inputs in producing housing. Together with other data on sales prices of new single-family houses and the incomes of their buyers, these relative input cost data permit one to analyze the substitution of current inputs for real estate services in housing production.

The substitution of capital for current inputs may have important implications for many issues in housing policy, so my interest in it is more than mere whim or idle curiosity. A common complaint about the federal public housing program, for example, is that such housing is frequently provided in massive high-rise buildings which are poorly maintained. Since the subsidy to public housing has taken the form of a subsidy to capital costs, this is precisely the kind of result an economist would expect. Quantitatively, though, the effects of the subsidy depend upon the ease of substitution of real estate for current inputs in producing housing. Though in Section III I find the elasticity of substitution between them to be rather small, perhaps .2, when coupled with a subsidy to real estate costs of 95 percent, the implications for the public housing program are nonetheless of substantial practical importance. In Section IV I calculate that, because of the form of the subsidy to public housing, real estate inputs per unit of housing are 37 percent greater, current inputs 25 percent smaller, and the resource cost of public housing dwellings about 20 percent greater than they would be if the rental payments of residents of public housing were subsidized directly.

The substitution possibilities of current inputs for real estate in producing housing are also of crucial importance for the short-run supply curve of housing. The latter is of great importance in determining whether general income or rental subsidies will enable their recipients to acquire better housing on the private market or whether these subsidies merely "line the pockets of landlords." The latter view is probably the most common popular and even professional one. However, during the 1950s the quality of the private housing stock improved markedly as incomes rose. (The evidence for this is discussed in my *Cities and Housing*.[1]) In addition, in a recent study Warren Farb has estimated that elasticity of the supply of substandard dwellings relative to the total housing stock is of the order of +10.[2]

The short-run supply curve for housing derived in Section V suggests a means of resolving this apparent conflict. It implies that in the vicinity of long-run marginal housing cost the short-run marginal cost curve is indeed highly inelastic because of the limited substitution possibilities between real estate and current inputs. At rates of output roughly half that associated with long-run marginal cost, or smaller, however, which may well correspond to that in formerly better quality housing converted to lower income occupancy, the short-run marginal cost curve becomes highly elastic.

The implications drawn in this paper are subject to one caveat, perhaps an important one. The data from which my estimates are drawn refer to single-family housing, yet applications I make of these findings refer primarily to multifamily housing. These two types of housing differ principally, however, in the relative proportions of land and structures used in producing real estate. Whether the latter affect the substitutability of larger rooms for more frequent redecorating or more efficient heating systems for fuel is a matter for which I have little feeling. Still, the findings of this paper suggest that, under certain conditions at least, the substitution of real estate for current inputs is too important to be dismissed in considering housing policy issues.

1. Richard F. Muth, *Cities and Housing* (Chicago: University of Chicago Press, 1969) , esp. pp. 124–25 and 280–81.

2. Warren Edward Farb, "An Estimate of the Relative Supply and Demand of Substandard Rental Housing in Major U.S. Cities" (Ph.D. diss., Washington University, 1970) .

II

Before presenting the estimates and implications of my model in later sections, I wish briefly to describe the model here. Let R, the services of real estate or land plus structures, and C, current expenditures, be the inputs used in the production of housing services, Q. The maximum quantity of housing services producible from given inputs of real estate services and current inputs is given by a production function $Q = Q(R,C)$. This function incorporates both technical substitution possibilities and the consumer's willingness to substitute one attribute of the bundle of services called housing for others. Thus, it reflects not only the possibility of using more efficient furnaces and less fuel, but also better heated and lighted rooms instead of larger ones. Q is assumed to be homogeneous of degree one and to possess the usual first and second order differentiability properties of production functions. Later on, in Section IV, I will assume that the production function is of the constant elasticity of substitution variety, or

$$Q = [\alpha R^{-\beta} + C^{-\beta}]^{-1/\beta}$$
$$\text{where } \sigma = 1/(1 + \beta).$$

The empirical results presented in Section III, though, are in no way dependent upon the specific form of the production function.

The annual costs of real estate and current inputs are denoted by r and c, respectively, and housing services are sold at a unit price p, by the owner to himself in the case of owner-occupied housing. I assume further that firms producing housing services are competitive in product and factor markets, so that

$$\frac{\partial Q}{\partial R} = \frac{r}{p} \quad \text{and} \quad \frac{\partial Q}{\partial C} = \frac{c}{p}.$$

Finally, the demand function for housing per family is given by

$$Q = \xi\, p^{\eta_p} y^{\eta_y},$$

where y is income per family. The price and income elasticities of housing demand are η_p and η_y.

Under these conditions it is relatively easy to solve for Q, R, C, and p in terms of given values for r, c, and y.[3] The results which I use here are

$$(rR)^* = \{1 - (k_c\sigma - k_R\eta_p)\}r^* + k_c(\sigma + \eta_p)c^* + \eta_y y^* \text{ and} \qquad (1)$$
$$p^* = k_R r^* + k_c C^*, \qquad (2)$$

3. For the method of derivation see Muth, "The Derived Demand for a Productive Factor and the Industry Supply Curve," *Oxford Economic Papers* 16 (July 1964) : 221–34.

where * designates the logarithmic differential of the variable so designated, σ is the elasticity of substitution of real estate for current expenditures in producing housing, k_R is the relative importance of capital expenditure in producing housing or rR/pQ, and similarly for k_C. (Since Q is homogeneous of degree one, $k_C = 1 - k_R$.) Equation (2) gives the implicit housing price index in terms of the unit prices of real estate and current expenditure and is included here for those readers who might wonder what is meant by p. (Q, of course, is defined by the production function in terms of arbitrary units selected for R and C.) The appropriate housing price index is seen to be a fairly conventional weighted average of input price relatives where the weights are fractions spent upon the input item in question.

Equation (1) is likewise a relatively standard result for the derived demand for a productive factor. It is expressed in expenditure rather than physical units, however, because the basic data used in Section III relate to expenditures on capital inputs. The coefficient of the rental value of real estate is thus one plus the derived demand elasticity for the services of real estate. The latter elasticity is a weighted average of the elasticities of substitution in production and the substitution of housing for other commodities in consumption. The coefficient of the price of current inputs depends upon the algebraic sum of these two elasticities, being positive or negative depending upon whether substitution in production is easier or more difficult than substitution in consumption. Knowing the coefficients of r and c in (1), estimates of σ and η_p may be derived, for

$$\lambda = 1 - k_C\sigma + k_R\eta_p \text{ and}$$
$$\mu = k_c(\sigma + \eta_p)$$

imply

$$\eta_p = \lambda + \mu - 1$$
$$\sigma = -\lambda + (k_R/k_C)\mu + 1.$$

III

The data used for the empirical estimates of this study are from two principal sources. Data on annual costs of real estate and current inputs were obtained from unpublished data on homeowner shelter costs in the spring of 1967 by the Bureau of Labor Statistics. These data were used in preparing estimates of the expenditures necessary to achieve three different standards of living published in BLS Bulletin 1570–5, *Three Standards of Living for an Urban Family of Four Persons* (1969). Data on sales prices of new FHA-insured homes and on the incomes of their buyers in 1966 were obtained from the Federal

Housing Administration.[4] Thirty-two cities were covered by both of these sources.

The BLS data used contain a detailed breakdown of the annual shelter costs of homeowner families at a moderate standard of living. Essentially, they cover the costs of owning and operating a standard or specified kind of house.[5] These costs include the capital costs of acquiring such a house in different cities, property taxes and the homeowner's insurance premium for a specified policy on it, repairs and maintenance, and certain costs of operating the house.[6] The capital costs measure given in the BLS data is mortgage payments on the specified house, purchased in 1959–60 with a fifteen-year first mortgage representing 75 percent of the purchase price. Also included in the BLS data was the estimated market value of the specified house in the spring of 1967.

Based upon my examination, the BLS ownership cost data are probably of as high quality as one might hope to find for a variety of places at a given time. In my judgment, however, they contain one serious conceptual shortcoming. This is the inclusion of mortgage principal repayment in capital costs. Principal repayment is, of course, savings. Its counterpart in the rental value of owner-occupied real estate is interest on the owner's equity. A better measure of home-owner capital costs would thus be interest on the estimated market value of the home.[7] The mortgage interest rate used in the calculations was not obtainable,[8] but it could be estimated from the given

4. U.S. Federal Housing Administration, *FHA Homes, 1966* (Washington, D.C.: Department of Housing and Urban Development, 1967) .

5. As defined in U.S. Bureau of Labor Statistics, *Three Standards of Living for an Urban Family of Four Persons,* BLS Bulletin 1570-5 (Washington, D.C.: U.S. Government Printing Office, 1969) , this is a five or six room house with one or one and one-half baths and fully equipped kitchen, with hot and cold running water, electricity, and central or other installed heating. Such a house was located in a neighborhood with access to public transportation, schools, grocery stores, children's play space, and was "free from hazards and nuisances."

6. Operating costs include those for heating fuel, electricity and gas for non-heating uses; water, sewage and refuse disposal, and replacement for equipment—refrigerator, range and space heaters—where required.

7. Such a measure, of course, neglects possible differences in the homeowner's discount rate and the mortgage rate of interest arising out of limitations on mort-gage loan to value ratios.

8. I was able, however, to obtain estimates of rates on conventional first mortgages in July 1966, for thirteen of the thirty-two cities used here from the Federal Home Loan Bank Board. Using these rates together with the BLS estimated market value of the specified house to estimate capital costs resulted in regression estimates quite similar to those for the equation comparable to (B) , shown in Table 1, for the thirteen cities only.

data on principal and interest payments.[9] The resulting estimated rates, however, ranged from 9 to 10 percent, much too high for mortgages made in 1959–60, though not far from rates prevailing in the latter part of 1966. Because of this last difficulty, I used, alternately, capital cost estimates including the given principal repayment data and interest on the owner's equity as just described. These are designated as CAPTL1 and CAPTL2, respectively, in Table 4.1 and elsewhere in this paper.

Both measures of the rental cost of real estate include property taxes and the homeowner's insurance premium, as well as capital costs. Because of the federal personal income tax saving for homeowners, interest costs, including interest on the owner's equity in CAPTL2, and property taxes were multiplied by .86, which is one minus the first bracket marginal rate. It seemed more reasonable to me to treat expenditures for repairs and maintenance as current expenditures. It might be argued, however, that such expenditures are strongly affected by the amount of real estate used in producing a given level of housing services. For this reason, I defined another measure of the rental cost of real estate, called CAPTL3, which is CAPTL2 plus expenditures for repairs and maintenance. When using CAPTL3, current input expenditures were taken to include only what I called operating costs earlier, designated by OPERTN. When using CAPTL1 or CAPTL2, though, expenditures for repairs and maintenance were added to operating expenditures to obtain the variable CURENT.

The income measure used is that which the FHA terms "total effective income" less federal income taxes. Total effective income is current income adjusted in some unrevealed way, probably for certain transitory income elements. It is by no means clear that such a variable approximates normal or permanent income very closely. In addition, because the FHA imposes a fixed insurance charge, regard-

9. Using a continuous approximation for a level payment, fully amortized loan, where

$B(t)$ = unpaid balance at time t
P = constant rate of payment,
i = mortgage rate of interest, and
T = length of the mortgage loan,

$$B(t) = \frac{P}{i}[1 - e^{-i(T-t)}].$$

Hence,

$$-B'(t) = Pe^{-i(T-t)},$$
$$i = -\frac{1}{(T-t)} \ln[-B'(t)/P].$$

Table 4.1—Some Regression Results

Explanatory Variable	Dependent Variable			
	(Equation)			
	SALPRC			RENTAL
	(A)	(B)	(C)	(D)
Constant	1.60	1.66	1.50	−2.14
	(1.02)	(.92)	(.92)	(.94)
INCOME	.756	.698	.680	.804
	(.104)	(.096)	(.100)	(.098)
CAPTL1	.349	—	—	—
	(.069)			
CAPTL2	—	.363	—	.383
		(.059)		(.060)
CAPTL3	—	—	.370	—
			(.062)	
CURENT	−.179	−.136	—	−.0498
	(.090)	(.078)		(.0798)
OPERTN	—	—	−.0996	—
			(.0617)	
Std. Error of Estimate	.0592	.0533	.0541	.0542
η_p	−.831	−.773	−.729	−.666
	(.096)	(.089)	(.083)	(.091)
σ	.171	.180	.161	.449
	(.268)	(.282)	(.304)	(.286)

Definition of Variables (All variables in natural logs and weighted by the square root of the number of transactions)

SALPRC—Sales price of new, FHA-insured, single-family, owner-occupant homes

RENTAL—SALPRC multiplied by estimated rate of interest plus property tax rate, as described in text

INCOME—FHA adjusted family income of home buyers net of federal income taxes

CAPTL1—Annual cost of capital services defined to include principal repayment, mortgage interest and property taxes net of federal tax deduction, and homeowner insurance premium, from BLS survey data

CAPTL2—same as CAPITL1 except that interest on owner's equity net of federal tax deduction substituted for principal repayment

CAPTL3—CAPTL2 plus repairs and maintenance expenditures

CURENT—Repairs and maintenance expenditure plus OPERTN

OPERTN—Expenditures for heating fuel; electricity and gas for non-heating uses; water, sewage and refuse disposal, and replacement rate for refrigerator, range, and space heater.

less of the terms of the loan and characteristics of the borrower, and because of upper limits on the amount of an FHA-insured mortgage, I would think it probable that the income elasticity estimated, using the FHA income and sales price data, would be downward biased.[10] In addition, if housing prices are positively correlated with income, the estimated housing price elasticity would be biased toward zero as well.

The primary measure of the value of capital inputs used as the dependent variable in the regressions presented is the sales price of single-family, owner-occupant homes, SALPRC. This is the amount stated in the sales agreement, adjusted for any closing costs and other items, exclusive of real estate, borne by the seller. The annual value of capital services used, however, varies as well with the gross rate of return on real estate.[11] As an alternative measure of the annual value of real estate inputs, termed RENTAL, I thus used an estimated gross rate of return on residential real estate multiplied by SALPRC. The gross rate of return was estimated by the sum of the interest rate and property tax rates. The estimated interest rate used was described earlier, while the property tax rate was property taxes paid divided by estimated market value of the BLS specified house.

In the regressions presented in Table 1, all variables are in natural logarithmic form. The FHA data are averages of individual transactions for what essentially are standard metropolitan areas. The number of individual transactions per observation, however, varied

---

10. The reasons are spelled out in more detail in Muth, "The Derived Demand for Urban Residential Land," *Urban Studies* 8 (October 1971) : 243:54.

11. Where

R = annual value of capital services, assumed constant overtime
$V(t)$ = capital value at time t
T = length of life of the asset
i = the rate of interest
τ = property tax rate

$$V(t) = \int_t^T Re^{-i(v-t)} \, dv - \int_t^T \tau V(v)e^{-i(v-t)} \, dv + V(T)e^{-i(T-t)},$$

$$V'(t) = (i + \tau)V(t) - R, \text{ so}$$

$$V(t) = V(T)e^{-(i+\tau)(T-t)} + \frac{R}{(i + \tau)}[1 - e^{-(i+\tau)(T-t)}].$$

As $T \to \infty$ but $V(T) < \infty$

$$V(t) \to \frac{R}{(i + \tau)}.$$

Depreciation is omitted from the above, because repairs and maintenance were treated as current expenditure in the regression where the alternative dependent variable was used.

substantially—from about 30 to 1,000. Since it would seem that the residual variance per individual transaction would be more or less the same, the observations were weighted by the square root of the number of transactions per observation. The standard error of estimate for the regressions reported in Table 1 refers, however, to an observation based on the sample average number of transactions.

Table 1 summarizes the results obtained using alternative measures of the annual value of real estate inputs and their per unit costs. With one major exception, the results obtained using the alternative measures do not differ very much. Judged on purely statistical grounds, equation (B)—using SALPRC as dependent, including interest on owner's equity rather than principal repayment in capital cost and treating expenditures for repairs and maintenance as associated with current rather than real estate inputs—performed best. The standard error of estimate and most of the standard errors of the coefficients are lower for this equation than for any of the others.[12] And, indeed, for all save equation (D), when three regional dummy variables were included to account for possible differences in technology associated with climate, the standard error of the regression actually increased.

In all forms of the equation, the estimated price and income elasticity of housing demand vary from roughly .7 to .8 numerically. All tend to be highly significant statistically but significantly smaller than unity, which I think is much closer to their true values.

I have already indicated why I think these differences result. The one really important difference among the four estimated versions of equation (1) is in the estimated elasticity of substitution. In equations (A) − (C), this parameter is smaller than its standard error and averages about .2. In each case the coefficient of current expenditure cost is significant at about the two-tail 10 percent level or better. In contrast, in equation (D), the coefficient of CURENT is smaller than its standard error, while the estimated elasticity of substitution is about .45 and statistically significant at about the one-tail 5 percent level. While not estimated precisely, I am inclined to conclude that, though smaller numerically than the price elasticity of housing demand, some substitution is possible between real estate and current

12. In (D) the dependent variable, of course, is the log of the gross rate of return plus the log of SALPRC. Hence, it is equivalent to the regression with log of SALPRC dependent and the coefficient of the gross rate of return forced to equal minus one.

inputs in the production of housing. In the following two sections, I will demonstrate that even for σ as small as .2, in certain instances the substitution between current inputs and real estate may have important practical implications for housing policy issues.

IV

In the federal public housing program, as in most housing and in many other governmental subsidy programs, the implicit price to consumers of the service produced has been reduced through a subsidy to capital costs. Long-term financing of public housing projects is through bonds issued by the Local Housing Authority (LHA). These bonds are exempt from federal personal income taxation and, consequently, are issued at rates roughly half those of taxable bonds. More important, the federal government contracts with the LHA to pay 90 percent of the capital costs of the project. Thus, the LHA pays about 5 percent of the opportunity cost of capital for the public housing projects they develop and manage.[13]

In appraising the effects of the interest rate subsidy to public housing, I will make use of the constant elasticity of substitution form of the housing production function mentioned in Section II above. From this function,

$$\frac{R}{Q} = \alpha^{1/\beta} \left[1 + \alpha^{-1} \left(\frac{C}{R} \right)^{-\beta} \right]^{1/\beta}. \tag{3}$$

By equating the ratio of marginal physical products to the factor price ratio and solving,

$$\frac{C}{R} = \alpha^{-1/(1+\beta)} \left(\frac{r}{c} \right)^{1/(1+\beta)}. \tag{4}$$

Substitution of (4) into (3) then yields

$$\frac{R}{Q} = \alpha^{\sigma/(1-\sigma)} \left[1 + \alpha^{-\sigma} \left(\frac{r}{c} \right)^{(\sigma-1)} \right]^{\sigma/(1-\sigma)}. \tag{5}$$

Normalizing by taking $r = c = 1$, (4) also implies $\alpha^\sigma = (k_R/k_C)$.

For the sample used in Section III, the ratio of the geometric

13. Public housing projects are also exempt from real property taxes, but some payments in lieu of taxes are made by the LHA to local governments. I have not been able to determine the effective property tax rate resulting from these arrangements and will neglect property taxes in what follows. The program has been amended recently to permit federal contributions toward current expenditures as well. Most projects, however, were built prior to this change.

means of CAPTL2 and CURENT was approximately 3. Thus, $\sigma = .2$ implies $a = 243$ and (5) becomes

$$\frac{R}{Q} = 3.95 \left[1 + \frac{1}{3} \left(\frac{r}{c} \right)^{-.8} \right]^{.25}.$$ (5′)

On substituting $r = c = 1$ into (5′), $R/Q = 4.24$. For $r = .05$, $c = 1$, however, (5′) implies $R/Q = 5.80$. Thus, assuming that LHA's produce public housing efficiently given the factor prices they must pay, the quantity of real estate and its value at market prices per unit of public housing would be about 37 percent greater because of the way it is financed. Elsewhere I have estimated that building public housing dwellings upon cleared slum land has increased the average capital expenditure per public housing unit by about 21 percent, so together with the interest rate subsidy, the average capital expenditure per unit of public housing would be about two-thirds greater than if no units were built on cleared slum land and rentals subsidized directly.[14] It is not surprising, then, that capital expenditures on public housing seem high, or that public housing is frequently provided in monolithic high-rise structures.

To determine the effects of the interest rate subsidy to public housing on its resource cost, it is necessary to determine this subsidy's effects upon current inputs as well. In essentially the same way as (5) was derived,

$$\frac{C}{Q} = \left[\alpha^\sigma \left(\frac{r}{c} \right)^{1-\sigma} + 1 \right]^{\sigma/(1-\sigma)},$$ (6)

so for $a = 243$, $\sigma = .2$,

$$\frac{C}{Q} = \left[3 \left(\frac{r}{c} \right)^{.8} + 1 \right]^{.25}.$$ (6′)

Consequently, for $r = c = 1$, $C/Q = 1.41$, but for public housing where $r = .05$, $C/Q = 1.06$. The interest rate subsidy to public housing would thus reduce the use of current inputs in public housing production by about 25 percent, which is certainly consistent with the frequent complaint that public housing is poorly maintained. For either set of factor prices the opportunity cost of the resources used is $r = c = 1$. Thus, the resource cost of the public housing program is $(6.86/5.66 - 1)$ $100 = 21$ percent greater than it would be if the LHA were to bear the full capital costs of public housing, but the rental payments of public housing residents were subsidized.

14. Richard F. Muth, "The Derived Demand for Urban Residential Land," *Urban Studies* 8 (October 1971) : 252–53.

Stated differently, under an equivalent rental subsidy, roughly five public housing units could be provided for the same resource cost as four are under the interest subsidy.

Assuming that rental payments of public housing tenants cover the costs which LHA's must bear, it is fairly easy to determine the housing price subsidy to tenants which results from the interest rate subsidy. Substituting (5) and (6) into $p = r(\frac{R}{Q}) + c(\frac{C}{Q})$ yields

$$p = (\alpha^\sigma r^{1-\sigma} + c^{1-\sigma})^{1/(1-\sigma)}. \tag{7}$$

Inserting the values used above for a and σ, (7) becomes

$$p = (3r^{.8} + c^{.8})^{1.25}. \tag{7'}$$

For $r = c = 1$, $p = 5.66$, while for $r = .05$, $c = 1$, $p = 1.35$. Consequently, the interest rate subsidy by itself reduces the unit price of housing services to public housing tenants by about three-quarters.

V

The nature of the substitution possibilities between real estate and current inputs in the production of housing also has important implications for the private market's short-run supply curve of housing. By short-run supply, I mean the variation in the rate of output of housing services that results from varying the level of current inputs but holding real estate inputs constant. The nature of this response, in turn, is critical in determining the effects of income or rental subsidies on the housing consumption of their recipients as well as for the effects of policies such as rent control on private housing output from the controlled housing stock.

The short-run marginal cost function for producers of housing is

$$\frac{\partial K}{\partial Q} = c / \frac{\partial Q}{\partial C} = cQ^{-(1+\beta)}C^{(1+\beta)}. \tag{8}$$

From the production function itself

$$C = [Q^{-\beta} - \alpha \bar{R}^{-\beta}]^{-1/\beta}, \tag{9}$$

where $\bar{R}$ is the fixed level of real estate inputs. Consequently, substitution of (9) into (8) gives

$$\frac{\partial K}{\partial Q} = c[1 - \alpha\rho^{(1-\sigma)/\sigma}]^{-1/(1-\sigma)}, \tag{10}$$

where $\rho = Q/\bar{R}$. From (10) it is easy to see that marginal cost is an increasing function of Q. Further, short-run marginal cost approaches

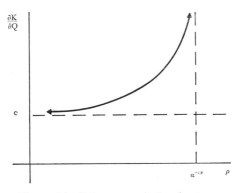

Figure 4.1—Private market's short-run
supply curve of housing.

c asymptotically as Q goes to zero and plus infinity as Q goes to $a^{-1/\beta}$. Its qualitative properties are shown in Figure 4.1. Thus, regardless of the values for a and σ, the short-run marginal cost function is very flat for small enough outputs and very steep for large ones.

The practical implications of the shape of the short-run marginal cost function for housing output depends critically upon where along this function the market is operating. This can be determined in part by substituting the values $a = 243$, $\sigma = .2$ and $c = 1$ Section III into (10), yielding

$$\frac{\partial K}{\partial Q} = [1 - 243\rho^4]^{-1.25}. \tag{10'}$$

This function, in turn, is tabulated in Table 4.2. The upper asymptote to the flow of housing services per unit of real estate is .253. Long-run marginal cost as determined from equation (7') is 5.66, and the flow of services per unit of real estate is .236 at this level of marginal cost. In addition, reducing the rate of flow of housing services in the short-run by about 15 percent from the long-run level reduces short-run marginal cost by about two-thirds. Thus, in the neighborhood of long-run marginal cost, the short-run marginal cost and supply function for housing services tends to be quite inelastic. Though rent control may provide an incentive for landlords to reduce their expenditures on current inputs and such reductions may give the appearance of physical deterioration, controls would appear to have relatively little effect on the rate of flow of housing services in controlled dwellings over fairly wide limits.

Table 4.2—Short-Run Marginal Cost Function for Housing

p	$\partial K / \partial Q$
.253	∞
.236	5.66[a]
.2	1.85
.15	1.18
.1	1.03
.05	1.002
0	1.

[a] Long-run marginal cost assuming $r = c = 1$.

On the other hand, as the flow of housing services becomes small enough, the private market, short-run supply becomes highly elastic. At a rate of output which is about half the long-run equilibrium rate, short-run marginal cost is only about 10 percent above its lower asymptote. One circumstance of decided practical importance where the private market may be operating in this range is the case of slum housing or private lower-income housing generally. Such housing in cities of the United States is rarely newly built as such. Rather it is typically produced by converting higher-income housing, partly through actual physical conversion of larger to smaller dwellings and partly through reducing expenditures for repairs, maintenance, and operation. If such conversions of higher- to lower-income housing reduce the flow of housing services per unit of real estate far enough —and a reduction by one-half is by no means unlikely in some instances, I feel—then the private market's supply may indeed be in the highly elastic range. Even if such were the case, econometric measurements, if made in the vicinity of long-run equilibrium would never reveal this fact. In the elastic range of the short-run supply function, of course, rental or general income subsidies to lower-income families would tend substantially to improve their consumption of housing services, there being little dissipation of the subsidy in the form of higher unit housing prices even in the short-run.

ACKNOWLEDGMENTS

I wish to thank Charles Levin and Jerome Rothenberg for their comments during an earlier oral presentation of this material.

5 *Robert F. Boxley and William D. Anderson*

THE INCIDENCE OF BENEFITS FROM COMMODITY PRICE-SUPPORT PROGRAMS:
A CASE STUDY OF TOBACCO

The flue-cured tobacco price-support program, along with most other parts of current agricultural price support and production adjustment programs, has its roots in the economic crises leading to the Great Depression of the 1930s. Economic difficulties for the agricultural sector actually began with the collapse of commodity prices following World War I.[1] Throughout the 1920s and 1930s the federal government undertook a number of steps of increasing directness and intensity in an effort to reverse the decline in farm prices and income.[2] Public support for these efforts was based on a number of considerations, including the presumed contribution of a strong agricultural sector to overall economic recovery and the judgement that farmers as farmers were deserving of help. This judgement, and the implied policy prescription of redistributing income from nonfarmers to farmers,[3] was based on the proposition that farmers were generally

1. Murray R. Benedict, *Farm Policies of the United States 1790–1950* (New York: The Twentieth Century Fund, 1953), pp. 171–206; Chester C. Davis, "The Development of Agricultural Policy Since the End of the World War," in American Farm Economic Association, *Readings on Agricultural Policy* (Philadelphia: The Blakiston Company, 1949), pp. 56–75.

2. For a concise discussion of the development of price-support legislation, see *A Brief History of the Committee on Agriculture and Forestry United States Senate and Landmark Legislation 1825–1970*, S. Doc. No. 91–107, 91st Cong., 2d sess., 1970, p. 31 [hereafter cited as *A Brief History*].

3. James T. Bonnen, "The Absence of Knowledge of Distributional Impacts: An Obstacle to Effective Public Program Analysis and Decisions," *The Analysis and Evaluation of Public Expenditures: The PPB System*, I, 438, 91st Cong., 1st sess. (Joint Committee Print, 1969) (a compendium of papers submitted to the Subcommittee on Economy in Government).

poor and, as a group, received less for their labor and resources than nonfarmers. Thus, the concept of "parity" evolved as a policy objective and it continues to be a dominant goal.[4]

Early farm policy debates and empirical economic studies focused on questions of how parity was to be obtained. However, the issues also attracted the attention of economists interested in the distributional consequences of the programs within the agricultural sector. Today much of our knowledge of the nature and incidence of benefits from governmental programs of all types can be traced to early studies of agricultural programs.

Many of the pioneering investigations into the distribution of farm program benefits were of the flue-cured tobacco price support and acreage allotment program.[5] Research on this program has been facilitated by the fact that it has operated essentially unchanged and uninterrupted since the late 1930s. In addition, flue-cured tobacco production is geographically concentrated. This has aided empirical inquiry and prompted research by state and regional groups.[6] Because of the program continuity and research investment, we can now piece together a relatively detailed view of the program and its effect on farm operators, landlords and laborers, and on the regional economies of flue-cured tobacco production areas.

Tobacco Production: The Institutional Setting

In the United States, tobacco is grown in at least eighteen states. Production ranges from the speciality cigar binder and wrapper tobaccos of the Connecticut valley and Wisconsin to the perique to-

4. Parity, in its original sense, would restore to farmers purchasing power equivalent to that of agriculture's "golden age," 1910 to 1914, a period in which agriculture experienced unusually favorable terms of trade with the rest of the economy. (The base period for tobacco was 1919–1929.) Subsequently, policy discussions have focused on parity of income, as well as parity of price. For general reading, see John D. Black, "The Evolution of Parity," and H. R. Wellman et al., "On the Redefinition of Parity Price and Parity Income," both in *Readings on Agricultural Policy*, pp. 91, 203; *A Brief History*, p. 35.

5. For a brief summary of the economic studies of the flue-cured tobacco program through 1968, see James A. Seagraves, "Capitalized Values of Tobacco Allotments and the Rate of Return to Allotment Owners," *Am. J. Agric. Econ.* 51 (May 1969): 320–34; see esp. p. 320 n. 1.

6. Primarily by the Virginia and North Carolina Agricultural Experiment Stations and by the Agricultural Policy Institute, North Carolina State University. Regional research has been sponsored by the Southern Land Economics Research Committee. The Economic Research Service, U.S. Department of Agriculture, has cooperated in much of this work.

bacco production of Louisiana. In total, about 625,000 farm families derive income from the production of some type of tobacco.[7] Flue-cured tobacco is the dominant type produced in the United States and it accounted for about 63 percent of total tobacco acreage and 58 percent of total tobacco production in 1969. Burley is the next most important tobacco type.[8]

Compared to other farm marketings, flue-cured tobacco is a relatively minor cash crop; receipts from flue-cured tobacco sales in 1969 made up less than 4 percent of total farm receipts from crop sales in that year. Tobacco sales are quite important, however, in the few areas where production is concentrated; it also is an important export crop.

Characteristics of Tobacco Producing Regions

North Carolina is, by far, the leading state in the production of flue cured tobacco, followed by Virginia, South Carolina, Georgia, and Florida. Most flue-cured tobacco is produced in two areas: the coastal plains of North Carolina and the Piedmont of North Carolina and Virginia. These two flue-cured tobacco areas are among the most heavily populated rural areas in the United States.[9] The coastal plain in particular is ideally situated with regard to soil, climate, and labor supply for intensive cultivation of flue-cured tobacco. The area contained 38,427 farms with tobacco allotments in 1968. The average allotment was 4.55 acres, with 30 percent of the allotments less than 2 acres and 65 percent less than 4 acres (Table 5.1).

The Piedmont is the nation's oldest growing belt for flue-cured tobacco and is also the center of the processing and cigarette manu-

7. Economic Research Service, U.S. Department of Agriculture, *Tobacco Situation,* TS-136 (Washington, D.C.: Government Printing Office, June 1971), p. 29 [hereafter cited as *Tobacco Situation*].

8. U.S., Department of Agriculture, *Agricultural Statistics, 1970* (Washington, D.C.: Government Printing Office, 1970); the production of burley tobacco is a major source of farm income in Kentucky and Tennessee and in parts of West Virginia, Virginia, and North Carolina. The burley program operates in the same manner and under the same basic legislation as the flue-cured tobacco program and the economic effects of the two programs have been comparable.

9. These areas correspond to Census of Agriculture Sub-Regions 17 and 18. Tobacco is also produced in some Tidewater counties of North Carolina (Census Sub-Region 15). For a full definition of commonly used area designations, see Economic Research Service, *Potential Mechanization in the Flue-Cured Tobacco Industry with Emphasis on Human Resource Adjustment,* Agric. Econ. Rpt. no. 169 (Washington, D.C.: Government Printing Office, 1969), pp. 4, 1 [hereafter cited as *Potential Mechanization*].

Table 5.1—Distribution of Flue-Cured Tobacco Allotments, by Size Groups, Coastal Plains, North Carolina; and Piedmont, North Carolina and Virginia, 1968.

Size of allotment	Percentage of all farms	
	Coastal plains	Piedmont
Acres:		
Less than 2.00	30.4	40.1
2.01 to 4.00	34.5	35.7
4.01 to 6.00	15.0	13.0
6.01 to 8.00	7.5	5.2
8.01 to 10.00	4.0	2.4
10.01 to 20.00	6.4	2.9
20.01 to 50.00	1.9	0.6
Over 50.00	0.3	a
Total	100.0	100.0

Source: Economic Research Service, *Potential Mechanization in the Flue-Cured Tobacco Industry with Emphasis on Human Resource Adjustment*, Agric. Econ. Rpt. no. 169 (Washington, D.C.: Government Printing Office, 1969), pp. 21–22.

a Less than 0.1 percent.

facturing industries. The Piedmont, relative to the coastal plain, has more uneven terrain and farms are smaller. Allotments also are smaller, averaging 3.25 acres, with 40 percent under 2 acres and 76 percent under 4 acres. In 1968 there were about 45,000 farms with tobacco allotments in the Piedmont.

The current organization of tobacco farm units, particularly in the coastal plains, is a legacy from the break-up of the plantation system. Tobacco cultivation requires high labor inputs and thus encourages production units scaled to labor supply. Even today, farms —whether owner-operated or sharecropper units—tend to be organized around family labor and hence tend to be small. The Piedmont area is characterized by small owner-operator farms or single-cropper units. In the coastal plains, farms tend to be larger and to have developed more multiple-cropper units.[10]

10. Rupert B. Vance, "Human Factors in the South's Agricultural Readjustment," *Law and Contemp. Prob.* 1 (1933–34) : 259–74; see esp. pp. 262–66. Although details may vary, sharecropping generally refers to a form of tenancy where the landlord supplies the land and workstock and perhaps a share of the seed and fertilizer; the tenant supplies mainly his labor, and output is shared in agreed proportions. A multiple-cropper unit refers to a landlord's holding that has been subdivided into more than one cropper unit (pp. 267, 268). Here the terms tenants and sharecroppers will be used interchangeably.

Table 5.2—Distribution of White and Negro Tobacco Farm Operators by Gross Farm Sales, 1964 (Percent) *

Sales class	White	Negro	All
$10,000 and over	28.8	12.7	24.3
$5,000 to $9,999	30.6	37.6	32.5
$2,500 to $4,999	25.0	31.3	26.8
Less than $2,500	15.6	18.4	16.4
All	100.0	100.0	100.0

Source: U.S. Department of Commerce, Bureau of the Census, *United States Census of Agriculture: 1964*, vol. 1, *Statistics for the State and Counties*, pt. 24, Virginia; pt. 26, North Carolina.

* Data refer to commercial farms, defined as farms with gross sales of $2,500 or more, or as farms with sales of $50 to $2,499 where the operator was under 65 years of age and did not work off-farm more than 100 days during the year. These data are available at the state level only and include some tobacco farms outside Census Sub-Regions 17 and 18.

Both areas traditionally have had high rates of farm tenancy. In 1964, almost 40 percent of farm operators in the Piedmont and coastal plain were classified as tenants.[11] Another 25 percent (classified as part owners) operated both owned and rented land. Slightly over 25 percent of the farm operators were Negroes. Gross sales from tobacco farms are relatively low but more evenly distributed than for other types of farms in Virginia and North Carolina (Table 5.2). In 1964 less than a fourth of the commercial tobacco farm operators reported sales of more than $10,000.[12] Most farms did not greatly exceed the $10,000 sales level; only 552 farms (less than 1 percent of all commercial tobacco farms) had sales of more than $40,000. Nationally, over 40 percent of all commercial farms had sales of more than $10,000 in 1964, and 7 percent had sales of more than $40,000.

11. U.S. Department of Commerce, Bureau of the Census, *United States Census of Agriculture: 1964*, vol. 1, *Statistics for the State and Counties*, pt. 24, Virginia, pt. 26, North Carolina.

12. The conventional sharecropping arrangement in the area is one-third of returns to the landowner and two-thirds to tenants, and this share ratio has remained unchanged over time. Assuming the tenant supplies mainly labor and "downward" mobility in tenure status (for example, full owner-operators have the option of renting some or all land they operate), then the economic class data for tobacco farms can be approximately translated into a net labor return equivalent at two-thirds of gross sales. J. L. Hedrick, G. S. Tolley, and W. B. Back, *Effects of Flue-Cured Tobacco Programs on Returns to Land and Labor*, ERS-379 (Washington, D.C., June 1968), p. 7.

Negro farm operators do not fare quite so well in the distribution of gross sales as whites. In particular, fewer Negro operators have sales over $10,000 (Table 5.2). Nevertheless, the divergences in gross sales distributions by race are considerably less than can be observed for white and Negro farmers engaged in other types of agriculture.[13]

Nature of the Flue-Cured Tobacco Program

Modern tobacco control programs grew out of the major swings in production and prices for tobacco in the early years of this century, although earlier efforts by government to control tobacco production date to the colonial period.[14] The precursor to federal intervention in tobacco production and marketing was the agricultural cooperative movement of the early 1900s which, in the tobacco regions, emerged largely in response to the extreme concentration of buyer power in the industry. The cooperatives attempted to counter this concentration by means of five-year supply control contracts with producers.[15]

Geographic concentration of production facilitated the organization of cooperatives, and by the early 1920s the three largest cooperatives in the United States were tobacco cooperatives. In terms of supply control, the Burley Tobacco Growers Cooperative Association was the most successful, controlling 70 percent of the 1922–23 crop. The Tri-State Association, which operated in the flue-cured tobacco area, was never as successful. In particular, it had trouble controlling the production of its members and production by nonmembers increased significantly.[16]

Efforts were made in the early 1930s to promote cooperatives under the Agricultural Marketing Act of 1929, but these efforts also failed. The experience with tobacco cooperatives appears, however, to have

13. There were about 31,000 Negro operators of commercial farms in Virginia and North Carolina in 1964. Of this number, 22,710 were tobacco farmers.

14. W. D. Toussaint, "Alternative Production Control Programs," in *The Tobacco Industry in Perspective,* API Series 11 (Raleigh: Agricultural Policy Institute North Carolina State University, 1964), p. 155; John Hanna, "Agricultural Cooperation in Tobacco," *Law and Contemp. Prob.* 1 (1933–34) : 292–324; see esp. p. 293.

15. From 1903 until 1911, when a Supreme Court decision required dissolution of the company, there was essentially only one buyer of tobacco in the chief producing areas of the United States. Efforts to gain producer power in the market eventually led to substantial acts of violence attempting to terrorize nonmembers of cooperatives and the tobacco manufacturing trust. Hanna, "Agricultural Cooperation," pp. 302, 303.

16. For example, in Georgia where the association did not operate, production increased from 6 million pounds in 1922 to approximately 40 million pounds in 1926. Ibid., p. 317.

impressed farmers with the need for joint action and probably explains the broad support for the federal programs that were to follow.[17]

The first attempt by the federal government to control flue-cured tobacco production came under the Agricultural Adjustment Act of 1933. Under the act, tobacco growers could contract with the Agricultural Adjustment Administration to limit production in return for payments to be made from proceeds of a general processing tax. In addition, the government made a rental payment for acreage taken out of production. Between December 4, 1933, and April 1, 1934, about 98 percent of the growers in the five principal flue-cured tobacco states signed production adjustment contracts.[18]

Despite the high level of voluntary cooperation at the outset of the program, there was concern that participation would drop if noncontracting growers continued to receive the benefits of higher prices without bearing the burden of restricting production. This concern led to the Kerr-Smith Tobacco Act of 1934 which added to the general processing tax of the 1933 act a specific levy of 33.3 percent on the "first" sale of tobacco by noncooperators under the federal program.[19] The Kerr-Smith Tobacco Act was repealed following the Supreme Court decision in *United States* v. *Butler*[20] which invalidated the general processing tax under the Agricultural Adjustment Act of 1933.

During 1936 and 1937 the only federal program for controlling flue-cured tobacco production was the Soil Conservation and Domestic Allotment Act of 1936.[21] Under this act payments were made for diverting acreage used in the production of soil-depleting crops to soil-conserving crops and for carrying out soil conservation practices. Tobacco was

17. R. Charles Brooks and J. C. Williamson, Jr., *Flue-Cured Tobacco Programs 1933–1958*, A. E. Inf. Series no. 66 (Raleigh: Dept. of Agric. Econ., North Carolina State College, 1958) , p. 14.

18. For a detailed description and analysis, see Joseph G. Knapp and L. R. Paramore, "Flue-Cured Tobacco Developments Under the AAA," *Law and Contemp. Prob.* 1 (1933–34) : 325–49; see esp. pp. 325, 341–44, 347.

19. David F. Cavers, "Production Control by Taxation," *Law and Contemp. Prob.* 1 (1933–34) : 349–61; see esp. pp. 349, 359. The Secretary of Agriculture had the option of setting a lower rate, but not less than 25 percent.

20. 297 U.S. 1 (1936) . The decision in the Butler case thwarted efforts by Congress to control agricultural production by means of the taxing power under the Constitution. However, because of the repeal of the Kerr-Smith Tobacco Act, the so-called "penalty tax" issue was not decided at that time. See generally, Elbert P. Tuttle, "Control of National Agricultural Production and Consumption Through Taxation," *Cornell Law Quarterly* 23 (1938) : 117–30.

21. Brooks and Williamson, *Tobacco Programs 1933–1958*, pp. 26–29.

designated as a soil-depleting crop. The current program legislation, which started with the Agricultural Adjustment Act of 1938, incorporated amendments to the Soil Conservation and Domestic Allotment Act and these remain as an operative element in the price support program.

A major feature of the 1938 act as it affects tobacco was the introduction of marketing quotas aimed at restricting production and the provision of civil penalties for growers who exceeded marketing quotas.[22] The national marketing quota, proclaimed by the Secretary of Agriculture, must be approved by a two-thirds favorable vote in a referendum of farmers engaged in the production of tobacco in the preceding year.[23] Farmers have approved the marketing quotas in every referendum except 1939.[24]

In general, the national marketing quota is allocated among the states on the basis of prior production. State quotas, in terms of poundage, are converted to state acreage allotments.[25] The state marketing quota and acreage allotment is then allocated through local committees to individual farms based on each farm's history of tobacco production.

Before 1965, the limit on production by individual farms was solely in terms of acreage allotments. This created incentives to substitute other factors of production for land, and the per-acre yields increased dramatically. The yield increases, in turn, required compensating cuts in state and individual acreage allotments and created further incentives to adopt yield-increasing technology. Tobacco quality also suffered since producers had incentives to market all of the plant, regardless of grade.[26] To counter these forces, the flue-cured tobacco program was shifted to an acreage-poundage program in 1965.[27]

22. Ibid., p. 30.

23. The constitutional issues and administrative aspects of the legislation are discussed by Neil Brooks and Donald A. Campbell, "Marketing Quotas Under the Agricultural Adjustment Act of 1938," *Geo. Wash. L. Rev.* 26 (1958) : 255–75 [a symposium issue on the regulatory functions of the Department of Agriculture].

24. U.S. Department of Agriculture, Agricultural Stabilization and Conservation Service, *Results of Tobacco Quota Referenda* (Washington, D.C., May 1971) . Quotas are set for each of three successive marketing years.

25. U.S. Department of Agriculture, Agricultural Stabilization and Conservation Service, *Farm Commodity and Related Programs*, Agric. Handbook no. 345 (Washington, D.C.: Government Printing Office, 1967) , p. 28.

26. William O. Shofner, "Market Behavior, 1964–1967," *Tobacco Mechanization and Marketing*, API Series 29 (Raleigh: Agricultural Policy Institute, North Carolina State University, 1968) , p. 68.

27. Agricultural Stabilization and Conservation Service, *ASCS Commodity Fact Sheet: 1971 Flue-Cured Tobacco* (June 1971) , p. 1.

Originally the allotment was tied exclusively to the farm or to the land and not the owner or operator.[28] However, in 1962 the legislation was amended to provide for the lease and transfer of flue-cured tobacco allotments on an annual basis to an owner or operator of a farm in the same county that also had a current flue-cured tobacco allotment, subject to a specific acreage limitation on the amount leased.[29] With some modifications, leasing continues to be a significant aspect of the program.[30]

The price support feature of the program for flue-cured tobacco establishes minimum prices (based on a parity formula) for each grade of tobacco. Tobacco buyers must pay at least 1 cent per pound above the support price to acquire a given lot of tobacco. If such a price is not bid, the grower receives the support price, and the tobacco passes into the hands of the Flue-Cured Tobacco Cooperative Stabilization Corporation. This is a producer organization that handles, processes, stores, and offers for resale flue-cured tobacco acquired under the price support program. Flue-cured tobacco received by the Stabilization Corporation has ranged from 4.2 to 22.6 percent of net sales in the marketing seasons since 1960.[31]

Program Effects on Land Values

Since the times of Ricardo and Marshall, economists have had the necessary theoretical tools to predict the consequences of an output control program that limits access to a formerly competitive industry. In the Agricultural Adjustment Acts of 1933 and 1938, land was generally designated as the access point. In the case of flue-cured tobacco, access to the benefits of price supports was made conditional on possession of the right to produce as embodied in the acreage allotment. Since the allotments were originally distributed to production units, or

28. Brooks and Campbell, "Marketing Quotas," p. 262.

29. David Westfall, "Agricultural Allotments as Property," *Harv. L. Rev.* 79 (1966) : 1180–1206; see esp. pp. 1180, 1199, 1200. Legal scholars have been particularly interested in the trend toward authorizing the transfers of allotments separate from the land because the effect is to create a new and valuable type of intangible property from what was originally a regulatory device. See also, Charles A. Reich, "The New Property," *Yale L. J.* 73 (1964) : 733–87; and Brainerd S. Parrish, "Cotton Allotments: Another 'New Property,'" *Texas L. Rev.* 45 (1967) : 734–53.

30. See generally, *Potential Mechanization*, p. 8. In 1970, producers leased about one-fifth of the total poundage quota and the prospects were that the proportion would increase. *Tobacco Situation*, p. 14.

31. *Potential Mechanization*, p. 8.

farms, possession of the right was ultimately conveyed to the owner of the unit, whether owner-operator or landlord.

There can be little doubt that the various production adjustment and price support actions of the 1930s substantially improved the lot of the typical farm operator or that the high price-support levels of the immediate post–World War II years helped cushion the readjustment from a war-time economy. In the case of flue-cured tobacco, the strongly favorable producer support of the program is, in itself, presumptive evidence that benefits have arisen under the program.[32] There is also strong evidence that, over roughly comparable pre- and post-program periods, the tobacco program has resulted in both higher long-run average prices and greater price stability.[33] For a commodity that has been plagued by overproduction and widely gyrating prices since colonial times, this latter achievement should not be minimized.[34]

Empirical Studies of Allotment Capitalization

As early as 1945, evidence of capitalization of tobacco allotments in the burley and flue-cured tobacco producing regions was accumulating. Mason, studying sales handbills, advertisements, land deeds and contracts, concluded that farms sold with tobacco allotments in 1945 were enhanced in market value by $300 to $600 per allotment acre.[35] During the fifties, awareness of agricultural program effects on land values in-

32. Since the referendum of 1946, favorable votes have exceeded 95 percent for every triennial referenda except 1965, when producers first voted on acreage-poundage controls. Agricultural Stabilization and Conservation Service, U.S.D.A., *Results of Tobacco Quota Referenda.*

33. Frank H. Maier, James L. Hedrick, and W. L. Gibson, Jr., *The Sale Value of Flue-Cured Tobacco Allotments,* Tech. Bull. no. 148 (Blacksburg: Agricultural Experiment Station, Virginia Polytechnic Institute, 1960), compared flue-cured tobacco prices prior to the program (1909 to 1916 and 1921 to 1929) with those during the program (1940 to 1942 and 1947 to 1958) and found that the average real annual prices (1947 to 1949 dollars) was $0.46 per pound during the program compared with $0.31 per pound prior to the program. The coefficient of variation was 9.1 percent during the program compared with 19.7 percent prior to the program; which is evidence that the program contributed to price stability.

34. Seagraves presents evidence that, through 1962, tobacco prices since World War II have generally stayed within a range of 50 to 70 cents per pound, in constant 1957 to 1959 dollars. Net revenues per pound of tobacco also have remained fairly stable within a range of 15 to 35 cents per pound. Of course, net revenue *per acre* increased steadily as yields increased during this period, but the net revenue of a given size farm remained fairly constant as the number of allotted acres was reduced. Seagraves, "Capitalized Values of Tobacco Allotments," p. 324.

35. John B. Mason, "Acreage Allotments and Land Prices," *J. Land & P. U. Econ.* 23 (May 1946): 176–81.

creased generally.[36] In the early 1960s Maier, Hedrick, and Gibson completed a landmark study of the tobacco program's effect on land values. Using multiple regression techniques to analyze actual farm sales in several flue-cured production regions of Virginia and North Carolina, they obtained estimates of allotment values ranging from $962 to $1,290 per acre in 1954 to $1,673 to $2,500 per acre in 1957, depending on the relative importance of tobacco production to the farm economy of the study areas. A major part of the rise in allotment values between 1954 and 1957 was attributed to a one-third reduction in individual allotment acreages that occurred during this period.[37]

Seagraves, in 1969, used econometric techniques to estimate net revenue and capitalized values of the right to produce a pound of flue-cured tobacco for each year from 1934 through 1962 in eastern North Carolina. His results indicate that, in constant dollars, net revenues from tobacco production were relatively constant between 1934 and 1962, increasing from an average of 19.2 cents per pound of tobacco in the first decade of the program to 25.6 cents per pound for 1943 to 1952, and falling to 23.7 cents per pound in the third decade. Capitalized values, on the other hand, steadily increased from 34.5 cents per pound of tobacco to $1.51 per pound in the last decade studied. Seagraves attributes the continued rise in capitalized values of allotments over the decades of 1943 to 1952 and 1953 to 1962, relative to near constant net revenues, to increasing confidence in program continuation and to the possibility that buyers and sellers of farms only gradually become aware of the high net incomes possible from tobacco. In current dollars, his estimates of capitalized values per pound of tobacco were equivalent to per acre values ranging from $92 in 1934 to $3,281 in 1962.[38]

Subsequent studies have reported estimated allotment values consistent with those found by Seagraves and Maier et al. A study in South Carolina,[39] for example, estimated a flue-cured tobacco allotment to be

36. See, for example, Calvin B. Hoover and B. V. Ratchford, *Economic Resources and Policies of the South* (New York: Macmillan Company, 1951), pp. 356–60; and Murray R. Benedict and Oscar C. Stine, *The Agricultural Commodity Programs* (New York: The Twentieth Century Fund, 1956), p. 87.

37. Maier, Hedrick, and Gibson, *Sale Value of Flue-Cured Tobacco Allotments,* p. 3. All estimates were of the value of the allotment separate from the value of any associated cropland.

38. Seagraves, "Capitalized Values of Tobacco Allotments," p. 328.

39. Henry C. Gilliam, Jr., and John W. Hubbard, *An Analysis of Agricultural Land Values in Selected Cotton-Producing Counties of the South Carolina Coastal Plain,* Bull. 554 (Clemson: South Carolina Agricultural Experiment Station, Clemson University, 1971).

worth $3,100 an acre in 1963–64. Westfall in 1966 reported the results of a survey he conducted of attorneys, bank officers, and landowners which yielded estimates ranging between $3,000 and $5,000 per acre.[40] Comparable levels of capitalization have also been observed under the acreage allotment programs for peanuts and for burley tobacco.[41]

Policy Implications of Capitalization

The early evidence that benefits from the tobacco program were being capitalized into land values had sober implications for long-run program consequences. Maier was among the first to trace out these consequences.[42] At first, he noted, farmers who hold title to land when a program is initiated will get most of the price-raising benefits flowing from the program. Over time, however, a shifting of program benefits between sellers and buyers will occur. Persons who buy land after the future price-raising benefits of the program have been capitalized into farmland values will be paying in advance for a part of the future benefits of the program. These future benefits become windfall gains to sellers who were original owners of the land. Vested interests in the program will be created as people come to expect its continuance, and any disruption in the program would mean sudden capital losses for persons who had purchased farmlands with acreage allotments at prices that reflected the expected future benefits of the program.

Maier was careful to avoid stating that *all* program benefits would be capitalized into land values—landowners obviously attach some uncertainty to program continuation, for example—but the trends over time were clear. This reasoning introduced a pessimistic note to farm policy literature since it was obvious that, over time and with a continuing program, capitalization would eventually wipe out any successful attempts to raise farm income. T. W. Schultz viewed these price and income consequences as regressive in their effect on the personal distribution of income among farm families, and proposals to deal with

40. Westfall, "Agricultural Allotments as Property," p. 1188.

41. James L. Hedrick, "The Effects of the Price-Support Program for Peanuts on the Sale Value of Farms," *J. Farm Econ.* 44 (December 1962) : 1749–53; Robert F. Boxley, Jr., and W. L. Gibson, Jr., *Peanut Acreage Allotments and Farm Land Values*, Tech. Bull. 175 (Blacksburg: Agricultural Experiment Station, Virginia Polytechnic Institute, 1964) ; Milton Shuffett and Josiah Hoskins, "Capitalization of Burley Tobacco Allotment Rights into Farmland Values," *Am. J. Agric. Econ.* 51 (May 1969) : 471–74.

42. Frank H. Maier, "Land and One of the Farm Programs," in *Yearbook of Agriculture, 1958* (Washington, D.C.: Government Printing Office, 1958) , pp. 310–14.

the "capitalization problem" were being put forward as early as 1954.[43]

Others, however, downgraded the significance of the capitalization problem. Wilcox argued that because of the low rates of ownership transfers through bona fide sales (he used the figure of 1.1 percent per year), the increase in land values was hypothetical and unrealized for most farm families, while the program benefits in the form of increased income were real and enjoyable.[44] Schmid argued that capitalization was to be expected and that arguments over how much of program benefits are capitalized diverted attention from more important policy questions which he identified as "overcapitalization of income streams."[45] Aines also used the low rate of turnover in ownership of farmland to discount the importance of capitalization of benefits.[46]

Program Implications for Intertemporal Wealth Distributions

From a longer perspective than that available to Maier and other earlier writers, it is not clear that the pessimistic evaluation of the consequences of land value capitalization is fully warranted. In particular, Gibson found that relatively high discounts were required for both tobacco and peanuts in order to equate estimated marginal allotment values and sale prices in the late 1950s and early 1960s.[47] Sea-

43. T. W. Schultz, "Agricultural Policy for What?" *J. Farm Econ.* 41 (May 1959): 189–93; George K. Brinegar and Steward Johnson, "On Letting Go of the Bear's Tail," *J. Farm Econ.* 36 (February 1954): 30–43.

44. Walter W. Wilcox, "How Much of Farm Program Benefits are Lost to Farm Operators via Capitalization into Land Values?" *J. Farm Econ.* 46 (February 1964): 246–47.

45. A. Allan Schmid, "Capitalization of Farm Program Benefits: Further Comment," *J. Farm Econ.* 46 (August 1964): 687–88. Overcapitalization refers to the valuation of an asset higher than can be justified in terms of annual income streams from the asset and the prevailing opportunity cost of capital used to purchase the asset.

46. Ronald O. Aines, "Farmland Valuation and Farm Programs," *J. Farm Econ.* 46 (December 1964): 1253–59. A rejoinder is that a low-turnover rate may delay but cannot, in itself, avoid any problems associated with capitalization. Unfortunately, the point of the low-turnover argument was never made clear.

47. W. L. Gibson, Jr., C. J. Arnold, F. D. Aigner, *The Marginal Value of Flue-Cured Tobacco Allotments,* Tech. Bull. no. 156 (Blacksburg: Agricultural Experiment Station, Virginia Polytechnic Institute, 1962); F. M. Halsey and W. L. Gibson, Jr., *Peanut Allotments—Comparison of Sale Value and Capitalized Net Income,* Bull. 574 (Blacksburg: Agricultural Experiment Station, Virginia Polytechnic Institute, 1966). The estimated discount rate in these studies varied with assumptions regarding size of farm, available operating capital, and allotment size but, in the absence of severe capital rationing, discount rates of 15.3 to 24.0 percent were implied for tobacco and from 14.2 to 20.2 for peanuts.

graves has calculated rates of return to tobacco allotment values in North Carolina for every year from 1934 to 1962.[48] Averaged approximately by decades, his estimates are 56 percent annually between 1934 and 1942; 40 percent between 1943 and 1952; and 16 percent between 1953 and 1962. Seagraves also converted these estimates of annual rates of return to implied time horizons, assuming that the riskless rate of return was between 4 and 6 percent for the period. His calculations indicate that the average time horizon lengthened from 1.5 years in 1945 to 9.5 years in 1959–60 and then declined to 8 years in 1961–62. The number of years in the planning horizon was virtually constant from 1957 to 1962, which suggests stabilization in expectations about the future of the program during this period.

These findings at least suggest that land buyers and sellers hold basically conservative attitudes toward the permanence of the program, despite the seemingly "high" prices being paid for allotments. Any definitive evaluation of the indicated rates of returns to allotment purchasers would require knowledge of their opportunity costs but, by all conventional measures, the rates of return are greater than those generally obtained on agricultural capital or equities.[49] Thus, Seagraves' data indicate that any windfall gains have been imperfectly captured by allotment sellers, especially those selling in early program years. Some unknown number of allotments have never been transferred through the market. Together, this suggests that intertemporal wealth transfer (up to 1962) attributable to capitalization of windfall gains has been relatively mild—at least compared with statements in the literature implying instantaneous and complete capture.[50]

48. Seagraves, "Capitalized Values of Tobacco Allotments, pp. 321, 329.

49. Scofield estimates the rate of return to owned capital used in agricultural production in the United States was 9.7 percent in the decade of the 1940s and 5.6 percent in the decade of the 1950s. Returns to owned real estate capital were slightly higher at 10.6 and 5.8 percent respectively. William H. Scofield, "Returns to Productive Capital in Agriculture," *The Farm Real Estate Market*, ARS 43–118 (CD-54) (Washington, D.C., February 1960). Others have estimated rates of return to asset equities as 7.1 percent in 1945 to 1949, 4.8 percent in 1950 to 1954, 2.9 percent in 1955 to 1959, and 3.6 percent in 1960 to 1964. Economic Research Service, *The Balance Sheet of the Farming Sector, 1969*, Agric. Inf. Bull. no. 340 (Washington, D.C.: Government Printing Office, 1970). The determination of rates of return in agriculture involves a number of complex problems in measurement and imputation. See, for example, Scofield.

50. For example, Baum and Heady concluded in 1957 that "because the tobacco program has been in existence and its income effects have been capitalized into land values for such a long period of time, the program *per se* now has no more than minute effects on mobility of persons entering the nonagricultural labor

It would be useful to have data on tobacco allotment sale and rental values over the last decade but this information has not yet reached the literature.[51] We might speculate that provisions for the leasing of allotments since 1962 have broadened the market and thus improved price communication. This should result in higher levels of capital values. Increasing uncertainties associated with future program continuation, however, have probably had a greater (negative) influence on allotment sale prices.[52]

Program Effects on Labor Returns

In contrast to the investigations of program effects on land values, relatively little attention has been given to the effects of the tobacco program on labor returns. Among researchers, it was argued that the program effects on wage rates and prices of other inputs were either slight or nonexistent.[53] It was generally accepted, therefore, that most program benefits were received as windfall gains by landowners.

At the firm level, the tobacco program itself does not regulate the supply of labor, nor is there reason to argue that restrictions on the land input necessarily increase the firm's total demand for labor (although labor may be used more intensely on the allotted acreage). Thus, any program effects on labor earnings at the firm level would have to occur through the distributive mechanism; in this case, tenure arrangements between landlords and croppers, tenants, and laborers.

Hedrick, Tolley, and Back found that tenure arrangements, including share-rates, in the flue-cured tobacco regions of Virginia and North

force." E. L. Baum and Earl O. Heady, "Some Effects of Selected Policy Programs on Agricultural Labor Mobility in the South," *So. Econ. J.,* 25 (January 1959): 327–37; see esp. p. 329.

51. Shuffet and Hoskins report a study of burley tobacco allotment values, based on 1957–59 farm sales, in which they project estimated sale values to 1967. They estimated the 1967 discount rate (based on projected land values) to be 11.1 percent. Shuffet and Hoskins, Capitalization of Burley Tobacco Allotment Rights," p. 472.

52. *The Washington Post,* 25 January 1970, reports that burley tobacco producers in Kentucky are suing the national television networks for damages from antismoking commercials ". . . because farm real estate with tobacco allotments has declined in value. . . ."

53. John E. Floyd, "The Effects of Farm Price Supports on the Returns to Land and Labor in Agriculture," *J. Pol. Econ.,* 73 (April 1965): 148–58. W. B. Back, James L. Hedrick, and W. L. Gibson, Jr., "Effects of Acreage-Allotment, Price-Support Programs Upon Farmland Values," *Incidence of Benefits and Costs of Selected Public Programs Affecting Agriculture,* Bull. 576 (Blacksburg: Agricultural Experiment Station, Virginia Polytechnic Institute, 1966), p. 53.

Carolina have remained essentially unchanged since the 1920s.[54] This might be taken to suggest that labor has shared proportionately with land in the benefits of the flue-cured tobacco program. Hedrick et al. propose an alternative hypothesis that, in the long run, labor used in flue-cured tobacco production has received returns approximately equivalent to its opportunity returns regardless of the tobacco program or tenure arrangements. The only data on tenant opportunity returns available to the researchers were farm wage rates, and on this evidence they accept the alternative hypothesis. They recognized, however, that farm wage rates as well as cropper returns could be affected by the program.

Back and Wunderlich, in an important theoretical paper, also accept the view that landowners captured most of the benefits of the program with increased income to labor just sufficient to parallel increased opportunity returns to this labor over time.[55] They conclude, therefore, that the program has been neutral with respect to tenancy. Additionally, they suggest that overall employment in the farm sector may have been reduced by the program because of the lack of alternative farm enterprises with comparable labor requirements, but that adjustments in labor supply probably have been sufficient to leave income per farm laborer about what it would have been without a program.

In a long-run dynamic framework, consideration needs be given to the substantial shifts in farm labor supply that have occurred in the southeast in recent decades. The flue-cured tobacco region, in particular, has been marked by high and continuing rates of labor out-migration in response to a shortage of suitable off-farm employment in the area and the pull of employment possibilities in northern cities.[56] As we suggest below, the tobacco program may have acted to retard structural adjustments in farm size and numbers. This combination of organizational rigidities and shifts in labor supplies may have affected the relative bargaining positions of tenants and landlords and, hence, the distribution of program benefits between land and labor. Tenure data from the Census of Agriculture are suggestive of the changes that may have occurred.

Perhaps because it is conceptually tidier, there is a tendency to view

54. Hedrick, Tolley, and Back, *Effects of Flue-Cured Tobacco Programs*, p. 2.

55. W. B. Back and Gene Wunderlich, "Distributional and Redistributional Effects of Flue-Cured Tobacco Programs," *Income Distribution Analysis*, API Series 23 (Raleigh: Agricultural Policy Institute, North Carolina State University, 1966).

56. "Leaving Home Blues: An NBC News White Paper on Rural Migration," transcript of a broadcast given August 27, 1971, 130 Cong. Rec. S14081 (daily ed., 10 September 1971).

Table 5.3—Distribution of Tobacco and Other Commercial Farmers, by Race, Tenure and Economic Class of Farm, Virginia and North Carolina, 1964

Race and tenure	All commercial farms	Gross sales classes, percent			
		$10,000 or more	$9,999 to $5,000	$4,999 to $2,500	less than $2,500
		Tobacco farmers			
White:					
Full owners	32	14	26	41	58
Part owners	33	45	33	28	19
Tenants	35	41	41	31	23
Negro:					
Full owners	15	3	5	18	37
Part owners	19	17	17	22	20
Tenants	66	80	78	60	43
		Other commercial farmers			
White:					
Full owners	60	43	54	66	79
Part owners	31	47	36	26	14
Tenants	9	10	10	8	7
Negro:					
Full owners	28	10	11	25	47
Part owners	25	37	25	28	19
Tenants	47	53	64	47	34

Source: U.S. Department of Commerce, Bureau of the Census, *United States Census of Agriculture: 1964,* vol. 1, *Statistics for the State and Counties,* pt. 24, Virginia; pt. 26, North Carolina.

the tobacco program in terms of an agriculture made up of owner-operated units. In fact, however, full owner-operators of tobacco farms are in the minority (Table 5.3). Furthermore, full ownership tends to be associated with small farms and low gross farm sales. For these full owners, therefore, total returns to allotment, land, and labor are low.[57]

On the other hand, there is a strong and positive relationship between the proportion of tenancy and high gross farm sales. This is especially true for Negro farm operators—for example, 97 percent of

57. It is particularly interesting to speculate about the very low proportion of white full owners on tobacco farms with sales of more than $10,000. The low proportions would be consistent with a hypothesis that capitalized allotment values create barriers to farm access through full ownership. It is possible that the tobacco program has acted to restrict large scale ownership opportunities for (white) farm operators in the tobacco producing region in the same way that some other factor (for example, capital rationing) has restricted Negro farm ownership opportunities generally.

the Negro operators with gross sales of $10,000 or more are either tenants or part owners. Thus, if gross sales can be taken as an index of success, a high proportion of successful tobacco farm operators have claims only to labor and management returns.

Another indication that tobacco farming (and farmers) differs substantially from other types of farming can be found in data on the age distribution for tobacco farmers (Table 5.4). Tobacco farmers of both

Table 5.4—Distribution of Tobacco and Other Commercial Farmers, by Age and Economic Class of Farm, Virginia and North Carolina, 1964

	Operator age					
Type of farm and gross sales	under 25	25 to 34	35 to 44	45 to 54	55 to 64	65 and over
Farm operators (thousands)						
Tobacco	2.5	9.5	19.6	26.6	20.0	4.7
Other commercial	0.7	4.8	12.7	19.6	22.5	6.8
Gross Sales:						
Tobacco farms (percent)						
$10,000 or more	13	27	32	27	17	13
$5,000 to $9,999	28	33	34	34	29	32
$2,500 to $4,999	35	27	23	24	27	55
less than $2,500	24	13	11	15	27	a
Total	100	100	100	100	100	100
Other commercial (percent)						
$10,000 or more	31	46	44	32	19	28
$5,000 to $9,999	20	19	19	19	14	26
$2,500 to $4,999	19	19	18	19	17	46
less than $2,500	30	16	19	30	50	a
Total	100	100	100	100	100	100

Source: U.S. Department of Commerce, Bureau of the Census, *United States Census of Agriculture: 1964*, vol. 1, *Statistics for the State and Counties*, pt. 24, Virginia; pt. 26, North Carolina.

a These farms are classified as part-retirement farms.

races are, on the average, younger than the operators of other commercial farms, and young operators are entering tobacco farming at a faster rate. In 1964 there were over three times as many tobacco farmers under 25 years of age and twice as many between the ages of 25 and 34 as for other commercial farmers.

Tolley has recently examined the relationships between age, entry rates, and earnings within agriculture.[58] Viewing agriculture in the ag-

58. G. S. Tolley, "Management Entry into U.S. Agriculture," *Am. J. Agric. Econ.* 52 (November 1970): 485–93.

gregate, he finds that management adjustments have been both age-selective and management-selective. One sector of American agriculture is characterized by aging managers with relatively low gross farm sales. As these managers gradually leave agriculture, they are being replaced by fewer numbers of younger managers entering agriculture with expectations of considerably higher earnings. These relationships seem to hold for commercial farmers other than tobacco farmers in Virginia and North Carolina. For example, nearly a third of "other" commercial farmers under 25 years of age have gross sales of $10,000 or more (Table 5.4). Conversely, the older farmers predominately operate farms in the lowest gross sales categories.

On the other hand, the distribution of tobacco farm operators by sales classes does not appear to vary significantly with age. The majority of tobacco farmers operate farms with gross sales between $2,500 and $10,000, regardless of age. These data suggest that, in contrast to other types of farming, young entrants into tobacco farming probably do not have earnings expectations substantially higher than those of older tobacco farmers.

Neither the tenure nor age data necessarily support inferences about the effects of the flue-cured tobacco program on labor earnings. This would require data on off-farm opportunity costs and on net returns to tobacco farming with and without the program—data which we do not have. However, the sector's ability to attract (or absorb) new entrants, together with the greater mobility usually associated with tenancy, suggests that relative bargaining strength between landlords and tenants may be competitive enough to ensure labor a share of the benefits arising from the tobacco program.

Program Effects on the Regional Economy

Observers of the tobacco program seem unanimous in their judgment that the program has benefited the states of Virginia and North Carolina. Seagraves, observing the program as it operates in North Carolina, states: "The program clearly has helped the State, and some of its land owners, a great deal."[59] Given the general nature of the organization of tobacco farms into small, locally owned units, it is likely that most benefits, whether received by landowners or laborers, have accrued to residents of the area and thus contribute directly to regional income.[60]

59. Seagraves, "Capitalized Values of Tobacco Allotments," p. 320.
60. To the extent that benefits captured by landowners are capitalized into land values, further capture and redistribution of program benefits may occur by local

Back and Wunderlich have examined the flue-cured tobacco program as it may have affected the personal distribution of income within the local or regional economies of the production regions. Data limitations, unfortunately, restrict their analysis to statements of hypotheses for further testing but, in general, they find no evidence that the program has resulted in major concentrations of income among landowners within the farm sector or within the local trade area.[61] Back and Wunderlich also suggest that "a major effect of the flue-cured tobacco program on many local economies might have been to prevent their emergence as economically depressed areas. Many communities in the Piedmont probably would have lost tobacco acreage to the coastal plains without the acreage allotment program."[62] Studies of tobacco production budgets for North Carolina also suggest that, with free transferability of tobacco allotments, tobacco production would tend to move to the eastern and southern boundaries of the flue-cured tobacco belt.[63] The legislative restriction on transfer of allotments across county lines by lease was, in part, included to allay fears (particularly of Piedmont producers) of major shifts in production to the coastal plains or to other southern states.[64]

---

governments through the property taxation system. Bradford and Toussaint note that one consequence of creating transferable tobacco allotments would be a probable reduction in the property tax base of some counties in the old and middle tobacco belts. G. L. Bradford and W. D. Toussaint, *Economic Effects of Transferable Tobacco Allotments*, A. E. Inf. Series no. 89 (Raleigh: Dept. of Agric. Econ., North Carolina State College, 1962), p. 50.

61. Back and Wunderlich were writing of the program as it operated prior to the 1962 amendment permitting the lease and transfer of tobacco allotments. Allotment leasing has since increased rapidly (nearly a fourth of all flue-cured tobacco acreage was under lease in 1970). This change would appear to increase the chances for concentration of control over allotments and, hence, concentration in the distribution of allotment-related income.

62. Back and Wunderlich, "Distributional and Redistributional Effects of Tobacco Programs," p. 257.

63. Bradford and Toussaint, *Economic Effects of Transferable Tobacco Allotments*, pp. 3–5.

64. To say that the locus of tobacco production probably would shift (either within the traditional production region or further south) is to say that unrealized production efficiencies still exist. Whether such a shift would improve personal income distribution within the region would depend on the welfare position of producers losing and receiving the allotments. Bradford and Toussaint found the relatively highest degree of underplanting of allotments occurred, in 1960, in areas with greatest off-farm employment opportunities. Since the off-farm employment opportunities are generally greatest in the Piedmont, a shift of production to the coastal plain need not imply a net welfare loss.

Ideally, an evaluation of the flue-cured tobacco program and its effect on the regional economy should give consideration to the effect that the program may have had in preserving earning opportunities that otherwise would have been lost. This is a difficult issue to evaluate. Relative to other areas of both Virginia and North Carolina, the number of farm operators and the acreage of land in farms in the flue-cured tobacco region have declined less rapidly. In the major tobacco-producing counties of Virginia and North Carolina (Census Areas 17 and 18) the number of farms in 1964 was 58 percent of the number in 1930, while the acreage of the farms was 80 percent. Corresponding percentages for all other counties in these two states, which include some tobacco farms also, was 48 and 75 percent, respectively. In 1930 farms in Areas 17 and 18 accounted for 35 percent of all farms in the two states; by 1964 they accounted for over one-half (50.4 percent).

In part, of course, the tobacco region has been sheltered from the more explosive rates of urbanization occurring in other areas of the two states; nevertheless, the tobacco region has not experienced the same degree of farm consolidation and growth in farm size that other agricultural sectors have experienced. In Census Areas 17 and 18, average farm size increased from 71 acres in 1930 to 98 acres in 1964. Outside this area, farm size rose from 80 acres to 124 acres during the same time period.

Traditionally, tobacco production has been organized around small production units because high labor and management requirements limit the amount of tobacco a farm family can handle. In the absence of mechanization of tobacco production, the labor supply condition alone may have limited adjustments in farm size and farm numbers, with or without the tobacco program. Whatever the past effects of the program, however, it is clear that the program as it now operates serves as a major barrier to the mechanization of tobacco harvesting and the organizational changes that must accompany mechanization.[65]

Recently developed harvesting systems now have the potential of reducing the labor input in tobacco production by about half. According to a USDA Task Force that has studied it, mechanization becomes financially feasible when the machines can be operated at capacity of about 40 acres of tobacco and when wage rates exceed a level of about $1.35 per hour. Of these two conditions, the acreage requirement is the major barrier, and if substantial mechanization is to occur,

---

65. *Potential Mechanization*, pp. iii–vi. During 1967, around 295 million man-hours of labor were required to produce the nation's flue-cured tobacco crop.

fragmented allotments must be combined.[66] Current harvesting and curing systems require a capital outlay of at least $52,000, in addition to the cost of land and other production inputs. If, in addition, producers are required to acquire and consolidate economic-sized allotments in the market, the capital barrier is formidable. It is likely, therefore, that pressures for a change in the tobacco program will increase.

The tobacco workers' stake in such a change is substantial. One reported estimate indicates a potential loss of 150,000 farm jobs if relatively full mechanization is achieved by 1975. This estimate may be conservative, because a great number of tobacco workers who are seasonally employed are not included. In other cases, family income may decline even though the principle wage earner continues to be employed in tobacco production. If the human resources made surplus by mechanization of tobacco production can be productively reallocated, there may be a net social gain from such a technological change. However, it appears that, in the short-run, there will be substantial barriers to effective reallocation of many of these workers.[67]

Program Costs

Given the income redistribution objectives implied or explicit to most farm programs, the notion of program costs raises some conceptual difficulties. Here, we consider "costs" in terms of the efficiency with which the redistribution has been achieved. These efficiency costs are an issue apart from any redistribution burden and its incidence.

The Agricultural Stabilization and Conservation Service (ASCS) classifies the national farm programs it administers into eight basic types, ranging from acreage allotment and marketing quota programs, to land retirement and to surplus removal programs.[68] We would judge that, as these federal programs go, the acreage allotment and marketing quota programs operate with relatively low costs.[69] The direct

66. Ibid., p. 11. In 1968, less than 1 percent of all farms (nationwide) with flue-cured tobacco allotments had allotments exceeding 20 acres; 96 percent had 10 acres or less.

67. Robert C. McElroy, "Manpower Implications of Trends in the Tobacco Industry" (Talk presented to the Association for Public Program Analysis Conference, U.S. Civil Service Commission, Washington, D.C., June 16, 1969), p. 6. McElroy attributed the estimate of 150,000 jobs to Bruce Biossat, writing in the Washington Daily News. See also the transcript of the NBC White Paper, "Leaving Home Blues."

68. Agricultural Stabilization and Conservation Service, *Farm Commodity and Related Programs*, p. 2.

69. General stabilization and price-support programs statistics are available in Ch. XI of *Agricultural Statistics, 1970* (Washington, D.C.: Government Printing

treasury costs of the program have probably been quite low. These would involve costs such as program administration by ASCS county officials and the assumption of some costs of operating the Flue-Cured Tobacco Cooperative Stabilization Corporation which handles price-support loans. A major part of the corporation's expenses, however, are covered by service charges to producers.[70] Most marketing and storage functions of the corporation would, of course, still have to be performed in the absence of the program.

To the extent the program has raised average prices of tobacco, the price effects have probably been passed on to final users or to export markets.[71] Thus, domestically, the redistribution has been from tobacco users to tobacco producers. This incidence of cost bearing is consistent with the value judgments implied in excise taxation of tobacco products. (If, however, the main effect of the program has been price stability, the program has probably reduced inventory and other hedging costs to manufacturers sufficiently to offset, at least partially, higher tobacco prices.) Finally, the allotment program undoubtedly has generated certain production inefficiencies (for example, by creating some allotments too small to utilize available farm labor fully or by impeding intercounty or state production shifts) that might have been avoided under alternative programs. These costs have not been measured and may be large. Offsetting this, on the other hand, are instances where the program may have provided employment for labor and capital resources with no long-run employment alternatives.

Summary

There can be little question that the flue-cured tobacco price-support program has been a major force in shaping the economic and

---

Office, 1970). It should be noted, however, that data on value of tobacco placed under loans and related statistics overstate program costs because the tobacco is later sold out of storage.

70. Agricultural Stabilization and Conservation Service, *Farm Commodity and Related Programs,* p. 11.

71. Paul R. Johnson, "The Social Cost of the Tobacco Program," *J. Farm Econ.* 47 (May 1965) : 242–55. Johnson estimated that in 1960 the United States held substantial monopoly power in world markets for flue-cured tobacco. Over time, however, the high world prices generated by U.S. trade policies have encouraged other producing countries to increase their tobacco marketing. Presently, U.S. tobacco sales are facing increasing competition in world markets. Malcolm Seawell, "Development of Foreign Market for Tobacco," *The Tobacco Industry in Perspective,* API Series 11 (Raleigh: Agricultural Policy Institute, North Carolina State University, 1964) , p. 165.

social milieu of flue-cured tobacco production over the last thirty-odd years. The program clearly has brought price stability to tobacco markets, and it seems evident that the program has succeeded in maintaining or increasing aggregate returns to tobacco producers over what otherwise would have prevailed.

From the nature of the organization of tobacco farms (geographically concentrated with few large-scale or absentee landowners),[72] it appears likely that most program benefits to producers, whether received by landowners or laborers, have accrued to residents of the areas in which tobacco is produced and thus have contributed directly to regional income. The program has probably also been a factor in providing or preserving jobs in agriculture during a period in which general off-farm migration has been heavy and, in the opinion of many, has exceeded the assimilative capacity of urban areas.[73]

It is clear that the allotment provision created windfall gains for those people owning land at the time the program was initiated or when it first obtained a degree of permanency in producers' eyes. The evidence indicates, however, that these gains have been imperfectly captured by many allotment sellers.

To the extent that *any* capitalized values are actually realized, a portion of the future stream of program benefits is transferred to the seller. As Schmid points out, however, any increased residual stream, whether originating in subsidies, increased demands, or new and more productive inputs, will be capitalized into the price of the fixed factor which controls access to the income stream.[74] There is perhaps a tendency to view allotment capitalization as a unique phenomenon, but it obviously is not; rather, there is strong evidence that farmland is the residual claimant to the benefits of nearly all government farm programs or actions affecting agriculture.[75] If all sources of uncertainty could be sorted out and measured (uncertainty of program continua-

72. Precise support for this statement is not available, but a 1960 survey of land-ownership in the southeastern states found that 95 and 93 percent of landowners in Piedmont and coastal plain subregions, respectively, resided within the state in which they owned land. Roger W. Strohbehn, *Ownership of Rural Land in the Southeast*, Agric. Econ. Rpt. no. 46 (Washington, D.C.: Government Printing Office, 1964).

73. See, for example, The President's Task Force on Rural Development, *A New Life for the Country* (Washington, D.C.: Government Printing Office, 1970).

74. Schmid, "Capitalization of Farm Program Benefits," p. 687–88.

75. John E. Reynolds and John F. Timmons, *Factors Affecting Farmland Values in the United States*, Research Bull. 566 (Ames: Agriculture and Home Economics Experiment Station, Iowa State University, 1969). See especially the bibliography for additional references.

tion, uncertainty of reactions by other producers of the commodity or potential entrants, and so on), "high" tobacco allotment prices should create no greater barriers to entry into tobacco farming nor have more adverse distributional consequences than do "high" land prices generally.

As to the future, however successful or unsuccessful the tobacco program may be judged to date, pressures for change are building. One major factor is the health and smoking issue. Although trends are still not entirely clear, the long-run prospects are probably for stable or modestly declining U.S. tobacco consumption.[76] The health issue has accelerated the switch to filter cigarettes which require less tobacco, and progress is being made in developing "puffed" or freeze-dried tobacco which promises to reduce substantially tobacco requirements for cigarette manufacture. In export markets, American tobacco is facing increasing competition from foreign producers. Finally, we may expect pressures from farm machinery interests and from some growers to consolidate tobacco allotments.

Back and Wunderlich make the point that the incidence of program effects generally are not reversible and that future program changes (especially program elimination) may result in a new set of income gains and losses of unknown magnitude and incidence.[77] Already some who foresee a phasing out or abandonment of the allotment program are expressing concern over the incidence of the resultant "decapitalization" of allotment values, and as a result allotment purchase programs to ease the transition have been suggested.[78] Thus policy-makers may soon have to face substantial new questions of equity and fairness in formulating a future flue-cured tobacco program.

76. William Greider, "A New Leaf for the South," *The Washington Post,* 25 January 1970.

77. Back and Wunderlich, "Distributional and Redistributional Effects of Tobacco Programs," pp. 253–54.

78. Editorial, "Phasing Out the Tobacco Industry," *The Washington Post,* 27 January 1970; Ernest W. Grove, "Irrelevance Is Where You Find It: Reply," *Am. J. Agric. Econ.* 53 (February 1971): 138–40.

6 *Roy A. Ballinger*

THE BENEFITS AND BURDENS OF THE UNITED STATES SUGAR QUOTA SYSTEM

The United States sugar industry is protected by a quota system which controls the total supply marketed and the quantity produced for consumption in the United States by various domestic and foreign sources. This supply control is the principal factor determining sugar prices in the United States. The domestic sugar industry also receives the protection of a tariff, but the rate of duty is low enough that its economic effects are insignificant in comparison to those of the quota arrangement. They will not be considered in this article.

The purpose of this paper is to identify the groups receiving benefits and those bearing the costs of the sugar quota program and, where feasible, to give some indication of the magnitude of the costs and benefits accruing to the groups involved.

Important Features of the Quota System

The quota system operates under the provisions of the Sugar Act of 1948, as amended, and it is administered by the United States Department of Agriculture. It may reasonably be described as a government sponsored cartel. Under the law the Secretary of Agriculture is directed to determine for each calendar year the "consumption requirements" for sugar within the United States. The Secretary can revise this determination as often during the year as he thinks desirable. The "consumption requirements" set the maximum quantity of sugar that can be marketed in the United States in any year.

The quota law also specifies in detail the manner in which the requirements are to be divided among the various domestic sugar producing areas and among foreign countries. The total of the quotas must always equal the "consumption requirements." The law

105

also contains general rules to be followed by the Department of Agriculture in apportioning the quota in each domestic area among producers in that area. The governments of foreign countries usually provide some means of dividing their quota for sugar to be exported to the United States among their own producers.

Successful operation of the quota system is dependent, among other things, on the ability of the federal government to control, that is, to limit, the production of sugar in domestic areas. This is done by means of subsidy payments made to growers of sugar beets and sugarcane. The receipt of the payments is in part contingent on the grower's conformation to certain requirements concerning acreage planted or harvested, as specified by the Department of Agriculture, and as authorized in the Sugar Act of 1948.

An excise tax is also imposed on all sugar used in the United States, regardless of whether the sugar was produced domestically or imported. Originally the receipts from the tax were to be used to pay the subsidy to growers. The tax and subsidy are legally separate but remain connected in a political sense. For instance, industry spokesmen frequently still argue that the sugar quota system does not burden United States taxpayers because the receipts from the tax are larger than the subsidy payments, ignoring the fact that the treasury would benefit even more if the subsidy were reduced or eliminated.

Effect of the Quota System on Sugar Prices and Production

A major effect of the Sugar Act, as it has been administered, has been to raise sugar prices in the United States substantially above those in the world markets except on a few occasions when some unusual circumstances caused world prices to rise to unusually high levels (Table 6.1). This has been done by restricting supplies sufficiently to achieve the desired price effect. Not only do the quota actions of the United States affect sugar prices in this country, they also have a considerable effect on prices in the world market. In this context the world market refers to sales of sugar exported to countries where the exporting nation receives no preferential treatment in tariff duty or quotas over sugar from any other nation. It accounts for only about 10 percent of world sugar production.

The United States is by far the world's largest importer of sugar. When sugar prices in the United States are raised by decreasing marketable supplies (consumption requirements), imports as well as domestic marketings are reduced. This makes more sugar available for the world market, forcing prices there downward. Several countries export sugar

Table 6.1—Average Annual Prices of Sugar in the United States and World Markets (Cents per Pound)

Year	U.S. price[a]	World price[b]	Adjust- ments[c]	U.S. price above world price
1948	5.54	4.23	.90	.41
1949	5.81	4.16	.87	.78
1950	5.93	4.98	.84	.11
1951	6.06	5.67	.99	−.60
1952	6.26	4.17	.91	1.18
1953	6.29	3.41	.86	2.02
1954	6.09	3.26	.88	1.95
1955	5.95	3.24	.95	1.76
1956	6.09	3.48	.99	1.62
1957	6.24	5.16	.94	.14
1958	6.27	3.50	.86	1.91
1959	6.24	2.97	.89	2.38
1960	6.30	3.14	.95	2.21
1961	6.30	2.91	.94	2.45
1962	6.45	2.98	.89	2.58
1963	8.18	8.50	.91	−1.23
1964	6.90	5.87	.92	.11
1965	6.75	2.12	.95	3.68
1966	6.99	1.86	.96	4.17
1967	7.28	1.99	.96	4.33
1968	7.52	1.98	.98	4.56
1969	7.75	3.37	1.00	3.38
1970	8.07	3.75	1.13	3.19

Source: Statistics published by The Sugar Division, ASCS, USDA.

[a] Raw sugar, duty paid, New York.

[b] Spot price for sugar in Caribbean ports for shipment to world market.

[c] Includes freight, insurance, duty, etc.

to both the United States and to world markets, so that higher prices for exports to the United States, even when somewhat reduced in volume, enable sugar producers there to accept lower prices in the world market without reducing to unprofitable levels the average price received for all exports. This helps to maintain world production and keep world prices below those in the United States.

Various attempts have been made to quantify the price and production effects of the United States sugar quota system. These customarily involve estimates of demand and supply elasticities and of international transportation costs. They usually have been designed to provide comparisons with what would be expected under conditions of free trade. Some estimates have been confined to the effects of the United States quota system; others include an analysis of the effects of removing all restrictions on international trade in sugar throughout the world. Many other countries also provide protection for their domestic industries, which affects their domestic production and price and influence markets in other countries.

A recent study[1] of the effects of the United States sugar quota system indicates that:

1. The estimated cost of sugar for United States consumers in 1970 would be reduced 31 percent if free trade in sugar were substituted for the present quota program.

2. Removal of all trade restrictions on sugar would reduce the share of United States consumption provided by domestic producers to 15.7 percent of the total supply from 41.8 percent under the Sugar Act.

The same study shows that, if domestic price supports and international trade restrictions were removed throughout the world, the effects would include:

1. A reduction in sugar production in the United States of about 65 percent. Production in the USSR would decline about 30 percent.

2. Substantial increases in production in Central America and the Caribbean area.

3. Price declines in the United States and the Philippines. Prices would rise in South America, Taiwan, and Cuba.

The economic effects of Sugar Act subsidies and of the excise tax on sugar are much smaller than those directly related to supply limitation. The basic rate of subsidy payments to growers of sugar beets and sugarcane is 80 cents per 100 pounds of sugar recoverable from the beets or cane produced by the grower. Growers producing relatively small quantities of beets or cane receive payments at the basic rate. The rate is progressively reduced for growers with larger outputs. Most beet growers operate on a scale small enough to receive payments at the basic rate. A number of sugarcane growers, however, operate on a scale large enough that the average payment received is considerably below 80 cents. Thus there is some differential effect among growers in the benefits received from subsidy payments.

The excise tax on sugar is imposed at the rate of 50 cents per 100 pounds on all sugar used in this country. With minor exceptions the

1. Thomas H. Bates and Andrew Schmits, *A Spatial Equilibrium Analysis of the World Sugar Economy*, Gianninis Foundation Monograph No. 23 (Berkeley: California Agriculture Experiment Station, 1969).

tax is paid by cane sugar refiners and sugar beet processors who produce and sell refined sugar. Neither class of operators receives any subsidy payments under the Sugar Act unless it also grows sugar beets or sugarcane.

Total Sugar Act subsidy payments, all going to domestic producers, have averaged about $90 million annually in recent years. Sugar excise tax collections have amounted to around $108 million yearly, of which about $50 million represent payments on imported sugar.

Distribution of Benefits and Burdens of the Quota System

The burden of higher sugar prices in the United States is generated by the sugar quota system and is borne by sugar consumers. This is true whether the sugar is purchased for household use or by industrial food processors who sell their products to consumers. Such processors are in a position to increase the prices of their products sufficiently to offset the higher price paid for sugar, since all processors are affected by the quota system in the same degree. The quantity of sugar used by consumers may be reduced somewhat by higher prices, although the demand for sugar in an affluent country, such as the United States, is relatively inelastic.

The largest change in sugar consumption that can logically be considered a result of higher sugar prices is that arising from the increased use of sugar substitutes. Two classes of substitutes are important. One, commonly known as noncaloric or nonnutritive, consists of products which taste sweet but have no food value. Available evidence suggests that only about one-third of the quantity of these sweeteners used in the United States replaces sugar.[2] The remainder is consumed by persons who would not have consumed sugar if no noncaloric sweetner had been available. Market prices of noncaloric sweeteners generally are considerably lower, per unit of sweetness, than those for sugar, and there appears to be little price competition between sugar and the noncalorics.

The other type of substitute for sugar consists of the starch or corn sweeteners, commonly called corn syrup and dextrose. The consumption of these during the past decade or more, particularly corn syrup, has been increasing more rapidly than the consumption of sugar and

2. Roy A. Ballinger, *Noncaloric Sweeteners: Their Position in the Sweetener Industry,* Agricultural Economics Report No. 113 (Washington, D.C.: Economic Research Service, United States Department of Agriculture, 1967), p. 13.

the price has declined relative to the price of sugar.[3] Corn syrup accounted for 8.2 percent of the total quantity of sugar, dextrose, and corn syrup consumed in the United States in 1957. In 1968 the percentage was 11.8. The New York price of sugar, refined wholesale, rose from 9.15 cents per pound in 1957 to 10.84 cents in 1968. The comparable price of corn syrup, dry basis, declined from 9.17 cents to 7.85 in the same period.

Recent technological improvements have made possible the production of sweeter syrups from starch than the corn syrup now generally available to users of sweeteners. If the corn sweetener industry succeeds in producing these syrups at low enough cost, they could become much more important than they now are. In any event, producers of corn sweeteners have benefited materially from the high sugar prices which have prevailed under the Sugar Act, since they have not been subject to regulation under the quota law and have been free to take full advantage of high sugar prices by expanding their sales to those who might otherwise have used sugar.

Capitalization of Sugar Act Benefits

At the time the Sugar Act first became effective in 1934, farmers who were growing sugar beets and sugarcane undoubtedly benefited by whatever higher price they received for their beets or cane because of the operation of the Act. When the owners and prospective buyers became convinced that the Sugar Act would remain in effect for some time, the increased returns were capitalized. Moreover, the process has tended to be repeated each time returns from the sugar crops have increased relative to what the farmer could expect from growing other crops.

Few studies appear to have been made which attempt to measure the extent of this capitalization process, but general observation seems to support the general conclusion stated. Attempts at measurement frequently encounter difficulty because of other factors which affected land prices during the period when increasing sugar prices were being capitalized. The situation is especially complex in the case of sugar beets. Beets are grown in rotation with other crops, and the profitability of the crop depends partly on how well it fits into a feasible rotation. Stated in another way, it depends on the comparative returns that may be obtained from growing sugar beets or some other crop.

3. Roy A. Ballinger, *A History of Sugar Marketing*, Agricultural Economic Report No. 197 (Washington, D.C.: Economic Research Service, United States Department of Agriculture, 1971), p. 107.

For instance, tomatoes grown for processing is one crop that competes with sugar beets for land in central California. In the mid-1960s a machine which successfully harvested tomatoes came into general use, thus reducing materially the cost of harvesting tomatoes. Sugar beet acreage in the area, at least partly as a result of this development, was reduced substantially and has not yet returned to its former peak. Under such circumstances whatever capitalization of Sugar Act benefits there may once have been in an area tends to disappear, although land values may rise.

The situation in the Red River Valley of Minnesota and North Dakota is quite different. Alternate crops return much less per acre to growers than do sugar beets. Many farmers would like to grow a larger acreage of beets than they are permitted under the quota system. To grow beets they must have a contract with the only processor in the area and, in some years, an acreage allotment from the federal government. For various reasons some farmers have secured contracts for larger acreages of beets than others have. In addition, distribution of the acreage under contract for beets tends to remain relatively stable from year to year among farmers. Unpublished reports from work done at the North Dakota State University Agricultural Experiment Station indicate that the per acre value of farms with relatively large acreages of sugar beets is recognizably higher than that of nearby farms with smaller or no acreage in sugar beets.

The situation in areas growing sugarcane is simpler in some respects than that in beet-growing areas. Cane is commonly grown continuously on the same fields without any crop rotation. In many areas the next best use for the land is substantially less profitable than sugarcane. Under these circumstances a large share of land values represents capitalization of benefits received from the sugar quota system. Land value would decline drastically if the production of sugarcane became unprofitable. The sugarcane area in Louisiana provides an example of this. In the 1920s, when the sugar industry was protected by tariff, Louisiana sugarcane was seriously affected by disease and the acreage declined to a low level. Some land was abandoned and returned to swamp worth only a dollar or two an acre. In a few years new disease-resistant varieties were developed and acreage increased, reaching a level above its previous peak. Sugarcane land in Louisiana is once more highly valuable.

Various factors have caused the acreage of sugarcane in Puerto Rico to decline substantially during the past fifteen years. Failure to maintain a rate of technological progress in mechanization, plant breeding, fertilization, and so on, that is competitive with that of Louisiana,

Florida, and Hawaii, together with higher wages which Puerto Rican labor can earn in New York and in other industries in Puerto Rico, made sugarcane growing unprofitable in large areas in the island, in spite of the high prices received for sugar. Presumably without the benefit of higher prices resulting from the sugar quota system, sugarcane acreage in Puerto Rico would have declined at an even faster rate.

Some Effects of the United States Sugar Quota System in Foreign Countries

The United States is by far the world's largest importer of sugar, nearly all of it reaching this country in raw form in bulk cargoes in vessels which are unloaded at a few ports where sugarcane refineries operate. Imports under the Sugar Act are received from thirty-one countries, of which five—the Philippines, Mexico, Brazil, the Dominican Republic, and Peru—supply about 70 percent. More than one-fourth of all imports comes from the Philippines. Imported sugar sells at the same price in the United States as that produced in domestic areas, and producers of sugar exported to the United States benefit from the generally higher prices prevailing here.

The Philippines represent an extreme case in this respect. More than half the sugar production of the Philippines is exported, and practically all of the sugar exported comes to the United States. Under these circumstances Philippine producers have benefited substantially from the United States sugar quota system, although not so much as producers in the United States.

Some sugar exporting countries, however, are clearly injured by the United States sugar quota system. Taiwan is an excellent example. More than half the sugar produced in Taiwan is exported, but only about one-fifth of the exports comes to the United States. The remaining exports go to the world market at prices well below those in the United States.

As was previously noted, an important factor keeping prices in the world market lower than would otherwise be expected is the high price of sugar in the United States. This is illustrated by the situation in the Dominican Republic which exports about three-fourths of its sugar output, with half going to the United States and half to the world market. Obviously the returns received by producers in the Dominican Republic are essentially determined by a blend of prices in the United States and world markets. The higher the price in the United States, the lower the world price can go and still provide an average price high enough to maintain production in the Dominican Republic. This arrangement of prices provides Taiwan producers with lower returns than those of producers in the Dominican Republic, and even lower than those received by producers in the Philippines.

A general conclusion reached from these examples is that the effect of the United States quota system on foreign sugar producers exporting to this country is highly variable and depends chiefly on the proportion of exports which are allowed to enter the United States. Under these circumstances every country, including the Philippines, which presently exports sugar to the United States plus all those who would like to do so, is continually attempting to get a larger United States sugar quota. These efforts come to a peak periodically when Congress is considering a revision of the Sugar Act, the last time in 1971. Foreign efforts to affect the Sugar Act lead to the employment of lobbyists by numerous countries and even to rumors of scandal. However, the employment of lobbyists is not confined to foreign countries. Every segment of the domestic industry uses them.

A basic difficulty in the allotment of quotas, both domestic and foreign, is that no suitable economic standard is available for determining them. As a result quotas are politically determined, and this has led to considerable capriciousness in their distribution among countries, areas, and individuals and, consequently, in the distribution of the economic benefits obtained from the system.

Perhaps the greatest difference between the sugar cartel and other cartels in this and other countries is to be found in the wide international scope of the economic effects of the sugar arrangement. In other ways, such as higher prices, the encouragement of the production of substitutes, and disagreements about shares among producers whose output is partly or wholly under the sugar system, the sugar cartel is quite similar to many others.

Part III. Transportation, Water, and Other Factors Affecting Location Value

7 *Martin O. Stern and Robert U. Ayres*

TRANSPORTATION OUTLAYS
WHO PAYS AND WHO BENEFITS?

Introduction

The discussion below aims at being illustrative and methodological rather than comprehensive, empirically oriented rather than theoretical, and order-of-magnitude rather than accurately quantitative. We believe that such an approach, coupled with mathematical simulation techniques, can shed considerable light on the forces at work when a transportation improvement is made. We concentrate on passenger transportation, and the main focus of this paper is on central business district transportation.

A brief summary of the financial statement for the most common U.S. transportation systems reveals no glaring inequities between users and nonusers per se. As has been previously shown, while some users are perhaps somewhat subsidized while others carry more than their share of costs, nonusers are not assessed beyond what might be considered reasonable from the point of view of a reservation charge. With the possible exception of an urban-rural inequity (which is not adequately discussed in the paper), the national, overall inequities in transportation appear less glaring than those, say, in compulsory education. In the case of the automobile, the private and voluntary annual investment in car purchases, car operation, and maintenance far outweighs public investment in roadways, for instance. Urban-rural or urban-suburban inequities, on the other hand, appear real and major.

Other user costs to be considered in trip-making can be subsumed under the headings of time and physical and emotional stress. Assuming a "reasonable" time cost for various trip purposes, we can calculate an annual time budget for different transportation modes. For air travel, the annual investment in time is well below the dollar outlays; for automobile travel, time and dollar outlays are comparable, provided private investments in automobiles and their operation are included; for rail travel, and especially for mass transit systems, the annual outlay in time far outweighs dollar outlays. Since mileage costs are roughly comparable for all modes, this clearly indicates the need for technological improvement in speed for mass transit and rail, if they are to compete with the automobile. The total time in man-hours spent traveling in 1970 by all modes could reasonably be assigned a value of $\sim$\$170 $\times$ 10^9.

If we now focus on urban movement, benefits due to incremental improvements in transportation (either in cost, time, or stress) between residence and work in a centralized city such as New York seem to be reflected fairly unambiguously in increases of residential rent and land values. Thus, the user benefits only marginally unless he is also the landowner at his residence; as a renter, he may even be put at a disadvantage.

The benefits from an improvement in transportation designed to foster central business district synergism can be much more striking. We illustrate this with figures taken from a study carried out for Lower Manhattan, where a quasi-equilibrium transportation model was built to derive a quantitative concept of accessibility. Changes of accessibility can be deduced from transportation improvements (for example, savings in time and stress) and related to changes in land values. It is found that the leverage exerted by an effective transportation improvement can be very high, resulting in windfalls exceeding the investment by sizable factors.

The implications of the foregoing for various affected user and non-user groups are discussed. Transportation investments can cause major shifts in location of residential as well as business sectors. Benefits due to an improvement are capitalized almost exclusively into land values along the way, unless user costs or land taxes are raised concomitantly. If it is true that ground rent (reflecting land value) is not a prime motivator for land improvement, taxing away at least the part of rent that is due to the transportation improvement would appear highly justified, and could contribute to maintenance, amortization, and continual improvement of transportation technology, as well as to the orderly development and upkeep of the area. It may even provide considerable excess revenue for other social purposes.

I. Who Pays for Public Transportation Investments?

To answer this question, aggregated financial statements for various common U.S. transportation systems are presented in Tables 7.1 and 7.2. The tables are compiled for the year 1970 and involve a number of approximations or assumptions indicated in the footnotes. In some

Table 7.1—Disbursements, 1970 (Billions of Dollars)

	New investments	Operation, maintenance, and financial charges	Total	Reserves	Grand total
Airlines	2.1[a]	7.021[b]	9.121	0.549	9.670
U.S. passenger railroads	0.011[c]	0.946[d]	0.957	0.377	0.580
Rural state-federal highways	5.812[e]	3.511[f]	9.323	0.272[g]	13.442
Municipal extensions of state highways	2.890[e]	0.957[f]	3.847		
Local rural roads	1.152[e]	2.450[f]	3.602	0.154[g]	3.756
Local municipal roads and streets	1.082[e]	1.923[f]	3.005	0.198[g]	3.203
Total (Highways)	11.204[h]	8.886[h]	20.090[h]	0.624[i]	20.401[i] 20.714
Urban mass transit	Bus, Subway .146 Comm. Rail .007 [k] $\overline{.153}$	1.498[l]	1.653	0.082	1.735
Primary and secondary education	4.15[m]	39.10[n]	43.25	1.65	41.6

a. Telephone interview, Air Transport Association. This figure represents estimates of expenditures for equipment and property.

b. *Air Transport, 1971,* The Annual Report of the U.S. Scheduled Airline Industry (Washington, D.C.: Air Transport Assoc. of America, 1971) pp. 32–33. Included in this figure are expenses for domestic trunk airlines and all other U.S. scheduled airlines minus cargo and international lines.

c. Telephone interview, Association of American Railroads. This figure represents total equipment installed during 1970 minus freight train cars, locomotives, and work equipment.

d. *Statistics of Railroads of Class I in the United States, Years 1960 to 1970,* Statistical Summary JJ (Washington, D.C.: Association of American Railroads, 1971), p. 3. This figure includes total expenses for maintenance of way and structures for passenger service (0.089), total maintenance of equipment for passenger service (0.245), and total operation of trains for passenger service (0.484). The total for these is 0.818 billion dollars, to which we have added miscellaneous and general operations, yielding a grand total, including depreciation, of 0.946. (Total depreciation of property and equipment = 0.056.)

e. *1971 Automobile Facts and Figures* (Detroit, Mich.: Automobile Manufactures Association, Inc., 1971), p. 67.

f. Ibid. These figures include total disbursements for maintenance on the four major highway systems, as provided in the Auto Fact book. In order to add to these expenditures, additional expenditures for administration and research, highway police and safety, interest on debt, and debt retirement (par value), it was necessary to adopt some rationale for distributing the latter expenditures among the four systems. Therefore, the breakdown of funds in the four categories, for the four systems, was based primarily on the total vehicle mileage for each system, taking into account the disbursing agency, i.e., federal government, state agencies, counties and townships, and municipalities.

g. These figures were obtained from *1971 Automobile Facts and Figures*, pp. 66 and 68, by reducing the estimated 1971 surpluses, by agency, to the 1970 total of 1.474 billion dollars, and subtracting from the state-federal surplus (allocable to Highways and Municipal Extensions) an estimated 0.850 billion diverted by states to other areas.

h. *1971 Automobile Facts and Figures*, p. 67. Totals include outlays for roads in Puerto Rico and for unclassified systems, causing these figures to be slightly higher than the sum of the four figures above them.

i. This figure is obtained by subtracting an estimated 0.850 billion, diverted by states from highways to other uses, from the surplus of 1.474 billion.

j. The sums along row and column differ by the inclusion, in the row figures, of disbursements for Puerto Rico and for unclassified road systems.

k. Calculations from telephone interviews with the American Transit Association and the American Association of Railroads. Figure represents investments in new subway cars and buses and in new commuter rail cars. Capital investments for mass transit in 1970 appear small, but are not comparable from year to year because financing is done in spurts, with construction taking place continuously. The average annual level of investment will increase rapidly for the next decade because of passage of the Urban Mass Transportation Assistance Act of 1970, and implementation of other major transit projects including the Bay Area Rapid Transit System (BART), the Washington Metro, the PATH Tube, and the planned new Second Avenue subway in New York City.

l. *Transit Facts, 1970–71* (Washington, D.C.: American Transit Association, 1970, 1971), p. 3.

m. *Financial Status of the Public Schools, 1971*, National Education Association, p. 34. Figure applies to school year 1969–70.

n. Ibid., p. 28.

cases the "reserve" category had to be used to make total outlays and revenues match. Public education is included as a "straw man," for comparison purposes.

In Table 7.1, new investments and maintenance and operating charges are broken down separately, to give an idea of the relative activity in different systems. If we can assume that the ratio of investments (additions to the system) to operating charges (related to cumulative past investments) is a measure of dynamism, the system of municipal extensions of state highways (beltways and urban throughways) looks most dynamic, with the rural federal-state highway system, other roadways, and passenger airlines following in that order.

The picture looks somewhat different, however, if the total annual

Table 7.2—Revenue Sources, 1970 (Billions of Dollars)

	User charges, fares, tolls	General taxes and subsidies	Bond issues and other investment income	Total	Other user contributions	Grand total
Airlines	7.600[a]	1.293[b]	0.775[c]	9.670		9.670
U.S. passenger railroads	0.555[d]	0.025[e]		0.580		0.580
Rural state-federal highways	4.566[f]					
		0.107[g]	2.532[h]	11.024		
Municipal extensions of state highways	3.819[f]					
					65.5[i]	86.2
Local rural roads	2.892[f]					
		2.733[g]		9.690		
Local municipal roads and streets	4.065[f]					
Total (Highways)	15.342	2.840	2.532	20.714		
Urban mass transit	Rail 0.42[j] Bus 1.21 ‾1.63	0.105[k]	0[l]	1.735		1.735
Primary and secondary education		38.2[m]	3.4[n]	41.6	8.8	50.4

a. *Air Transport, 1971*, Air Transport Association, p. 31.

b. *Government Expenditures for Highway, Waterway, and Air Facilities, and Private Expenditures for Railroad Facilities*, Association of American Railroads, May 1971. Totals for 1970 taken from Tables 2, 3, and 4, showing expenditures to airways, airports, and to domestic airlines.

c. Ibid., Table 3. Sum of state and local expenditures for airports.

d. Conversations, Association of American Railroads.

e. This figure represents Department of Transportation outlays for high speed ground transportation. It covers more than railroads, therefore, and refers primarily to outlays for rail and commuter transportation in the Northeast Corridor.

f. User charges for the four major highway systems were derived by taking the total receipts in various categories, such as federal trust fund revenues, user imposts, tolls, and parking fees, and distributing them among the four systems on the basis of vehicle miles per system. Figures on total receipts were taken from *1971 Automobile Facts and Figures*, Automobile Manufacturers Association, p. 68.

. Ibid. The total of 0.107 for state highways includes an estimate of state road revenues diverted to purposes other than highways. Total funds in this category have been distributed to the various highway systems on the basis of estimates from the Automobile Manufacturers Association.

h. Ibid.

i. This number is approximate, includes only passenger vehicles, and can be justified in two ways. From *Automobile Facts and Figures, 1971*, p. 48, we get annual 1970 expenditure estimates of about 37 billion dollars for new and used car purchases, net of old car sales, and net of federal excise tax, with a 15% upward correction for business and government car purchases. Pp. 40 and 49 yield estimates of about 16 billion dollars for gas and oil (about 64 x 10⁹ gallons of gas, at 24¢ per gallon exclusive of federal and state taxes), 8 billion for tires, batteries and accessories, and 4.5 billion for service and repair labor. Yearly value added to total stock averages about 5 billion per year.

From Table 7.2, in "Transportation Projection: 1970 and 1980," Report to the Office of Systems Analysis and Information, U.S. Department of Transportation, mimeographed (Washington, D.C.: Jack Faucett Associates, 1970), we obtain 38.9 billion for the cost of passenger vehicle transport in 1958 dollars, or 27.8 billion net of state and federal imposts. With a rough across-the-board consumer price index of 1.35, this gives 37.5 billion dollars; it includes such services as commissions on car sales. Depreciation, figured at 20.6 billion for personal vehicles, 0.7 for government vehicles, and extrapolated to 6.5 billion for business passenger vehicles, yields 27.8 billion, or a total of 65.3 billion. The treatment of addition to car stock is not clear, and no inflator has been applied, so the agreement must be regarded as fortuitous.

j. *Transit Fact Book, 1970–71*, American Transit Association, p. 2.

k. Conversation, Urban Mass Transportation Administration, Department of Transportation. Total represents UMTA outlays for 1970. It includes funds for capital facilities and investment, 0.089; research, development, and demonstration grants, 0.0124; technical studies, 0.0023; and university research and training grants, 0.001.

l. Conversations with the Department of Transportation yielded information that no substantial bond issues were passed for mass transit in 1970 in major cities. See footnote b, Table 1.

m. *Estimates of School Statistics, 1970–71*, Research Division, National Education Association, p. 17. Includes federal, state, and local revenues.

n. Ibid., p. 18 (nonrevenue receipts).

o. Office of Education, Department of Health, Education and Welfare. Includes capital outlay of 1.1 billion and current expenditures of 7.7 billion for Fiscal Year 1969–70, in current unadjusted dollars.

private investment (in 1970) of some $65 billion in car purchases, repairs, and operating expenses is allocated, pro rata, to the various highway systems, with only automobile market growth (typically 3 or 4 percent per year) allocated to the "new investment" category. In that case, the passenger airlines emerge as the major passenger growth mode, not a surprising conclusion.

Table 7.2 gives sources of revenue, broken down by whether they come from user charges, general taxes and subsidies, or private financing. This tabulation is required if we are to decide who pays for the transportation system. User charges are obviously borne by users only, whereas general taxes and subsidies are borne by everyone.

As it stands, Table 7.2 is not an adequate representation of the allocation of transportation *costs*. To make it so a category for *indirect* public (that is, nonuser) costs should be added, which would include such items as damages resulting from air pollution and noise, municipal outlays for traffic control, tax benefits resulting from the exemption of public facilities (streets, highways, airports, and so on) from local real estate taxes (an exemption not available to railroads, for instance), and uncompensated individual losses associated with the taking of urban land for highway construction. Most of these costs are extremely difficult to quantify, though the real estate tax benefit is probably calculable in principle if one could settle on an appropriate methodology. We feel certain that the annual value of all indirect costs noted above is significant in comparison with the direct costs.

Subject to the omissions mentioned, Tables 7.1 and 7.2 can be combined to yield a first estimate of (1) how charges are allocated to users and nonusers, and (2) whether user charges are allocated to the systems that produced them.

Results of these considerations are shown in Table 7.3. In general, nonuser charges (subject to the caveats above) are small enough compared to user charges to seem appropriate for a reservation charge or a payment for "unexercised options."[1] (In the case of the four road systems, the nonuser charges must, of course, be added up for those who neither ride nor drive, and in a less simple way for other nonusers of more than one road system.) This is especially true if one compares the situation in transportation to that in primary and secondary education.

In the latter case, taxpayers without children pay as much as those whose children avail themselves of public education. Those who resort to private education similarly pay for both public and private education. (In our rough calculations, no allowance is made for the fact that childless households tend to pay higher taxes for a given income because of lower exemptions, but tend to have lower incomes.) That there are real benefits to everybody, including those without children, in having a good public education system can hardly be in question. Whether, in that case, the unexercised option price is fair, and provides sensible incentives for population control goals, is another matter. In any case, the user-nonuser inequities in transportation averaged across the population as a whole do not seem to warrant too much further consideration.

1. J. R. Meyer, J. F. Kain, and M. Wohl, *The Urban Transportation Problem* (Cambridge: Harvard University Press, 1965), pp. 347–49.

Table 7.3—User-Nonuser Incidence

	Percentage paid by users	Per-centage paid by nonusers	Annual dollar revenue per household derived from	
			Average user	Average nonuser
Airlines[a]	89.2	10.8	502.0	20.2
U.S. passenger railroads[a]	96.1	3.9	88.2	0.4
Rural State-Federal Highways[a,c]	89.7	10.3	147.3	50.9
Municipal Extensions of State Highways[a,c]	103.9	−3.9	86.9	−6.0
Local Rural Roads[c]	82.8	17.2	196.5	13.7
Local Municipal Roads and Streets[a,c]	106.7	−6.7	72.2	−13.6
Urban Mass Transit[a]	95.2	4.8	130.7	1.7
Primary and Secondary Education[b]	33.2	23.0 43.8	604.0	3280.0 604.0

Table 7.3 Explanation. This table is intended to show how various systems are supported through user charges, as opposed to charges or subsidies levied against the general public. It involves an estimate of what fraction of the U.S. 63,200,000 households of 1970 (incidentally also approximately equal to the number of people filing and paying a federal income tax return) were users and nonusers, and therefore contains a subjective element. General taxes and subsidies are allocated to all households, user charges to estimated user households. These sums are obtained from the first two columns of Table 7.2, with bond issues and other investment income ignored except in the highway system. Thus the calculation is straightforward for airlines and U.S. passenger railroads.

a. Users are estimated by the authors to constitute
   25% of all U.S. households for airlines,
   10% of all U.S. households for U.S. passenger railroads,
   75% of all U.S. households for rural state-federal highways,
   65% of all U.S. households for municipal extensions of state highways,
   25% of all U.S. households for local rural roads,
   75% of all U.S. households for local municipal roads and streets,
   20% of all U.S. households for urban mass transit, and
   46% of all U.S. households for primary and secondary education.

b. 54% of all households have no children under 18 (American Almanac, 1971, pp. 36–38), and are taken as nonusers of education. Of the remaining 46%, it is estimated (conversation with the National Education Association, 1968 figures) that 11.4% of the offspring are or will be using private education, the rest public education. The same breakdown is allocated by household, so that 54% are nonusers, 5.2% users of private education, and 40.8% users of public education.

In the second and fourth number columns for Education, the upper numbers refer to users of private education, who pay for both systems, the lower numbers to users of neither system.

   c. For the highway and road system, the computation method is more complicated, since we wish to show transfers of user charges from systems on which they are collected to others where they are spent. These transfers can then be exhibited as nonuser contributions. It must be kept in mind that the groups of users and nonusers are neither distinct nor completely overlapping, so vertical addition for the four systems in a column is not meaningful. Negative numbers in the second and fourth columns imply that nonusers are being subsidized by users for the given system in question.

   The numerical entries are obtained as follows: Use the "grand total" column of Table 7.1 as the total of expenditures on each system, with the reserve of 0.272 allocated to municipal extensions, to be on the conservative side. From the four categories of expenditure subtract (1) the user charges (first column of Table 7.1); (2) general taxes and subsidies, prorated according to total expenditures between the two systems for which they are lumped; (3) bond issues and other investment income in a sufficient amount ($2.219 billion) to balance receipts with expenditures, and prorated between Highways and Extensions in the ratio of total expenditures. The difference between receipts and expenditures for each system then becomes a deficit (or surplus). It is assumed that users pay the user charges, and users plus non-users the algebraic sum of deficits and general taxes and subsidies.

The situation is somewhat different concerning the allocation of user funds. Especially in the case of urban users, funds raised are not reinvested to a full degree in urban facilities, but transferred in part to rural federal-state highway systems. Transfer to urban mass transit, in which user fees barely supported operating expenses, was small in 1970, but it fluctuates, and may exhibit a growth trend in the future.

Four other issues, one of them already mentioned above, are not dealt with in Tables 7.1–7.3. One of these relates to possible inequities between peak-hour and off-peak-hour users. The question arises whether different user groups bear their fair share of the capital investment and operational charges for a given road system. Extra capacity has to be installed to accommodate peak (commuting) traffic, for which this traffic does not bear aditional costs (except for extra gas and oil consumed as a result of congestion). This point has been discussed at length in Meyer, et al.[2]

The same basic issue also arises with respect to congestion costs (primarily time delays) and leads to the question of optimal pricing strategy for use of the roads. This interesting problem has been dealt with

2. *Ibid.,* pp. 64–70.

by a number of authors, including Vickrey,[3] Walters,[4] Smeed,[5] and Johnson.[6]

Third, the automobile is a major polluter, imposing damage to health, agriculture, and structures estimated at several billion dollars annually, on user and nonuser alike, with the highest concentration of external costs imposed on highly urbanized areas and their immediate environs.

Finally, as already discussed, there are other large (but so far unquantified) indirect costs of urban automotive transportation.

In summary, then, it would appear that a serious urban-rural inequity exists. In effect, the heavy reliance on automotive transportation in central cities results in a significant redistribution of benefits from (1) direct subsidy of rural highways by gasoline taxes collected in urban areas, and (2) indirect subsidy to suburban users of urban roads, whose indirect costs fall almost exclusively on urban residents (that is, taxpayers) alone. This is a topic that deserves further exploration.

II. Other Costs: Time

Out-of-pocket costs are not the only social costs borne by trip-makers. Other cost components can be subsumed under time spent and (physical and emotional) stress expended. Although we have done some work on evaluating stress on short intraurban trips, which will be discussed below in Sections IV and V, we shall here confine ourselves to time.

Table 7.4, using passenger miles on various transportation modes as a point of departure, derives the yearly man-hours spent on these modes. In the case of airlines, an allowance in effective speed is made for "portal-to-portal" travel. The man-hours are then translated into dollars with the help of estimated breakdowns of trips by purpose, and time-money equivalents by purpose. The latter were derived in earlier work and are also discussed in Section IV. The results are quite startling, in that: (1) The ratio of the value of annual time spent traveling to annual outlays for travel (exclusive of new investment,

3. Wm. S. Vickrey, "Pricing in Urban and Suburban Transport," *American Economic Review* 52 (May 1963) : 452–65.

4. A. A. Walters, "The Theory and Measurement of Private and Social Cost of Highway Congestion," *Econometrica* 29 (1961) : 676–99.

5. *Road Pricing: The Economic and Technical Possibilities,* "The Smeed Panel Report" to the Ministry of Transport (London: HM's Stationery Office, 1964) .

6. M. Bruce Johnson, "On the Economics of Road Congestion," *Econometrica* 32 (1964) :137.

Table 7.4—Other User Costs, 1967 (Billions of Dollars)

	Billions of passenger miles	Average trip length (miles)	Average speed (mph) millions of hours	Annual time investment, millions of hours	Annual[e] equivalent dollar investment (in bils.)	Ratio of annual travel time value to annual operating costs
Airlines	131.7[a]	700	185[b]	712	3.8[d]	0.5
U.S. passenger railroads	6.2[e]	79[f]	40.1[g]	154	0.7[h]	3.5
Rural state-federal highways	481[i]		55[j]	8,740	36.3[k]	1.8[l]
Municipal extensions of state highways	403[i]		45[j]	8,950	46.2[m]	2.8[l]
Local rural roads	334[i]		45[k]	7,430	23.4[n]	1.7[l]
Municipal roads and streets	456[i]		20[j]	22,800	49.1[o]	2.6[l]
Urban mass transit	17.6 Bus[p] 4.6 Rail 16.9 Sub. ————— 39.1		10[q] 30 15	1,760 156 1,120	6.7[r]	4.5

a. *Air Transport, 1971,* Air Transport Association, p. 26.

b. Obtained from *American Almanac,* Statistical Abstract of the U.S., U.S. Department of Commerce (New York: Grosset and Dunlap, 1971), p. 565, for 390 mph average domestic airline speed, and estimated for average trip length and connecting ground travel. The time for ground travel should be credited against other modes to avoid double counting, but since the correction is small, and taxis and limousines have not been included, the correction has not been made.

c. Leisure travel at $1.30 per hr; commuting at $3.00 per hr; business travel at $8.00 per hr. (Based on the calculations presented in Section V of this paper.)

d. $5.32 per hr for 60% business, 40% leisure; our estimate.

e. *Statistics of Railroads of Class I in the United States (1960–1970),* Association of American Railroads, September 1971, p. 7.

f. Ibid.

g. *American Almanac,* p. 557.

h. $4.65 per hr for 50% business, 50% leisure; our estimate.

i. Calculated from Highway Statistics, 1970, U.S. Department of Transportation, Federal Highway Administration. A multiplier of 1.5 was used to make allowance for passengers carried.

j. Estimates.

k. $4.15 per hr for 40% business, 10% commuting, 50% leisure; our estimate.

l. The denominators of these ratios are obtained by apportioning the sum of private annual investment ($60.5 billion, exclusive of annual average stock value increase) and road operation and maintenance charges ($8.9 billion) to each road system according to mileage (which is proportional to the first column of Table 4).

m. $5.16 per hr for 50% business, 30% commuting, 20% leisure; our estimate.

n. $3.15 per hr for 20% business, 30% commuting, 50% leisure; our estimate.

o. $2.15 per hr for 50% commuting, 50% leisure; our estimate.

p. The passenger mile figure was obtained by multiplying the billions of bus passengers in 1970, provided by Faucett, "Transportation Projection," section 3, p. 13, by our estimate of the average trip length: $(6.3 \times 10^9 \times 2.8$ miles $= 17.6 \times 10^9)$. The figure for rail was obtained from Faucett, "Transportation Projection," section 3, p. 13. The figure for subways was calculated by multiplying billions of commuter rail passengers by estimated average trip length: $(1.22 \times 10^9 \times 9$ miles $= 16.9 \times 10^9)$.

q. Estimates.

r. $2.99 per hr. for 60% commuting, 30% leisure, 10% business.

to serve as a surrogate for out-of-pocket cost) varies all the way from 0.5 (for passenger airlines) to 4.5 (for mass transit). (2) The total value of time spent on all modes in 1970 by this reckoning amounted to close to 170×10^9, that is, one-fifth of the GNP. This time is probably over 50 percent (but not entirely) unproductive, and represents a waste; 90 percent of it was spent in motor vehicles.

The out-of-pocket costs per mile do not vary nearly as much for different modes as do the time costs. They generally range from 3 cents per passenger mile (for railroads) through 5 to 6 cents per passenger mile for airlines, to 7 cents per passenger mile for private vehicles on uncongested freeways. (Congestion costs, especially at the margin, are another matter.)

Thus, the ratio of the value of time spent to out-of-pocket cost can be taken as a rough index of the need for technological improvement. In the case of railroads, it can be taken as an indication of what speed improvements are needed as a function of trip length, to make them competitive with cars, on the one hand, and with air travel on the other. In the case of mass transit, the need for improvement is most glaring of all. Whether such improvements can be made cost-effectively (that is, by using time saved to pay for research, development and, capital expenditures) is, of course, a central question.

III. Benefits: The Commuting and Shopping Residents

We shall consider benefits in the quasi-equilibrium context. That is, we consider that land uses have become somewhat stable and exhibit substantial market efficiency. We then ask ourselves what is the effect of a transportation improvement, such as the Second Avenue subway, to be built in Manhattan between 126th Street and the Battery. This subway, running for about twelve miles, will cost about $1.0 billion, and will carry, on a weekday, some 100,000 commuters and an about equal number of shoppers from the upper East Side to Midtown and Lower Manhattan. A smaller number of riders, but one increasing in time with land development response, will ride between Midtown and Lower Manhattan during the day, and a still smaller number within each of these areas, which are themselves small enough to offer competitive modes (walking, bus, and taxis).

We shall not here concern ourselves quantitatively with the difficult second-order effects of response to transportation in terms of land use changes (although these may be of the greatest importance in the long run), but deal only with increased activity due to change in accessibility. Further, we shall only deal with passenger movement, not goods and information flow. We shall also ignore congestion which will clearly impose some upper limits on first-as well as second-order effects, unless major technological changes take place. Such changes must either allow free people flow at much higher densities than at present, or they must provide attractive substitutes for going to places of work and for making direct contact with clients and colleagues that seems to be the rationale of central business districts (CBD's).

Is the incremental improvement cost-effective at least in the limited "neighborhood" sense that the net benefits, in terms of fares collected from and time saved for the ridership on the new system, outweigh the annualized investment plus operating and maintenance costs? For the Second Avenue subway, we have postulated a ridership of 400,000 for 300 days out of the year and assumed time savings to the average user of ten minutes per trip (worth about fifty cents) as compared to presently available and competing systems. In that case, fare box revenue might be about $36 million per year, and the value of time saved, about $60 million per year. From this point of view, the investment looks marginal, even with very low operating and maintenance costs.

If the line were owned privately, the owner would, of course, have to exert all his ingenuity to capture most of the consumer surplus in the form of time saved (by raising the *average* fare from, say, thirty cents to seventy-five cents, and making the fare dependent on trip length) in order to realize even this marginal return.

From the viewpoint of the city-wide Mass Transit Authority, as opposed to that of the neighborhood, the fares lost to preexisting systems because of customers' switching to the Second Avenue Line must be regarded as a loss, to be subtracted from the net benefit. Since, in the near term, almost all customers on the Second Avenue Line will be switchers rather than new riders, the new link is clearly not cost-effective in that sense, since only the yearly $60 million worth of time saved can be counted as a benefit. The returns to the public treasury will have to come partly from higher taxes on land benefiting in value from the new link, and partly, in the longer run, from the land development response, creating new localized densification, growth, and trip-making. This growth is partly offset by reduced growth, or stagnancy and decay, in regions not benefited by the transportation improvement. Such stagnancy and decay may be due only partly to decreased ability to compete as a result of a relative decrease in accessibility. In part it may be due to the present way of financing transit improvements, by imposing additional burdens (increased taxes and/or fares) not only on the area benefited, but on the city as a whole.

The reason for treating residential aspects of transportation benefits separately from those affecting the central work place will become clearer as we go along. For the moment, suffice it to say that rent is typically the same per person at work and at home, but work densities are generally about twice as high: in Manhattan, a worker may, on the average, occupy 150 square feet of office floor space, ranging in rent from $6.00 to $12.00 per year per square foot, or $75.00 to $150.00 per month per person. (Ground floor retail space, incidentally, rents for about one and one-half to two times the equivalent upper-floor office space, although there are wide fluctuations.) At home, say in Greenwich Village or Midtown East or West, he may occupy 300 square feet (or considerably more if living alone) and pay $3.00 to $6.00 per square foot per year, or again $75.00 to $150.00 per person per month. If a family is affluent enough that access to such superior goods as fashion stores, the theatre, art galleries, or a panorama is important, an additional rent premium would be paid in neighborhoods convenient to these amenities.

As the worker moves away from his place of work, rent seems to decrease in step with time added (since the cost changes slightly, if at all), in keeping with classical location theory. A move from Midtown to Washington Heights or to the Bronx, for example, is likely to add one hour per day to his round-trip commuting time, or $75.00 per month at $3.00 per hour, a cost that is justified in Section V. This is somewhat smaller than the average price differential for average-sized apartments in the locations discussed. The discrepancy is probably mostly explained by the fact that land close-in is relatively scarce, so that rents are successfully bid up by people who value their time at more than the average value of $3.00 per hour. Stress differences may contribute additionally, but we have found commuting trips to be relatively stress-inelastic.

From this equilibrium picture, it seems reasonable to conclude that an incremental transportation improvement will result in time, money, and stress savings to the user that are more than fully reflected in increased rents and land values. Thus, if an improvement is cost-effective in the limited "neighborhood" sense, even the short-term neighborhood benefits appear to be sufficient to pay for its construction, operation, and maintenance.

Second-order effects may, of course, cause further and longer-range changes. For example, the improvement may be great enough that an entirely new ridership and clientele for certain terminus activities develops that previously did not exist (that is, people make more trips from their residences than heretofore). The terminus activities themselves will expand in response. These benefits may be reflected in additional rent increases. Another example: not all workers living in a given residential area act as if they valued their commuting time at $3.00 an hour. Thus, an increase in rent based on time saved at this value is likely to displace the lower-income worker to another, possibly less accessible or agreeable residence, with attendant dislocation expenses. If one pictures a city as a center with concentric residential zones, attractive housing close enough in may be sufficiently scarce to attract people whose commuting time value far exceeds $3.00 an hour, which would be reflected in much steeper rent differentials, as observed. A recent pertinent discussion on this point is that by Edel.[7]

In order to predict these second-order effects resulting from transportation changes, especially the important spatial shifts of economic, social, and racial groups, as well as employment categories, it is necessary to start with a thorough knowledge of where these groups live and work (or sometimes do not work) to begin with. It is for the prediction of the answers to such questions that simulation and urban modeling are useful. We shall now turn our attention to such a model, which was developed specifically to examine the effect of transportation on central business districts. We shall then deal with the benefits to CBD's with the help of the model.

IV. An Urban Transportation Model

We shall now briefly describe an urban transportation model, the Activity Accessibility Model (AAM for short), that was developed in

---

7. Matthew Edel, "Recent Land Use Conflict in American Cities," in *Readings in Urban Economics,* ed. Matthew Edel and Jerome Rothenberg (New York: The Macmillan Co., 1972), pp. 134–51.

1969–70 under auspices of the Department of Housing and Urban Development (HUD) to examine urban trip-making patterns and their effect on the economy of the area under study.[8] The model is intended as a planning model for decision-makers to examine first-order consequences resulting from changes in transportation or land use, which are due either to private or public investments or public policy changes. It is intended to be coupled to an Economic Impact Model (EIM). Both of these will be described next. Both models and the relations between them are schematized in Figure 7.1.

The AAM derives a demand for trip-making between two points. The two points may be street intersections in an urban neighborhood. The description of this neighborhood, to a degree of resolution or detail deemed practical, forms the main external input to the model. For example, transportation systems (including walking), with their routes, speeds, rates, stops and interchanges, can be completely described, as can the types of activities and numbers of people in various buildings, by street address or even floor for each building, or aggregated to blocks or zones.

For conceptual reasons a gravity formulation was chosen for the demand function. The demand depends on the population at the two points—the population at the origin generates trips, that at the destination attracts them. But instead of total populations at the two points, as in conventional gravity models, we consider population in specific activity sectors at the two points, such as retail or residential at the origin, banking or general office at the destination. For example, the sectors used for describing trips to and within the Lower Manhattan business district were:

Activity Sector

1. Households (outside of Lower Manhattan)
2. Business and Professional Services (outside of Lower Manhattan)
3. Goods and Supplies (outside of Lower Manhattan)
4. Other (outside of Lower Manhattan)
5. Business and Professional Services
6. Goods and Supplies
7. General Office
8. Government
9. Warehousing and On-Site Manufacturing
10. Restaurants and Eating Places
11. Retail
12. Parks and Plazas
13. Miscellaneous
14. Brokers
15. Exchanges
16. Miscellaneous Financial
17. Insurance
18. Banks

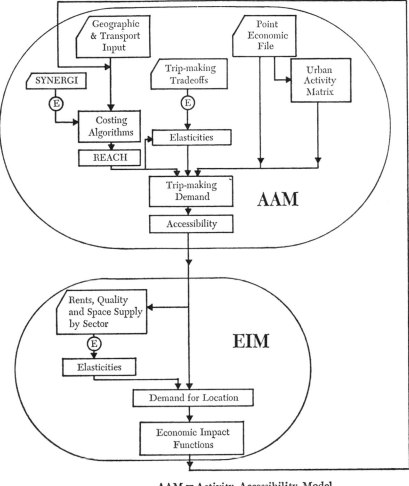

AAM = Activity Accessibility Model
EIM = Economic Impact Model
(E) = Numerical Estimation Procedure
Figure 7.1—Urban transportation model.

We multiply the product of the populations at the two points by a number which specifies how much trip-making, on the average throughout the neighborhood, is generated between the two sectors in question. This number is an element of what we call the Urban Activity Matrix (UAM).

In addition, the demand depends on the friction or impedance of trip-making between the two points, which is, in turn, related to how difficult it is to get from one point to the other by foot or with the help of whatever transportation systems are available. The degree of difficulty is determined by cost, time taken, and emotional and physical stress expended. One can think of out-of-pocket cost, time, and stress as the three components of a cost vector which is calculated for each route and mode available between the points, with mode-switching allowed. Stress is quantified through an opinion survey. If the stress is comprehensively defined and correctly quantified, and if the coefficients of relative importance of the three cost components ("elasticity coefficients") are carefully calibrated for all trip types of importance, we have then obtained an impedance which correctly reflects, in a statistical way, how people decide whether to make a trip, and what route and mode to take; that is, we have the basis for a quantitative demand function. Trips are grouped by types quite independently of the sectors generating or attracting them, different types being characterized by distinctly different sets of elasticity coefficients. We have considered six trip types:

Trip Type k	Description
$k = 1$	Journey to Work
2	Office-Based Business Trip (nonlunch)
3	Office-Based Business Trip (lunch)
4	Office-Based Personal Service Trip (lunch *and* nonlunch)
5	Home-Based Personal Service Trip
6	Goods Delivery Trip

Of course, only routes which offer competitive values of money cost, time, and stress need be considered. An infinity of noncompetitive routes is eliminated by a network selection algorithm called "REACH."

If we specify the demand for trips between one sector, say retail, at a given origin, and another sector, say banks, at all possible surrounding destinations, and then sum over all other destinations as well for which nonzero UAM elements exist, we obtain the number of trips indicating how much interaction with the surrounding area is created

by retail at the given origin point. This is the *accessibility* for the retail sector at that point. It can be divided by an average accessibility
for retail over the whole CBD, to give an "accessibility index." An index of unity indicates average accessibility. An index >1 means better
than average accessibility, either because the activities with which retail interacts most strongly are close by, or because the interacting activities are linked to the point by a good transportation system. Con-
versely, an index <1 implies below-average accessibility.

In summary, the accessibility index is a number that indicates how
suitable a given location is for carrying on a specific economic activity.
It quantifies the relative ease with which this activity interacts with
other activities in the area that are essential to its function.

Formally, the accessibility index $y_{2i}{}^{\eta}$ for sector η at origin point i
is given (with minor simplification) by

$$y_{2i}^{\eta} = \frac{\displaystyle\sum_{\eta,k} A^{\eta\mu,k} \tilde{m}_{\eta\mu} \sum_{j} B_j^{\mu} / \bar{R}_{ij}^{k}}{\displaystyle\sum_{\eta,k} \tilde{m}_{\eta\mu}^{k}}, \text{ where} \tag{1}$$

$\tilde{m}_{\eta\mu}^{k} = m_{\eta\mu}^{k} + m_{\mu\eta}^{k}$ = number of daily trips of type k between sectors
η and μ throughout the CBD (# of trips);

B_j^{μ} = fraction of activity μ at point j relative to that
throughout the CBD;

$A^{\eta\mu,k}$ = normalization factor, related to the average
impedance ($\simeq e \equiv 2.718 \ldots$ in value).

$$\bar{R}_{ij}^{k} = \exp. \sum_{p=1}^{3} \alpha_p^{k} X_{ij}^{p} \tag{2}$$

is the trip-making impedance averaged over
available modes, as a function of out-of-pocket
costs X^1, time X^2, and stress X^3; the exogenous-
ly derived coefficients α_1, α_2, α_3 indicate the
relative importance of the cost components.

By multiplying the trip demand between points by the cost—either
the out-of-pocket cost or the trip-type-dependent total 3-component
cost—before performing the sums, one can easily obtain the sector-
specific cost of access from a point. Any reduction of this cost has obvious implications for the competitive advantage of a given sector lo-
cating at that point.

The Economic Impact Model (EIM) is designed to quantify the determinants for demand and supply in a given location; that is, the variables which determine how desirable a given location is to a potential user, and how much space, and of what type, an owner is motivated to make available at that location. Once the "constitutive" equations of demand and supply are known, the effects of policy and investment decisions can be evaluated.

Of course, these constitutive equations are not observed in practice. What *is* observed, and has to do for purposes of derivation and calibration of these equations, is the structural relation between the identified variables on the surface representing the intersection between demand and supply, for the real world (say a neighborhood) under quasi-equilibrium conditions.

The EIM postulates that the salient variables are the (sector-specific) accessibility, derived from the AAM; the environmental quality characterizing a space and its surroundings (that is, the amenities, appearance and "image" presented by a building, its address, its occupants, and its surroundings); and the price (purchase or rent) of the space. Construction and maintenance costs for an improvement may be partial surrogates for quality; vacancy rate may also play an important role.

Once (1) a suitably large and well-distributed sample on price information in a neighborhood has been obtained (not always an easy task), (2) a panel of experts has provided a rating of quality, and (3) the AAM has been run to provide accessibilities, econometric methods can be used to provide a relation between these variables. Functionally plausible forms are then assumed for the constitutive equations (demand and supply must depend on the independent variables and their first and second derivatives in well-defined ways), and coefficients are deduced for them. These coefficients are again in the nature of elasticities, relating shadow prices, accessibility, quality, and demand or supply. While the coefficients of the constitutive equations can be subject to considerable uncertainties, one can have confidence that they yield sensible and reliable answers to questions of how the variables shift when changes are introduced in the neighborhood that cause not too large deviations from prevailing conditions.

The AAM is completely computerized and operational for Lower Manhattan, the EIM still requires some analytical work and programming, although the data base for Lower Manhattan is in hand. For this reason, a crude version of the EIM, formulated and calibrated during the HUD study, will be used below. In this version, the demand for space S is expressed as a function of rent y_1, and accessibility y_2, with coefficients calibrated from observations of rental space supplied and of rents paid at various Lower Manhattan locations; accessibility values are given by the AAM.

The design of these models was motivated primarily by a desire to understand trip-making and urban synergism *within* a central business district. The AAM was therefore calibrated and applied first in Lower Manhattan, and that is the location which will serve as illustration for our discussion of transportation benefits in a CBD. By reasonable aggregation, the same model can, however, describe home-based interactions with one or several CBD's or industrial areas. Such interactions would involve going to work, shopping, seeking entertainment, or taking advantage of other personal and social services.

V. Benefits: The Actors in the CBD

Here we shall be concerned mainly with the benefit accruing to land, businesses, and other CBD actors from a transportation improvement. Actually, a hypothetical improvement, in the form of a 10 mph continuous toll-free moving sidewalk surrounding the financial district, was implanted in our model. It would lead to improvements in accessibility of typically 10 percent for points nearby, corresponding to round-trip savings of about two minutes in office-based walking trips to other offices, as well as some decrease in stress. In order to understand this finding and its implications, we must go into some numerical detail. Two different (but not entirely independent) methods will be used to arrive at our results.

The more physically immediate method requires only the expression for accessibility and some typical numbers for business-oriented trips in Lower Manhattan, since we are interested in the effect of transportation change on urban synergism. A typical trip is one with impedance about equal to $c \simeq 2.72$. Trips from City Hall to Broad and Wall Street, for example, were rather typical. Costs were found to be as in Table 7.5 for a business trip. Money costs (in 10^{-4} \$) and time (in seconds) were obtained by observation, and stress (in "trolls") by structured panel survey.

Table 7.5—Cost Components, City Hall to Wall and Broad Streets

Mode	Money cost (X_1)	Time (X_2)	Stress (X_3)
Walk	0	508	272
Subway	3,000	652	293
Cab	10,500	502	173

The trade-off coefficients α_1, α_2, α_3 for trip types $k = 2$ or 3 that appear in $\bar{R}^k_{ij}$ and play a role akin to elasticities were obtained by a questionnaire, and are presented in Table 7.6. Note that these coefficients imply a trade-off of one hour against $8.00. Similar coefficients derived, for example, for a leisurely personal service trip laid a much higher emphasis on stress and gave $1.30 as the equivalent of an hour's time. For a commuter trip, $3.00 per hour was obtained.

Table 7.6—Trade-Off Coefficients for k = 2, 3

α_1	0.35×10^{-4}
α_2	7.25×10^{-4}
α_3	$22.5 \ \times 10^{-4}$

Source: Study of Major Urban Activity Circulation Systems and Their Impact on Congested Areas, IRT-R-29 (Washington, D.C.: International Research and Technology Corporation, 1970), p. 34, Table 7.

From Tables 7.5 and 7.6 we find that the trip described gave an impedance exp. $(0 + 0.37 + 0.61) \sim e$ for walking, and slightly higher (but competitive) values for the other modes, with time always contributing a factor of about $\exp(0.3)$ to $\exp(0.4)$. For cabs, for example, the exponent is $0.37 + 0.36 + 0.39 = 1.12$.

We shall now examine how accessibility relates to density of development, and density in turn to land value, in order to arrive at a direct relationship between accessibility and land value.

First, we imagine that the development in the immediate neighborhood of our point i of origin compacts in a little, from a density of ρ employes per acre to $\rho(1 + \epsilon)$ employes, where $\epsilon \ll 1$. If this change is made in a "quasi-equilibrium" way, leaving the bulk of the CBD unaffected, we see that the total number of trips $\tilde{m}^k_{\mu\eta}$ is virtually unaffected. If we also allow our mesh of points j near i to draw in at the same time (as if blocks just got smaller), the coefficients B^μ_j remain the same as before. Only $\bar{R}^k_{ij}$ changes, mainly because distances get shorter. Thus, in the absence of congestion, the time taken goes inversely with the square root of density, if we assume that employes at i remain "loyal" to their affiliations with sectors at j, as would be plausible from the viewpoint of intervening opportunities.

Stress (which, except for walking, is not strongly time-dependent) and dollar costs (which are almost distance-independent for short trips) can be assumed to change little with density.

Thus, our main change in accessibility from y_2^0 to y_2' is due to the average trip time factor $\exp(0.36)$ in the mean impedance of value e changing to

$$\exp. \frac{0.36}{\sqrt{1+\epsilon}} \approx e^{0.36(1-\frac{\epsilon}{2})}.$$

We can therefore write

$$y_2'/y_2^0 \approx e^{0.36}/e^{0.36(1+\frac{\epsilon}{2})} = e^{0.18\epsilon} \approx 1 + 0.18\epsilon$$
$$\approx (1+\epsilon)^{0.18}.$$

Accessibility thus varies with the fifth or sixth root of density *if changes in dollar costs and stress can be neglected.* In that case, for Lower Manhattan, we can normalize by writing

$$y_2 \approx 0.245\rho^{0.18}. \tag{3}$$

For walking, with walking stress proportional to time and somewhat dominant, the exponent will be closer to 0.5. For cabs, most of the stress is of the threshhold variety (related to waiting for and hailing the cab), hence distance-independent, but the fare is distance- or time-dependent, so that an exponent of about 0.33 results; for subways, similar considerations yield about the same exponent. We therefore adopt

$$y_2 \approx 0.075\rho^{0.33}. \tag{4}$$

This relationship is plotted in Figure 7.2. It is so normalized that an average accessibility index of 1.0 corresponds to the average observed density in the area (2,500 per acre). It is a gross average: we have found that banking and lawyers, for example, are so highly clustered as to indicate a predominantly pedestrian character. In that case the exponent should, indeed, be close to 0.5, but the coefficient would be reduced to yield an average accessibility index of 1.0 for a density of about 5,000 per acre.

In order to relate density to land value V, we obtained some land values (recent transactions where available, otherwise assessed values) in "prime" business districts and related them to employe densities (based on 150 square feet gross building floor space per employe). Wherever possible, a couple of close-lying buildings and parcel values were averaged. No correction was made for retail. Results are shown in Table 7.7 and plotted in Figure 7.3.

Most of the points of Figure 7.3 can be represented by a relationship

$$V = 1.1 \times 10^{-3}\rho^{1.5}. \tag{5}$$

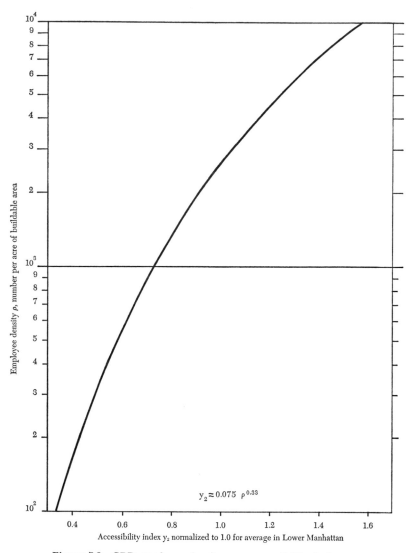

Figure 7.2—CBD employee density ρ vs. accessibility index y_2.

Table 7.7—Estimated CBD Land Values as Function of Employee Density, 1971

Location (Code, Fig. 3)	ρ, employees/acre	Dollar value (V) per sq. ft.
Lower Manhattan (M) (Chase-Manhattan Plaza area)	9,000	1,000
Washington, D.C. (W) (14-story Connecticut Ave. area)	2,700	150
Washington, D.C. (W) (8-story Connecticut Ave. area)	1,750	85 65
Denver, Colorado (D) (Downtown)	1,650	75
Pittsburgh, Pa. (P) (Downtown-Golden Triangle area)	7,600 5,000 4,400 2,600 1,900	49 54 49 20 20
Topeka, Kansas (To) (Downtown)	1,300 140	32 1.15
Trenton, N.J. (Tr)	2,900	9
Roanoke, Virginia (R)	580	21
Alexandria, Va. (A)	610	19
La Jolla, Calif. (LJ)	540 500	15 16

It must be emphasized that these land values are mere estimates and that the data are quite scattered. In particular, the Pittsburgh and Trenton data fall way off the curve. Both represent assessed values. In the case of Trenton, the sole building is not representative of surrounding densities (which are much lower), hence cannot meaningfully be related to accessibility. The same is true of the highest-density parcel in Pittsburgh, which represents by far the largest office building in that city. However, the other, more typical buildings in Pittsburgh also go with unusually low assessed land values. The explanation may be, in part, that land is underassessed. In part, it may

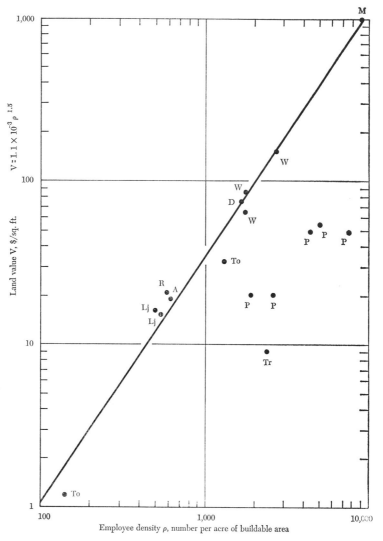

Figure 7.3—Land Value V in CBD's as a function of employee density ρ. Code for identity of location points is given in Table 7.7.

result from the fact that Pittsburgh is chronically depressed. Also, land is taxed at twice as high a rate as is improvement on the land. (This should have no depressing effect on its value, unless the assessor tries to offset the effect.) No conclusion may be drawn from these few points, except that they may warrant further study.

Combining (4) and (5), we obtain

$$V = 140\, y_2^{4.5} \tag{6}$$

which is plotted in Figure 7.4. We see that a 1 percent change in accessibility results in a 4.5 percent change in land values, or that a 10 percent change in accessibility (as in some of the property located near access points to our hypothetical moving sidewalk) leads to a 54 percent change in land values. In case of congestion effects, the leverage could be higher.

A second way to estimate the relationship between accessibility and land value is to make use of the rather primitive forms developed so far for the EIM. Coefficients were estimated from Lower Manhattan data, with the help of two functional relationships, one linear, the other exponential (Cobb-Douglas):

$$\underset{(1.4)}{S_i} = -6.8 \times 10^5 - \underset{(3.7)}{5.7 \times 10^3 y_{1i}} + \underset{(0.14)}{0.84 \times 10^6 y_{2i}}, \tag{7}$$
$$R^2 = 0.69;$$

and

$$S_i = e^{14.0}\underset{(5.8)}{} \underset{(1.18)}{y_{1i}^{1.37}} \underset{(2.8)}{y_{2i}^{9.5}}, \tag{8}$$
$$R^2 = 0.39.$$

Here S_i is the space "demanded" per block in square feet at point i, per unit rent and accessibility interval around rent y_{1i} (dollars per square foot) and accessibility (dimensionless), respectively, with average rent about \$12.00 per square foot at accessibility 1.0 (late 1969). (The assumption was made that space demanded was correctly reflected by that supplied.)

Note that y_{1i} and y_{2i} carry the right coefficient signs in both cases, although the coefficient for y_1 is far less well determined, and the explanatory power of Equation (7) appears superior to that of Equation (8). In these primitive relations we have aggregated over all sectors.

We can obtain an idea of the relation between accessibility and land value by forming the cross-elasticity of rent with respect to ac-

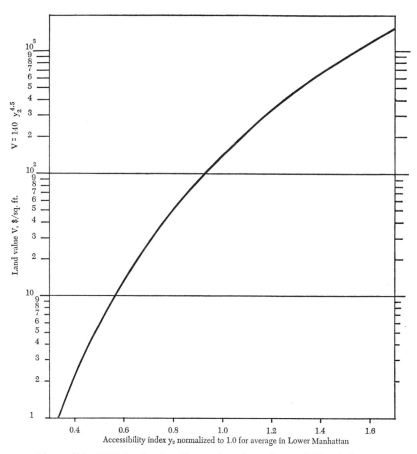

Figure 7.4—CBD land value V as a function of accessibility index y_2.

cessibility, keeping demand for space fixed. For Equation (7) this yields

$$(dy_{1i} / dy_{2i})(y_{2i} / y_{1i}) = (0.84 \times 10^6)(5.7 \times 10^3)^{-1} \times (1/12)$$
$$= 12.3.$$

For Equation (8) it gives $9.5 / 1.37 = 6.9$.

These models are too crude to have quantitative validity. They only corroborate that the effect of accessibility on land value is characterized by a large leverage factor, especially if one remembers that a percentage increase in floor rent corresponds to a greater percentage increase in ground rent, since part of the original rent had to cover debt amortization, depreciation, interest, operation, and maintenance on the buildings. We therefore adopt the more conservative Equation (6) for purposes of further discussion, but keep in mind that its exponent is probably at the low end of the spectrum. As in the case of private residences, accessibility is scarce and at a premium, and employers in sectors benefiting most from it are likely to bid up the rent beyond the confines of the average relations between land value and density, on the one hand, and density and accessibility on the other, described by Equations (4) and (5), respectively.

What are some of the implications of Equation (6)?

Consider a building of 1,200,000 square feet on an acre of ground, that is, typically a fifty-story building with a floor-area ratio of 27.5, and 8,000 occupants, imbedded in an area of similar density. The land may initially be $850 per square foot, the 1971 rent $12 per square foot. The number of daily (noncommuting) business-oriented trips to this building generated by its 8,000 occupants is typically 16,000 in this already highly synergistic area.

If now a publicly financed transportation improvement is made that causes an average accessibility increase of 10 percent (say because of average time savings of 2.0 minutes per round trip, and corresponding stress savings), this will cause total daily time savings of 533 hours per day, or $4,270 per day, 1.07×10^6 dollars per year. From the viewpoint of the occupants of this building, then, an investment of $10,-000,000 might be justified, and perhaps slightly more on account of stress savings, if the transportation investment is to be judged cost-effective (we assume that revenues enticed away from preexisting systems are just cancelled by riderships on the new system).

We have seen that a 10 percent change in accessibility might change land value by 54 percent or more. In this case, land value would therefore increase from $850 to $1,300 per square foot, with space rent going from $12 to perhaps $14 or $15. Total value of the acre would increase by about $20 million, or by about twice the maximum transportation investment (paid for by the public, and justified on grounds of overall social benefits).

In addition to the landowner's obtaining this tremendous windfall, it must be realized that part of the gain (for example, any reduction in stress that results) is retained by the trip-maker. Gains in time and out-of-pocket cost are likely to be divided between employees and employers, to the extent that employees are able to work more efficiently. The gain to the employer may be overshadowed by losses if the landowner raises his rent to the limit indicated by the EIM. Thus, the marginal downtown firm (that is, the one that has little to gain from an increase in accessibility) would be forced to move to a less desirable location, just as the marginal resident would be forced to move by an increase in rent. However, the effect is much stronger in the CBD. With an increase of rent beyond $14 to $15, the windfall land value gain would be even higher.

Two caveats should be noted: in spite of the relatively minor time savings discussed, the concomitant change in accessibility of 10 percent is probably quite large, and it is not clear that Equation (6) will be valid for such a large change. In the second place, a hypothetical increase in land value by 54 percent or more is large enough to make investigations of second-order effects mandatory. In fact, second-order consequences are quite likely to mitigate the first-order effects. Such large changes can only be handled by introducing various real-world constraints such as the limited total potential demand for various functions in a given area, costs of moving, inertial factors (for example, contractual relationships and leases that reduce mobility), and so on. Evidently a time-dependent analysis is called for. The first-order results obtained above merely suggest that there are very powerful forces underlying the spatial interactions in an urban activity area, and that much greater effort to explore these forces in a more sophisticated way seems warranted, both as to their first-order and their higher-order effects.

VI. Evaluation and Conclusions

It appears that an improvement in urban mass transportation resulting in savings of money, time, or stress almost never leads to a major fraction of these savings being passed on to the user as user. If, for example, a savings in time results and the transportation company is private (and unregulated), user out-of-pocket costs will be increased to maximize the return on investment. Residual consumer surpluses will be passed on to the users but this will, in turn, result in increased land rents. If the transportation company is public (and unregulated), user out-of-pocket costs could be similarly raised to pay for the improvement, with surpluses ultimately being translated, again, into land rents.

More commonly, an improvement, if carried out by a public entity, is financed by bond issues or general taxes or subsidies, and user out-of-pocket costs are kept competitive with those of preexisting systems, so that the surplus created by the improvement is largely "passed on." To whom is it passed on?

To avoid double counting, we should distinguish a transportation improvement benefiting home-based trips (commuting, shopping, personal services, recreation) from one benefiting office-based trips (that is, CBD synergism).

Consider first an improvement in home-based trips, resulting in, say, a net time savings. The actors are: system user residents (either renting or owning their homes); system nonusers (either renting or owning their homes); retail operators; business employers; residential landowners; commercial landowners; and owners of vacant land.

As we have seen, if the improvement is cost effective and user dollar cost is not raised to capture the savings in time, all users reap a benefit, dependent on how highly they value their time. Demand for residential—and probably also commercial—land goes up in such a way that the value of time saved is captured *at the margin* by the landowner, that is, land values and rents go up so as to retain the financially strongest residents, retail operators, or employers, those who value the improvement most highly. We suspect that land values generally go up at least by the amount invested in the transportation, but probably more.

Thus, the user who owns his home not only has a savings in time worth money, but additionally his land increases in market value. Of course he cannot enjoy—realize upon—both these benefits simultaneously; however, he has obtained the freedom of option to enjoy his time savings, or to move away and sell, or to rent his home at a higher price. Even while retaining his home, his borrowing—and therefore earning—capacity is increased.

The user who rents is only marginally benefited. If he values time highly, he may retain his location and realize some surplus of time saved over additional payments in rent (if the surplus were very large, he probably would not have lived there to begin with). The financially weaker renter would be forced to move farther out, thus suffering dislocation expenses as well as possible stress.

Among system nonusers, the homeowner obtains a windfall, elects to sell or rent at a higher price; or, again, he can borrow on the increased value. The nonuser who rents is most likely to lose. He may be a person who works (and/or shops and seeks services) in locations not served by the new system. Retail operators can tap a larger market; thus, the stronger ones, who are able to afford higher rents and can benefit from increasing returns to scale, will benefit and ultimately expand; weaker ones, especially the low-turnover neighborhood stores most of us love (but seldom use), are threatened with extinction.

As in the case of individual homeowners, owners of residential and commercial rental property (with the possible exception of land devoted to industrial or isolated office use) are likely to receive a windfall in the form of higher land values, as well as higher rents. Owners of vacant land may benefit similarly. The benefit to business or commercial renters from a more accessible labor supply may or may not outweigh their loss from increased rents. If there is a net loss, they are likely to be forced out, and thus to suffer displacement losses and moving costs as well.

Next, consider an improvement in office-based trips, again resulting in a time savings, hence increased accessibility and synergism. The actors are: employees; employers renting space; renters of retail space; owners of commercial space; and owners of vacant land. Employees, as we have seen, benefit marginally. Their time savings and part of their stress savings are passed on as benefits to the employer. The employer will probably have to pay additional rent. This means that the marginal employer, or one depending little for his return on accessibility to people (such as most manufacturing or warehousing sectors), will be forced to make room for a business which benefits from the increased productivity of space that accessibility provides. Retail operators with specialized, limited markets or lacking scale economies will also be forced out. Owners of commercial space and owners of isolated vacant space stand to benefit by large windfalls. In many cases the sum total of such increases in value far exceeds the original investment in transportation improvement.[8] For example, it is reported that property values in the area between Fifth and Seventh avenues from Twenty-third to Forty-seventh streets in New York City increased by over $60 million in 1901, after the plans for the Broadway Subway were announced.[9]

8. M. O. Stern, "A Planning Model for Transportation in Urban Activity Centers," *Highway Research Record*, no. 367, *New Transportation Systems and Concepts—12 Reports* (Washington, D.C.: National Academy of Sciences, 1971), p. 91.

9. Paul Latzke, "How Money Is Burned in N.Y.," *Saturday Evening Post*, 8 February 1902, reprinted in R. Brosseau, *Looking Forward—Life in the Twentieth Century* (New York: American Heritage Press, 1970).

The dislocations that could result from these pressures may be major and even self-defeating in their effects on the economics of the CBD, or they may merely cause a slow evolution away from its retail and commercial role toward that of a nerve center or information and idea exchange. The evaluation is complicated by multiple and unsymmetrical interlinkages between sectors: some sectors may need the stock exchange more than it needs them; many business services, such as accounting and law, are shared by many sectors, some of which do not exhibit markedly high sensitivity to accessibility, and so on. Most of all, the initial transportation investment, possibly highly multiplied, becomes frozen in new land value, where, except for rent increases, the possibility of bank borrowings, bond issues (recourse to which depends in part on macro-economic factors) and taxes, no cash flow for new investment is generated.

Land taxes are insufficient to recoup any major portion of adjacent public or private investments that affect its value. This is amply demonstrated by the frequency with which land is held in its unimproved state on the expectation that its value will rise faster than the product of consumer price index and current interest rate. We might therefore ask, as a first step, what would happen if landowners of a neighborhood were made to pay a share of a public transportation improvement benefiting this neighborhood.

A set of mathematical-econometric tools, such as our AAM and EIM, could be used to evaluate the incidence of benefits to different parcels. The contributions (which could be made over a period of years) would be allocated accordingly. The size of the benefits and of the levy that would help defray the costs of the improvement would, of course, depend on the effectiveness of the improvement. As we have shown, if it were barely cost-effective (in the restricted, localized free-enterprise sense explained earlier), it is likely that one could raise a major fraction, if not the total cost, by means of a neighborhood assessment in a high-density residential area. In a synergistic commercial area, it is likely that the whole cost could be financed by the neighborhood and yet leave substantial excess benefit to be capitalized into a land value windfall (which means that it is more than just marginally cost-effective from the social benefit point of view).

What would be some of the effects of such an assessment procedure? To begin with, the improvement costs would not become a burden upon citizens who do not benefit; such a burden would add insult to injury, since regions that are not benefited usually incur some competitive losses in any case. Moreover, windfalls would be reduced, with the difference available to the community treasury for other improvements. The yearly assessment charge, if sufficiently great, would have almost the same effect as an added tax: vacant lots would largely disappear; parking fees on remaining ones would be appropriately astronomical; and marginal land improvements would be replaced at a more rapid pace.

Windfalls may result not only from direct improvements, such as those in transportation, but also from indirect ones, such as the upgrading of surrounding land. As Gaffney puts it in an interesting paper,[10] the value of land is created by God, the public, and neighboring property owners, or, in his words, it "derives from natural advantage, public spending, and synergism." Is it possible to recoup this windfall?

Here it is not a question of taking up a collection to reimburse surrounding property owners for the costs incurred in creating the windfall benefit. Rather, it is a question of raising public revenue by taxing (to a greater extent than at present) the unearned rise in land value while at the same time creating a stronger incentive for land to be put to its highest and best use. The first step in the right direction is to shift the tax burden on improvements completely over to the land itself. If this were done without any attempt to increase total revenue, and if the assessed value of improvements bore a more or less constant relationship to that of land over the whole taxing district, there would be little effect on overall land values, since the earning capacity of land would be left, *on the average,* unimpaired. In finer detail, of course, the carrying charge on vacant or underimproved but valuable land would be increased, while that on land improved to high standards of quality and intensity would be decreased, thus providing some of the right incentives.

One can do even better. Vickrey has suggested[11] that the tax on the value of a piece of land be offset by a credit proportional to the quality (or cost) of the improvement erected on it. The only major theoretical problem (there are many practical problems with all such reformulations) with this approach is that it offers incentives for the most intensive marketable improvement under all circumstances, when under some real-life conditions the highest and best use of a piece of land may be a park or a low-density use.

Our models appear able to overcome this obstacle. With their help, it is possible to calculate (for, say, high-density residential or commercial areas) the value of a parcel of land (assumed to be vacant for the

10. Mason Gaffney, "Rent, Taxation and the Economists," *American Journal of Economics and Sociology* 31 (July 1972) : 241–58; see especially p. 247.

11. Wm. S. Vickery, as quoted in *The Assessment of Land Value,* ed. Daniel M. Holland (Madison: University of Wisconsin Press, 1970), pp. 275–87.

moment) derived from preexisting surrounding uses, and resulting from the accessibility and quality provided by them. A base tax would be levied on this value, which is a result of location, public improvements, and privately created synergism. It is then possible to test the effects of various improvements to be considered for the vacant parcel on surrounding land values; its highest and best use can be defined as one which adds the greatest value to all land in the neighborhood (including itself), and a credit (which need not be limited to the base tax) could be awarded in proportion to the value added. In this fashion all kinds of uses may be rewarded, especially if congestion is taken into account in the accessibility concept.

So far, we have limited ourselves to mitigating windfalls and to raising additional revenues only to cover direct public expenditures such as in transportation. However, since land values are created (at present) by the external factors mentioned, it becomes tempting to consider what would happen if all land appreciation were taxed away. In that case, land values would be stabilized more or less at present values by suitable adjustment of taxes. Such a policy would appear somewhat artificial and might considerably interfere with the functioning of the (presently somewhat less than perfect) land market. For example, land in areas of presently low demand would be kept at these low values by means of increasingly stiff carrying charges as the demand increases with time, although it is not apparent that such a policy would prevent demand from shifting and causing changing geographic patterns of development. Such a policy deserves further study, since it offers the promise of considerably higher revenue than that needed to cover direct public expenditures in areas where urban synergism is pronounced.

One can go even further and gradually raise the carrying charges on land (mitigated by incentive credits, as spelled out above) in such a way as to cause its market value to *decrease* gradually. It seems plausible[12] that land value per se bears no direct relation to the highest and best use to which it might be put and does not of itself provide an incentive for such use; on the contrary, it is the carrying charge or windfall tax that discourages speculation by hoarding and provides the incentive for optimal improvement.

What is the maximum revenue that could be raised by such a policy? The possibilities seem intriguing.[13] Is this maximum revenue obtained

12. Gaffney, "Rent, Taxation and the Economists," p. 246.
13. Mason Gaffney, "Adequacy of Land as a Tax Base," in *The Assessment of Land Value,* pp. 157–212.

for a tax rate that leaves land values not far below present ones? Or will land values tend toward zero as the amount of revenue increases, so that the tax *rate* approaches infinity? (The simplest formulation would indicate so.) In the latter case, will the economic consequences be equivalent, in terms of entrepreneurial behavior and public planning, to public ownership and private leasing of urban lands? Perhaps land will become a "hot potato" under these circumstances, to be acquired only if one has improvement plans ready for execution. Unforeseen changes in plans or status of the entrepreneur may make foreclosures by the community a common occurrence, and thus lead to increasing public repossession of unimproved land. If such a policy (or some other tax formulation) is found desirable, how is one to make the transition to the new steady state while holding economic shocks, dislocations, and inequities to a minimum? Clearly, economic modeling and careful empirical tests are required to reach an understanding of these complex but urgent questions.

In conclusion, we believe that we have demonstrated the plausibility of the following points; although we have not proved them:

1. The allocation of dollar costs for transportation as between users and nonusers as such shows no glaring inequities. Nonusers tend to pay a relatively minor charge for "unexercised options."

2. As for various user groups, the economic inefficiency arising from nonmarginal cost allocation under congested conditions has been documented elsewhere, and probably deserves serious effort at correction, all the more in view of the externalities (noise, pollution) arising from vehicular congestion.

3. A serious inequity does appear to exist between urban and other groups, with the urban nonusers of automobiles most severely penalized.

4. A consideration of time costs reveals that these are major indeed and far outweigh out-of-pocket costs in most transportation modes, particularly in urban mass transit. In fact, they are of the order of $200 billion yearly, that is, of the same order as annual transportation outlays, or 20 percent of our GNP. Being external to the market, these costs are, of course, excluded from the GNP, but they give an idea of the increase in productivity that might result, were it possible to reduce them. The same argument can be made about stress costs, which may approach the same order of magnitude.

5. This suggests that investments are justified in improvements, insofar as these can be achieved cost-effectively. The example of a new subway link used in the test illustrates the fact that the extension of conventional technologies is hard to justify economically in most cir-

cumstances. There is probably more promise in transportation innovation, substitute technologies (say, in communication), or deliberate rearrangements of work and residential patterns in cities.

6. By means of plausibility arguments based on empirical facts and extensions of these through mathematical models, we have shown that the benefits of transportation improvements ultimately become predominantly capitalized in increased rents and land values. The evidence suggests that the increase in land values in residential areas is at least of the same order as the neighborhood benefit from the transportation improvement; in synergistic CBD's the increase may be a multiple of the transportation benefit. Thus, if the improvement is cost-effective in the neighborhood-benefit sense, the increase in land values will be at least of the same order as the annualized capital and operating cost of the improvement; indeed, in CBD's it may be considerably higher.

7. It therefore becomes tempting to consider the possibility of having the landowners who benefit pay the cost of a public improvement, for example, local transportation. Assessment would be based on objective measures of benefit obtained from calibrated accessibility impact models like those described earlier. Benefits of such an assessment would include reduced land speculation, more timely improvement of vacant land, and more timely intensification of use of improved land, unburdening of areas that do not directly benefit, and the "freeing" of local frozen capital assets to create further improvements there or elsewhere.

8. From there it is only a step to considering the taxing away of all windfalls, whether they be due to direct improvements (such as investments in transportation) or indirect ones (such as upgrading the intensity or quality of development of the surrounding neighborhood). It is likely that large revenues can be raised in this fashion and that tax formulations can be devised in such a way as to bring the interests of the private entrepreneur more closely in line with that of the public. One possible such formulation has been suggested.

Any major restructuring of the property tax is likely to create economic shocks or dislocations. Thus, it is important not only to examine the long-range, steady-state consequences of a new tax structure, but also to make the transition from the old to the new as orderly as possible. In both instances, economic modeling, accompanied by carefully chosen and observed small-scale experiments, will be of great benefit in reducing the chance of false starts and in pointing us toward the right approach.

ACKNOWLEDGMENTS

We are indebted for helpful and stimulating discussions to several staff members and consultants of IR&T, notably George F. Brown, and to several professional colleagues, especially M. Mason Gaffney. Monique Cohen and Edgar Glick of IR&T helped gather some of the data of Table 7. Tables 1 to 4, as well as Table 7, derive most of their existence from the intelligent care and persistence of Susan Simon, and to her we owe very special thanks.

8 Robert E. Coughlin and Thomas R. Hammer

ESTIMATING THE BENEFITS
OF STREAM VALLEY AND OPEN SPACE
PRESERVATION PROJECTS

Introduction

Much attention has recently been focused on problems of degrada-
tion of the environment, and many projects have been proposed to
abate pollution and preserve environmental quality. The prospect of
a great increase in the number of such projects suggests that the marginal benefits of additional projects may diminish. This implies that
much improved efforts at benefit estimation are becoming more and
more necessary if proposals are to be evaluated properly and choices
made wisely.

Typically, the benefits of such projects consist in halting or revers-
ing the decline of the environmental quality which was enjoyed before
encroachment by urbanization. Thus, it is important to know something about the benefits obtained from environmental features in
their natural state. This question is obviously relevant for projects
which involve the decision of whether to preserve an area in natural
uses or to allow it to become developed.

This paper considers some of the aspects of benefit estimation for a
major class of environmental preservation projects which involve
maintaining the water quality of streams and keeping extensive areas
of land in an undeveloped state. The two objectives go hand-in-hand,
since the prevention of development will tend to prevent increased
frequency and extent of flooding, and corresponding erosion, sedimen-
tation, and channel enlargement.[1] The preclusion of development,
particularly development close to streams, will also tend to prevent the
deterioration of stream water quality which typically accompanies ur-

1. Thomas R. Hammer, "The Effect of Urbanization on Stream Channel Enlargement," *Water Resources Research* 8 (December 1972) : 1530–40.

banization.[2] In addition, the maintenance of high water quality will enhance the attractiveness and increase the usefulness of surrounding open space.

The physical changes resulting from such preservation projects are fairly straightforward, though they may be difficult to quantify. The value effects created by these physical changes, however, are hard to identify, since many of them do not involve direct monetary transactions. Table 8.1 suggests the relationships between the physical changes brought about and the value-related effects produced.

Table 8.1—Physical Changes and Value-Related Effects

Physical changes	More active use	More visual enjoyment	Eco-logical benefit	Reduced flood damages	Reduced need for water treatment
More open space	+	+	+	+	
Less pollution	+	+	+		+
More stable streamflow			+	+	

These value-related effects are measurable in various ways, as suggested in Table 8.2. The list of value-related effects could, of course, be expanded, but Table 2 gives an indication of the generic types of effects. The first two effects (active use and visual enjoyment) are peo-

Table 8.2—Measuring Value-Related Effects

Value-related effects	Number of users or user hours	Avoidance of mone-tary cost	Land value
More active use	+		+
More visual enjoyment	+		+
Ecological benefit			+
Reduced flood damages		+	+
Reduced need for water treatment		+	+

ple oriented and can be measured in numbers of people involved, although this measurement itself does not yield a dollar amount. The third effect (ecological benefit) makes its primary impact on the physical environment and the animal and plant life which inhabit it. The effects associated with reduced flooding and water treatment requirements can be expressed in terms of monetary costs. To some

2. Robert E. Coughlin and Thomas R. Hammer, *Stream Quality Preservation Through Planned Urban Development* (Washington, D.C.: Environmental Protection Administration, forthcoming), Chapter 3.

extent, these last two benefits are experienced downstream only, but to some extent (for example, the avoidance of increased water treatment costs which come with more intense urbanization) they are enjoyed widely by the people of the region.

An important fact is that all of the above effects may be registered in land values. This fact is particularly important, because measurement of numbers of users is difficult and can be transformed into monetary value only through the use of arbitrary assumptions of the value of a unit environmental experience. This paper will concentrate on the expression of environmental benefits in land values. In terms of the components listed above, the emphasis will be on people-oriented effects, namely, visual enjoyment and active use.

The Expression of Environmental Benefits in Land Value

It is worth while to consider at a general level the manner in which environmental benefits may be translated into land values. Basically, differential land values are created as a result of the importance of distance to an environmental amenity or other facility. Persons residing near the area in question can more easily derive benefits from its existence than persons living farther away. Presumably there is some distance beyond which persons derive virtually no benefit at all. Assuming that persons recognize the value of living close to the amenity, the price or rent of land close to the amenity should be bid up above what it would otherwise be. The amount that it is bid up comprises a location rent similar to the rent on a larger scale associated with proximity to a large city.

At a theoretical level, a case can be made that most or all people-oriented value-related effects created by an environmental amenity will be expressed in terms of location rent. Given that the critical factor is distance, and that distance is determined by residential location utilizing some minimum amount of land, then market forces should cause land value at each point to be bid up by an amount just equal to the environmental benefits obtained at that point. This location rent would be measurable as the difference, all else being equal, between the land price or rent at a point near an environmental benefit and its price at distances so great that no benefit cannot be enjoyed.

This analysis assumes that environmental features which yield benefits such as those discussed here are not a free good in an economic sense; that is, they are not ubiquitous and are not perceived as ubiquitous. The scarcity of environmental amenities is becoming increasingly obvious, at least in urbanized areas.

In order for a location rent gradient to be created in association with some amenity, the following things must be true of at least a portion of persons in the market for housing: (1) Persons considering a residential site near some amenity must be able to imagine the use and enjoyment of the amenity which they would derive from living there. (2) Persons must be willing to attach, at least implicitly, a money value to this use and enjoyment. This implies that persons recognize that environmental amenities are in scarce supply.

The first major portion of this paper deals with these points relating to the creation of location rent. A number of the studies which we have carried out are summarized. Most of them were designed to deal directly with the problem of water pollution and its effect on preferences. These studies provide indirect evidence concerning the general question of environmental benefits. Since the studies are fragmentary, our conclusions are rather conjectural. Relative to the two preconditions for location rent listed above, these studies suggest that: first, persons may not actually do a very good job of imagining how they would make use of an amenity if they lived nearby; second, even those who are currently enjoying the benefits of some amenity may not attribute a very high monetary value to it. The implication of these tentative findings is that environmental benefits may tend to be undervalued. The location rents created may be much lower than might be expected on theoretical grounds.

The second portion of this paper discusses a study which has attempted to estimate directly the value of location rent generated by a stream-valley park. Various issues relating to the comparison of such a value estimate with the opportunity cost of the park are discussed at that time.

The Response to Environmental Quality

In order to gain information relevant to the problem of environmental valuation, we have carried out a number of studies. The first series of studies was begun by taking a group of middle-class housewives to fifteen stream sites.[3] They then were asked to fill out a questionnaire which contained questions concerning overall preference (for example, "Assuming that you could have any type of house you wanted in this setting, how would you like to live here?" "How would you rate this site as a place to pass through and enjoy the scenery?"

3. Carla B. Rabinowitz and Robert E. Coughlin, "Analysis of Landscape Characteristics Relevant to Preference," *Regional Science Research Institute Discussion Paper Series: No. 38,* March 1970.

"How would you like to use this site for recreation?"). Questions were also asked concerning how much the respondent would like to use the area for wading, walking, picnicking, and so on, as were questions which required the respondent to rate the area on a set of semantic differential scales (for example, noxious-healthy, dull-picturesque, barren-lush, confining-spacious). The answers to many of these questions were significantly and positively correlated with characteristics of the areas, such as, the percentage of area covered by mowed grass, the percentage of foreground visible, the percentage of foreground that was firm ground, and with several variables denoting number and size of houses in view. Negative correlations were found with all variables denoting presence of junk and the percentage of area covered by twigs and brush. Characteristics of the stream itself, however, such as its pollution level or signs of flood debris, showed weak relationships with the use of, and preference for, the stream site as a whole.

A second study focused specifically on water quality.[4] In this study another group of middle-class housewives was taken to twelve stream sites which were chosen to be as similar physically as possible, but to have a wide range of water quality. These persons were asked specifically to rate the condition of the stream, the surrounding area, and the area as a whole. In addition, they were asked how much they would like to engage in a number of activities (picnicking, walking, wading, fishing, and so on) at each site, and to indicate their perceptions of the site by rating it on such terms as "pleasant," "healthful," and "inviting."

The study indicated that persons are able to identify water pollution reasonably well. Their perception of the degree to which a stream is "polluted" corresponded significantly with a number of chemically measured water quality characteristics. However, no significant correlations were found between chemical measures and preference ratings for the stream, its surrounding area, or the area overall. Thus, the connection between the objective level of water quality and liking for a site appears to be weak.

There was, however, some *indirect* association between preference ratings and chemical measures. Preference for a stream and its surroundings was related to the observers' perceptions of whether a stream is transparent, clean, inviting, or healthy. These perceived attributes, in turn, were correlated with the chemical measurements. Observers' judgments of whether a stream is suitable for certain water-

---

4. Ursula Scherer and Robert E. Coughlin, "The Influence of Water Quality in the Evaluation of Stream Sites," *Regional Science Research Institute Working Paper,* October 1971.

related activities were also correlated significantly with a number of chemical variables.

To this extent, there is a general consistency between chemical measures of water quality, perceived attributes, and preferences for the stream and surrounding area. However, the study does not indicate that water pollution is a strong determinant of preference for persons who visit a stream site but do not have a long or intimate knowledge of the site. Criteria other than water quality were evidently more important to such observers, who were generally agreed on the relative attractiveness of a stream.

The results of a third study were somewhat different.[5] This study involved questioning people about the streams they lived near, rather than bringing a given group of observers to a set of streams with which they were not previously acquainted. It consisted of questionnaire interviews of 312 households located near 29 stream locations for which detailed data on water quality were available. In this study, strong correlations were found between various chemical measures of water quality and most of the response variables. The better the water quality actually is, as determined by chemical analysis: (a) the less the stream appears to the residents to be polluted, (b) the better opinion they have of its general attractiveness, (c) the more suitable they consider it for nearly all activities listed (fishing, wading, picnicking, walking, sitting, bird watching), and (d) the more they engage in those activities. The respondents' desires to live close to the stream and their belief that property values are higher near the stream also tend to be stronger if the stream's water is clean. These relationships are illustrated in Figures 8.1 and 8.2. In both figures the quantity plotted on the horizontal axis is a water quality "index" obtained by extracting the first principal component from a set of sixteen water-quality variables.

The results of these last two studies suggest that although water quality is of little importance to people visiting a stream for the first time, it is a signficant factor for nearby residents in their determination of what the stream is suitable for, what they actually use it for, and the effect the stream has on nearby property values. The differences in outcomes of these two sets of studies suggest that persons living near a stream tend to view it somewhat differently from persons not living there. In particular, residents find themselves more sensitive

5. Robert E. Coughlin, Thomas R. Hammer, Thomas G. Dickert, and Sallie Sheldon, "Perception and Use of Streams in Suburban Areas," *Regional Science Research Institute Discussion Paper Series: No. 53*, March 1972.

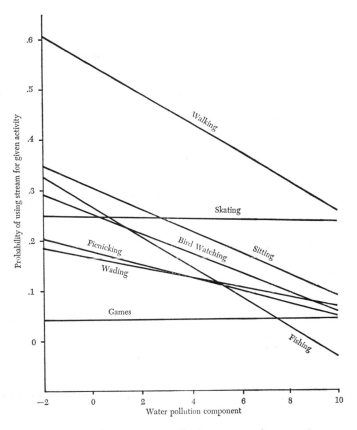

Figure 8.1—Effect of water pollution on use of stream sites.

to such factors as water quality than do persons who do not live nearby. One implication of this which is relevant to the issues discussed previously is that persons may be rather poor at estimating the use and enjoyment that they will obtain at a site before actually living there. This, in turn, implies that prospective residents of an area may not estimate correctly the value of the environmental amenities which it possesses.

This evidence is highly indirect and fragmentary. It does not indicate, for example, whether there is a systematic tendency for environmental benefits to be underestimated or overestimated. The general flavor of our research in this area, however, indicates that the value of environmental benefits accruing to residents of an area may not be easily appraised by prospective residents, that is, persons in the market

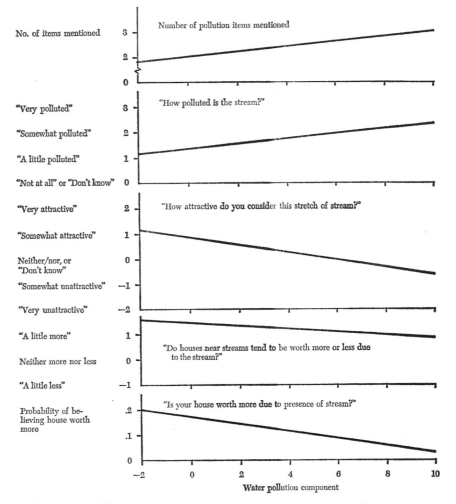

Figure 8.2—Effect of water pollution on perception of stream and house value.

for housing, who are unfamiliar with the area. We suspect that this may contribute to an undervaluation of environmental benefits, in the sense that the enjoyment of such benefits at nearby residential locations is only partially reflected in location rent.

Another related household survey concentrated on the effect of distance between house and stream. Perception of suitableness for use, actual use, and perception of effect on property value all declined regularly with distance. Curves illustrating the effects of distance are given in Figure 8.3, which graphs the use rate of residents living 100 feet from the stream as 100 percent. Note that by the time that distance between house and stream reaches a mile, the use rate has fallen to 20 percent or less for most activities.

The use gradients indicate the relative amount of use a resident is likely to make of the stream, depending on his distance from it. The gradient should, therefore, also indicate the relative value of the stream to a resident, depending on his distance from it. Thus, if the potential use of a stream is worth $100 dollars to a person if he lives within a

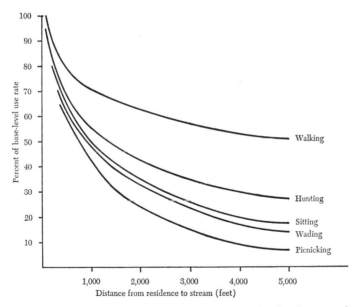

Figure 8.3—Percent of base-level use of stream site by distance of
residence from stream, for selected activities (distance
is straight-line distance from residence to nearest point
on stream).

hundred feet of the stream, it would be worth less than $20, if he lived a mile away.

The effects of distance and water quality, as determined through the household survey, are summarized in Figure 8.4. Use and attendant value of a stream are greater if the stream water is clean, and are greater for nearby residents than for those living farther away from it.

An interesting aspect of these studies is the apparent discrepancy between the amount of use and enjoyment obtained from the stream and the value which persons place on living near the stream. The general level of use is quite high: 94 percent of respondents in one sample indicated that they engaged in at least one activity at the stream, and the average number of activities was four. On the other hand, in response to a question asking whether houses close to streams are generally worth more or less because of their closeness to the stream, the mean response, as a numerical average, was half-way between saying

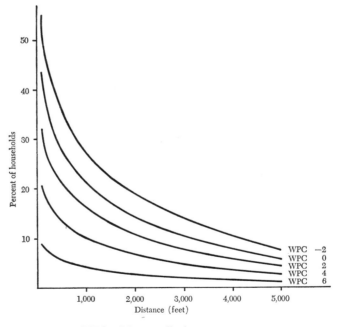

WPC = Water pollution component

Figure 8.4—Effect of water pollution and distance to residence on percent of households engaging in a typical activity at stream.

that the value of such houses is not affected by closeness to stream and that they are worth "a little more."

Additional evidence was obtained from questions asking how the respondent feels the value of his own house is affected by proximity to the stream, whether or not he would rather live closer to the stream (all else being equal), and whether his house would be worth more closer to the stream. Only 17 percent of respondents in one survey sample thought that proximity to the stream added to their house value. Approximately 25 percent of respondents in both samples expressed a desire to live closer to the stream, but only 8 percent thought that their own houses would be worth more if they were closer to the stream.

These results do suggest that people attach some value to streams as an environmental amenity. However, the weak response suggests that, in talking about value, people are considering primarily the direct visual amenity (that is, the value of having a stream in view from one's house), whereas the monetary value conferred by use of the stream may not be fully appreciated.

Direct Measurement of Location Rent

In general, a gradient of benefits can be expected to exist around an environmental amenity. Associated with the benefit gradient one would expect to find a location rent gradient; but, as indicated by the studies discussed above, this rent may not express the full value of the amenity enjoyed. Another study has attempted to identify directly the location rent associated with an environmental amenity, namely Pennypack Park, a 1,300 acre park in northeastern Philadelphia.[6] The area surrounding this park has been developed over the past twenty years—mostly with twin (two-family) houses at a density of ten dwelling units per acre.

One of the major difficulties in identifying location rent is the problem of isolating land value from the market value of property, which includes the value of buildings, utilities, and other structures on the land. Because much of the development around Pennypack Park was done on a large scale, however, relatively few basic types of houses were represented. Therefore, it appeared possible to isolate value com-

6. Thomas R. Hammer, Edward T. Horn IV, and Robert E. Coughlin, "The Effect of a Large Urban Park on Real Estate Value," *Regional Science Research Institute Discussion Paper Series: No. 51,* December 1971.

ponents by using a regression analysis, with overall sale price as the dependent variable, in which each type of house was represented by a separate dummy independent variable. The set of dummy variables would capture value of house and a base value of land, leaving the value of location rent to be explained by distance from the park, which would be entered as a separate independent variable.

A total of sixteen house types were identified from air photographs, field trips, and information in the Philadelphia Real Estate Directory. For example, one type group consisted of houses which looked identical on the air photograph, were semi-detached with basement garage, were two stories, brick and frame construction, and were assessed exclusive of land, at $9,200. In 1968 such properties were selling for about $19,500.

Such a house type classification cannot reflect improvements which have been made to the inside of a standard builder's house and which are neither visible from the outside nor accounted for in the assessed vaue of the house. Obvious outside additions, such as swimming pools, were observed and such properties were dropped from the sample. Dummy variables were also entered for year of sale, for whether or not the house was on an irregularly shaped lot, and for whether it abutted the park directly.

In order to eliminate influences other than the park, properties studied were limited to those which were closer to the park than to any other open space, and which did not adjoin any retail area or major highway. In addition, corner lots were excluded from the sample unless they bordered on the park, and these were identified specifically by dummy variables in the analysis.

The major focus of interest was upon the variables expressing distance to the park. Distance to the park was measured in two alternative ways: as the straight-line distance from the house to the nearest point in the park, and as distance along public ways to the nearest point of public access to the park. The variables expressing distance were in the form of negative exponential functions of distance (to which a small constant had been added to prevent domination by small distances). Two different exponents, -1 and -2, were tested; -1 was found to be more satisfactory. The negative exponential gives a gradient asymptotic to the distance axis, which was considered a desirable characteristic. The dependent variable (property value) was expressed in both log form and linear form, with similar regression results obtained for each form. Only the linear form will be discussed here.

In the regression analysis the sale price for each of 303 properties was related to a set of independent variables consisting of one or more distance variables and numerous dummy variables. The public access form of the distance variable proved to be the more significant statistically. The overall level of statistical explanation was quite high (multiple R = .902) but this was due primarily to the dummy variables. The distance variable was significant at the 1 percent level, however.

The magnitude of the estimated property value gradient is shown in Figure 8.5. The location rent can be calculated as the difference between the estimated property value at a given distance and the "base" property value (that is, the extrapolated value when distance from the park is infinite). The location rent gradient as estimated drops off rapidly with distance. The rent ranges from about $1,171 per property at 40 feet from the park to $104 per property at 2,500

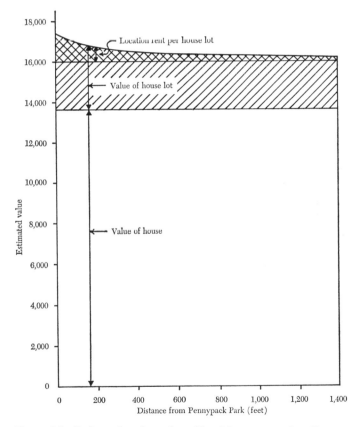

Figure 8.5—Estimated value of residential property by distance from Pennyback Park.

feet from the park. At first glance, this amount does not appear to be large. It is only 6.8 percent of total property price at 40 feet from the park, 1.4 percent at 1,000 feet, and 0.6 percent at 2,500 feet.

Location rent, however, must be considered in relation to land value, not to total property value. This is clear on a theoretical level, since the attribute of location is intrinsic only to land, not to the structures which may be built on it. As a practical matter, one would not expect the cost of constructing a standard house to vary with distance from a park or from any other facility which generates location rent (unless, of course, soil conditions, slope, or other characteristics also vary systematically with distance).

By subtracting a rough estimate of average house price from total property price, land price may be identified. This was done by observing that for the entire sample the tax assessment of the house was 83.2 percent of total assessment. The value of the average property, $16,386 multiplied by 83.2 percent, yields the average house value of $13,633, which is plotted on Figure 5. The remaining distance under the curve represents land value, part of which is location rent. Relative to total land value, location rent due to the closeness of the park is substantial. At 40 feet it accounts for 33 percent of land value; at 1,000 feet for 9 percent; and at 2,500 feet for 4 percent. In dollars per acre—recalling that on average there are ten houses per acre—location rent due to proximity to the park falls from $11,700 at 40 feet to $1,040 at 2,500 feet. These values would appear to lie in an expected and reasonable range.

An estimate of aggregate value of location rent generated by Pennypack Park can be made by multiplying the values per dwelling unit found in Figure 5 by the numbers of dwellings found at corresponding distances. This computation, which involved a total of 10,495 dwelling units, yields a net increase in aggregate real estate value of $3,391,000 which is attributable to the park.

It is interesting to compare this estimate of total value generated by the park with the value of the park itself in terms of what the land might bring on the market. Land value in the general part of the city where the park is located averages $25,000 to $30,000 per acre, with improvements. The 1,296 acres of the park are not all readily developable at densities typical of that portion of the city, however, since much of the land is in steep slopes. On the assumption that the average market value of the land in the Park is only $10,000 per acre because of its physical characteristics, the total market value of the parkland would be $13 million. This would represent, roughly, the opportunity cost of retaining the park. The discrepancy between the land value generated by the park and the opportunity cost of retaining it is impressive.

There are a number of minor reasons why the location rent may be underestimated, even assuming that the general estimating technique is correct. Most important is that no effect is computed for distances beyond 2,000 feet, although the curve of Figure 5 is asymptotic to distance, and, in fact, at 2,500 feet the location rent is still 4 percent of value of land.

In addition the estimating technique itself may lead to underestimation. The reasons for this would involve the difficulty of identifying an appropriate base-level land price. Although it is possible that overestimates of location rent might be obtained (that is, the base level may be set too low), it appears likely that the other result might more typically be true. For such a major amenity as Pennypack Park, the true location rent gradient may extend a great distance from the amenity itself, perhaps even affecting all the properties in the city. But in estimating the gradient, it is difficult to consider properties far from the amenity because of the confounding influences of other generators of land value. In addition, value effects may extend far beyond any distance at which use of the park is practical. The rent surface of the entire city may be elevated a small amount by the park, since to some extent the city comprises a single housing market, and the forces making land more attractive and values higher in one section will therefore tend to raise values elsewhere. Such a flat gradient would add only a small amount to the value of a single property but might extend so far that the aggregate additional rent would be substantial. Restricting the sample to properties near the amenity may then lead to base level being set too high and thus to great underestimation of the total location rent. In addition, the empirical method, of necessity, identifies differential location rent given that the park is in existence. If the park had never existed, or if it were to be built upon, one might expect a general lowering of prices.

Another probability is that value created by such amenities simply does not appear fully as location rent. Although this may be difficult to explain at a theoretical level, much of the benefit enjoyed by persons may be unrelated to distance. As indicated in the first section of this paper, there may be some tendency for persons to undervalue the direct benefits they receive from an amenity, or rather, to undervalue the importance of proximity to an amenity.

At any rate, the gap between our estimate of location rent generated by the park and the estimated market value of the park does not

necessarily lead to the conclusion that its cost greatly exceeds its benefits. The fact that there is no apparent movement to sell off urban
parks because opportunity costs have become too high suggests the possibility that there are value elements in having parks which are not
captured in land value.

9 Roy W. Bahl, Stephen P. Coelen, and Jeremy J. Warford

LAND VALUE INCREMENTS AS A MEASURE OF THE NET BENEFITS OF URBAN WATER SUPPLY PROJECTS IN DEVELOPING COUNTRIES

THEORY AND MEASUREMENT

I. Introduction

The subject of this paper is the extent to which the benefits of urban water supply projects are capitalized into land values.[1] Its focus will be the theoretical conditions necessary for such capitalization in a developing country context. In a later section of the paper, we present a brief anatomy of the kind of empirical approach which seems appropriate to test this model.[2]

It is generally acknowledged that the fundamental problem of cost-benefit analysis is that benefit measurement is either difficult or not possible in many sectors of activity. Economic rates of return, therefore, cannot be used to assist intersectoral allocation of funds. Moreover, the difficulties of benefit measurement vary considerably between sectors. In particular, it is alleged that water supply projects fare relatively badly according to such tests. This is in marked contrast to agricultural projects, for example, where demand can often be assumed to be perfectly elastic, or to transportation projects, where a large part of the benefits are often cost saving. In these cases, much, if not all, of the consumer's surplus area may be estimated.

The demand for water supply projects is generally thought to be

1. The views expressed in this paper are the authors' own and do not necessarily reflect opinions held by their respective institutions.
2. This paper is preliminary in the sense that it reflects our thinking in the early stages of a larger research project involving such empirical measurement in case studies of Nairobi, Kenya, and Kuala Lumpur, Malaysia. The larger research project is being undertaken through the Metropolitan and Regional Research Center of the Maxwell School at Syracuse University.

highly inelastic, and the consequent presence of consumer surplus on a large scale means that revenue from water sales—the benefit measure which is most often used—gives a considerable underestimate of true benefits. In addition, there is an observed reluctance of water authorities to charge prices for water that represent a true (that is, long-run marginal) cost of supply. Revenue, a conservative indicator of benefits at best, therefore becomes particularly inadequate. It follows that economic evaluation according to estimates of revenues likely to be derived provides a much less attractive view of water supply projects than of other projects.

The constancy of water pricing over time within an area, or over a cross section among several areas, further limits the type of benefit measurement possible. While the supply curve is most likely identified by observable market transactions, the constancy in the supply curve prohibits identification of the demand curve. Any attempts to estimate, by traditional demand-supply analysis, the willingness-to-pay area under the demand curve are thus thwarted.

The market for water services does not permit benefit estimation of the willingness of individuals to pay for public improvements in water; consequently, it is necessary to define a proxy market wherein preferences for these facilities are revealed. The residential land market may fit this need for water supply services. Water investments improve the quality of a particular site, thereby raising present values and increasing sales prices. From the point of buyers, these sales price increments would seem a reasonable measure of the market value placed on such improvements. Empirical analysis of these effects is more appropriate in developing countries where installation of these facilities often takes place after houses have been occupied, whereas in developed countries the facilities are installed before construction, and changes in land prices are more typically the outcome of bilateral monopoly bargaining where the resulting price has little welfare significance.

In general, the use of the housing market as a proxy for the water market implies the possibility that the consumers' surplus in the water market is transferred to the housing market. There are serious problems with developing such an approach. The immense empirical difficulties, which are not dealt with here, include a requirement to abstract from all other factors which could affect housing values. The conceptual difficulties, which are dealt with here, require the argument that the land market[3] is not characterized by imperfections

---

3. We will use the terms *land market, housing market,* and *property market* interchangeably. While distinctions between the terms can be drawn, it seems point-

which make it no better for these purposes that the water market. It is clear, however, that there are imperfections in the land market. Land is not generally homogeneous, knowledge and mobility are not perfect, and buyers and sellers may not be numerous. It is possible, on the other hand, that disaggregation of the land market into sub-markets (for residence, for businesses, for single family homes, for certain areas of the city) may increase the homogeneity of land and market knowledge to a point where the market might be relatively free of imperfections.[4] In general, we will take the position that the major imperfections, if they cannot be overcome for these purposes, can at least be taken into account in terms of estimates of their effects on the results of this analyis.

II. The Model

The basic assumption here is that supplying piped water to a home will raise its market value and that the increase will correspond to the present worth of the consumers' surplus that is expected to be derived from purchases in the water market. Assuming perfect rationability, a person would be willing to pay only an additional $100 for a house because it had water facilities, if the difference between the present worth of the utility he gets from the water and the present worth of the amount he expects to pay for the water (that is, the consumers' surplus) equals $100. If the amount that he expects to pay for water exactly corresponds to the benefits he personally derives from it, there is no reason to expect him to bid up the price of the house. Clearly, the area under the demand curve for property must increase by whatever amount the consumers's surplus in the water market increases. This is given by the traditional concept that the area under a demand curve for a good describes the willingness to pay.

The question that we now face is whether increasing values in the property market correctly capture the effects of the demand shift. That is, we assume that the increased consumers' surplus area in the water market is "transferred" into an equivalent shift in area under

---

less here. All increments in valuation are perceived to be attributable to the land itself. Increasing land values should have only limited effectiveness on increasing housing structure values, since the housing structures for developing countries are typically already built before the project is implemented. The exception is water supply delivery which encourages additions such as bathrooms to existing structures. This is probably of minor importance, and for our present methodological discussion we shall ignore it.

4. See John M. Copes, "Reckoning with Imperfections in the Land Market," in *The Assessment of Land Value,* ed. Daniel M. Holland (Madison: University of Wisconsin Press, 1970), p. 56.

the property market demand curve. We would like to determine whether expenditures on property also increase by this common amount. If they do, then the observations on property sales may identify for us the extent to which water benefits are undervalued by revenues derived from water sales.

A. Theoretical Framework

A simple and familiar model suggests that there are, at least, certain assumptions under which benefits and increased expenditures on property are equal. Consider the case where the consumers' surplus in the property market remains constant so that the following algebraic model is illustrative of full capitalization. In an area receiving new water supply (the project area), the housing demand function (before the project) is written generally as:

$$q_d = g(q_d) \tag{1}$$

and, again, for simplicity the housing supply is a constant:

$$q_s = k. \tag{2}$$

It follows that the market equilibrium price can be derived as:

$$p_e = f_1\{g(q_d), k\}. \tag{3}$$

A measure of consumers' surplus is:

$$c = \{_0\int^k g(q_d)\} - p_e k. \tag{4}$$

The effect of a water supply project providing each house with water can be shown through a shift in the demand curve from its initial position. For the same fixed quantity of housing, residents would now be willing to pay a higher rent—the demand curve has shifted upward. Let us assume that the new demand is:

$$q_d = h(q_d). \tag{5}$$

Consumers' surplus is now measured

$$c' = [_0\int^k h(q_d)] - p_e' k \tag{6}$$

where p_e' is defined:

$$p_e' = f_2[h(q_d), k]. \tag{7}$$

The increase in consumers' surplus between the two periods (Δc) is:

$$\Delta c = c' - c = [_0\int^k g(q_d)] - p_e' k - \{[_0\int^k h(q_d)] - p_e k\} \tag{8}$$
$$\Delta c = [_0\int^k g(q_d) - _0\int^k h(q_d)] - \Delta p_e k$$

where $\Delta p_e = p_e' - p_e.$

The increase in net benefits (ΔB) of the water project to residents of the area is equal to the increase in price times the quantity supplied ($\Delta p_e k$) plus any increase in consumers' surplus, that is,

$$\Delta B = \Delta p_e k + \Delta C = [_0 \int^k g(q_d) - _0 \int^k h(q_d)] - \Delta p_e k + \Delta p_e k \quad (9)$$
$$\Delta B = [_0 \int^k g(q_d) - _0 \int^k h(q_d)]. \quad (10)$$

If the shift in the housing demand function is such that ΔC is zero, that is, consumers' surplus remains constant, then from (8):

$$\Delta C = [_0 \int^k g(q_d) - _0 \int^k h(q_d)] - \Delta p_e k = 0 \quad (11)$$
$$\Delta p_e k = [_0 \int^k g(q_d) - _0 \int^k h(q_d)] \quad (12)$$

and from (10):

$$\Delta p_e k = \Delta B. \quad (13)$$

If the assumptions behind this simple model are valid, then the benefits of a water supply project will be fully measured in two steps. The first is revenues derived directly through sales in the water market. The second is a measure of the transferred consumers' surplus, from water to property markets, and is defined by equation (13). Their sum gives an unbiased measure of project benefits. In equation (13), ΔB is proportional to the increase in house prices, where the constant of proportionality is the stock of housing. If equation (11) does not hold, then there is both a change in housing prices and a change in consumers' surplus and the net benefits of the project are measured as in equation (10).

B. Required Demand and Supply Conditions

Since the total increase in benefits must be equal to the sum of the price increase and any increase in consumer surplus, a number of conditions must be present for the land value increment to exhaust totally the benefit increment. The first is that the slope of the demand curve for housing in the project area does not change, and a second is that the supply curve is perfectly inelastic. Consider the implications of these assumptions. First, if the demand schedule for housing in the project area changes, one would expect it to become relatively more inelastic—there are fewer good substitutes now that the house has piped-in water. That is, it would take a greater price increase to bid an individual away from a house with water than it would when the same house did not have public water supply. The implications of such a change in the slope of the demand schedule are that consumer surplus will increase, that is, the difference between the individual's and the market's valuation of the property will increase. This would mean that the sum of revenues from water sales and the property value increment due to a new water supply underestimates the true benefits of a water project. The unmeasured benefits are a return to labor—the consumer—since it is only he who can gain from the consumers' surplus as he lives on the property.

For the supply conditions, it is possible that a perfectly inelastic supply is unrealistic. Some elasticity to supply would imply that, as the price of properties in the affected area is bid up, property owners in the area would be induced to offer a greater amount of housing,[5] and *ceteris paribus,* causing land value increments to understate the increase in net benefits. More specifically, with any supply elasticity, the increase in demand (regardless of how the slope of the demand schedule changes) will be accompanied by an increase in total consumers' surplus. Whether average consumers' surplus, that is, the average return to a typical consumer, increases is not quite so clear. Similarly, we can be sure that with a supply curve having less than perfect elasticity there will be an increase in producers' surplus,[6] and hence a return to capital.

If either the supply or demand conditions in this simple framework are violated, it is quite likely that the sum of land value increments and revenue from water sales will be an inaccurate measure of true benefits of a water supply. The two measures together, however, will necessarily be more accurate than water sales revenue alone, and, on the basis of the arguments presented above, the error is likely to be on the conservative side.

III. Other Land-Value Studies

The use of land value models is not new, and the effects of infrastructure investment on land values has long been a subject of the literature in economics. Such a great deal of material has been written that it would be impossible to review it all. We shall attempt only to highlight a few studies and develop their relationship to the present work.

Early studies, such as that by Mohring and Harwitz on transportation,[7] neither looked at property value changes as a direct benefit

5. In this case, the offering of a greater amount of housing implies an increase in the number of occupancy units offered rather than an increase actually due to physical construction. The former could be accomplished by increasing the density of rental units, converting existing nonresidential to residential uses, and so on.

6. This type of analysis is applied to property taxes by R. E. Grieson, "The Economics of Property Taxes and Land Values," Working Paper 72, Department of Economics (Cambridge, Mass.: Massachusetts Institute of Technology, 1971).

7. Herbert Mohring and Mitchell Harwitz, *Highway Benefits: An Analytical Framework* (Evanston, Ill.: Northwestern University Press, 1962).

measure nor considered the effects of different capitalization rates on the model. Using Mohring and Harwitz's work as an example, however, we can transform these studies into a style that does explicitly treat land value changes. Further it is easy to expose implicit assumptions that point to a rather rigid consideration of capitalization models. Mohring and Harwitz explain observed variance in rent as a function of travel time differentials. Their treatment of the benefits of highway investments requires that the value of time savings be totally capitalized into land values. Their basic equation[8] describing such benefits is:

$$R_i - R_j = 2N(T_j - T_i)V_T \qquad (14)$$

where R_i, R_j = site rents at i, j

$$N = \text{number of trips taken to the central area}$$
$$T_i, T_j = \text{travel time from } i \text{ and } j \text{ to the central area}$$
and $\qquad V_T = \text{value of travel time.}$

While, empirically, many other considerations of site attractiveness must be entered into the equation, equation (14) can be solved for V_T,

$$\frac{R_i - R_j}{2N(T_j - T_i)} = V_T \cdot \qquad (15)$$

In this context, the benefits of a transport improvement—the value of time saved—may be described as:

$$\Delta T.V_T = \Delta T. \ \frac{R_i - R_j}{2N(T_j - T_i)} \qquad (16)$$

where ΔT is the reduction in time necessary to get from i or j to the central area.

The assumption of full capitalization of time-saving benefits into site rents is made clearer by assuming that i and j are the same property but i is before and j after the transportation project. The value of time is assumed to be a constant and the net change in total time spent in getting from the property in question to the central area is $2N(T_j - T_i)$, that is,

$$\Delta T = 2N(T_j - T_i). \qquad (17)$$

Applying (17) to (16) we can obtain time-saving benefits:

$$\Delta T.V_T = R_i - R_j = \Delta R \qquad (18)$$

8. Ibid., p. 147.

where ΔR is the land value increment associated with this property and due to the transportation project. All benefits are reflected in this increment, that is, there is an assumption of 100 percent capitalization of benefits.

Later studies have begun to relate increasing land values and investments in a more direct way. The types of investment involved have varied widely from Nourse's work on public housing;[9] Dobson,[10] Phares,[11] and Wihry[12] on racial integration; Paul on noise pollution;[13] Oates on property taxes;[14] and Spore[15] and Ridker and Henning[16] on air pollution. The list could easily be expanded both into different investment types and into different authors working within the same investment types. Only recently, however, have any of these studies worried about capitalization rates and land value changes.

Ridker[17] and Ridker and Henning, for example, have only recently come under attack for failing to consider capitalization. Ridker and Henning's results emphasize the negative effects of increasing pollution levels on land values.[18] They estimate an $83 and $245 increase in valuation per site as pollution levels are cut back by .25 mg per 100 cm[19] per day (but not below .49 mg per 100 cm² per day).[19] Two problems hamper interpretation of these results. First, property values are

9. Hugh O. Nourse, "The Effect of Public Housing on Property Values in Saint Louis" (Ph.D. diss., University of Chicago, 1962).

10. Allen Dobson, "Price Changes of Single Family Dwelling Units in Racially Changing Neighborhoods" (Ph.D. diss., Washington University, 1970).

11. Donald Phares, "Racial Change and Housing Values: Transition in an Inner Suburb," *Social Science Quarterly* 62 (December 1971) : 560–73.

12. David Wihry, "Price Discrimination in Metropolitan Housing Markets," *Proceedings of the American Real Estate and Urban Economics Association,* vol. 4, 1969, pp. 69–101.

13. M. E. Paul, "Can Aircraft Noise Nuisance Be Measured in Money?" *Oxford Economic Papers* 23 (November 1971) : 297–322.

14. Wallace E. Oates, "The Effects of Property Taxes and Local Public Spending on Property Values: An Empirical Study of Tax Capitalization and the Tiebout Hypothesis," *Journal of Political Economy* 77 (November–December 1969) : 957–71.

15. Robert L. Spore, "Property Values and Air Pollution Damage Costs: Some Results for the Pittsburgh Metropolitan Area" (Ph.D. diss., Pennsylvania State University, 1972).

16. Ronald G. Ridker and John A. Henning, "The Determinants of Residential Property Values with Special Reference to Air Pollution," *Review of Economics and Statistics* 69, no. 2 (May 1967) : 246–57.

17. Ronald G. Ridker, *Economic Costs of Air Pollution* (New York: Praeger, 1967).

18. Ridker and Henning, "Determinants of Residential Property Values," pp. 246–57.

19. Ibid., p. 254.

determined by an interaction between supply and demand for property. Benefits, on the other hand, are reflected only on the demand size. A capitalization model is required to relate the equilibrium market prices to benefit-related demand shifts. Without a capitalization model, it is impossible to separate supply and demand factors, and, consequently, to identify the land value-benefit relationship. Second, in a *ceteris paribus* regression analysis such as Ridker and Henning's, the coefficients must be interpreted as those that result when pollution levels are reduced on only one property—we cannot conceive of a simultaneous reduction in pollution levels over all areas with the model. Since pollution abatement projects will typically affect many properties, we must know how property values (within a wide, geographical area) change with a project.

Edel[20] and Freeman[21] each make the same criticism of the general land value approach. Freeman, on the first point argues:

In any urban area this relationship [property value-air quality] is the result of the interaction between the availability of land with different levels of air quality (supply factor) and tastes and preference, other prices, income and its distribution (demand factors). For any given set of demand factors different supply factors will lead to different patterns of property values and different regression results.[22]

On the second point Freeman continues:

The [Ridker and Henning regression] equation only purports to explain the variation in mean property values among observations. The air pollution coefficient can be used to predict the difference in property values between two properties within a system under *ceteris paribus* conditions, and these conditions must include no change in air quality over all other land in the system. But the regression equation cannot be used to predict the general pattern of property values or changes in the value of any given property when the pattern of air quality over the whole urban area has changed.[23]

Edel makes the same criticisms. In regard to the first object mentioned above, Edel relates nearly the same message as Freeman:

This regression analysis . . . can be interpreted in one of two ways. It may measure the costs imposed on households by pollution, estimated on the as-

20. Matthew Edel, "Land Values and the Costs of Urban Congestion: Measurement and Distribution" (Paper presented at "Man and His Environment," a Symposium on Political Economy of Environment, Paris, France, July 1971) .
21. A. Myrick Freeman, "Air Pollution and Property Values: A Methodological Comment," *Review of Economics and Statistics* 73, no. 4 (December 1971) : 415–16.
22. Ibid., p. 415.
23. Ibid.

sumption that the prices households bid for land will rationally reflect the true cost and disutility of dirty air. Or it may measure the extent to which the market and bid prices offered by families really capture these costs.[24]

For the second objection Edel continues:

If pollution in all districts of St. Louis were reduced to the 0.49 mg. "background" level, demand for space in formerly most polluted neighborhoods would certainly increase. But this increase might come at the expense of demand in census tracts that formerly had a unique advantage in low pollution levels. The $82,790,000 estimate assumes that demand will increase in the newly cleaned areas to equal demand elsewhere now, without the balancing effect of demand reduction. It is therefore almost certainly an overestimate.[25]

Many early studies on public investments and land values are difficult to interpret. Problems of interpretation notwithstanding, the Ridker and Henning study serves to exemplify what future changes in research methodology are required. However, little purely theoretical work has been attempted in this area. Strotz,[26] an exception, directly attacks some of the problems that are involved. Unfortunately several strong assumptions limit the realism and usefulness of his analysis.

Strotz's work approaches the second problem listed above in reference to the Ridker and Henning study. How do land values relate to welfare; how do offsetting land values in nonproject areas affect welfare. In building his model, Strotz hypothesizes an area where a pollution abatement project has had the effect of increasing land values by $1,000,000 in the project area and decreasing land values by $700,000 in the nonproject area. He makes the following assumptions:

(a) Air pollution affects every part of a region equally.

(b) A pollution abatement project changes the north half of the town for the better so that there is a shift in demand, causing rents to increase by $1,000,000 in the north and decrease by $700,000 in the south.

(c) There are no moving costs.

(d) Each person occupies some land in both the North and South (to assure convexity in the indifference surfaces).

24. Edel, "Land Values and the Costs of Urban Congestion," p. 10.
25. Ibid.
26. R. H. Strotz, "The Use of Land Rent Changes to Measure the Welfare Benefits of Land Improvements," mimeographed (Washington, D.C.: Resources for the Future, July 1966).

(e) Each person has an identical quantity, $\bar{x}$ of "bread" (all other goods-money) at his disposal.

(f) No land is owned, but is rented from the real estate company.

(g) Each person receives equal shares π and ρ of profits from the bread exchange and the real estate company, respectively.

(h) Each individual maximizes his utility subject to the budget constraint.

(i) The bread exchange buys bread at price, p, sells it at normalized price, l; r_n is the rental price of land in the North, r_s of land in the South.

(j) n^i, s^i, x^i are quantities of northern land, southern land, and bread, respectively, bought by the ith individual.

(k) a is an index of relative attractiveness of land in the north versus the south. a is assumed to shift in response to differential impact of public investments.

(l) The change in welfare (W) given a change in a is defined to be

$$\frac{dW}{da} = \Sigma \frac{1}{u_x{}^i} \frac{du^i}{da} ;$$

where $u_x{}^i$ is the partial derivative of u^i, the utility function for the ith individual, with respect to x.

Based on these assumptions he correctly concludes that the change in welfare, dW/da, will be obtained by adding the $1,000,000 increase in land values in the North to the $700,000 decrease in welfare in the South. Strotz therefore arrives at the somewhat surprising conclusion that the net effect is not, as might be supposed a priori, a net welfare gain of $300,000 or even $1,000,000, but one of the $1,700,000.

However, the Strotz assumptions, particularly with reference to property ownership— (f) and (g) —are questionable. These departures from reality, coupled with the assumption (d) that all individuals occupy land in both the North and South, produce the seemingly paradoxical conclusion which Strotz reaches. Residents are indifferent to the absolute level of prices; they are concerned only about relative prices. In effect, since there is no quality change in southern land, the southern land becomes a numeraire for the system. The quality change of northern land is judged by the relative change in its price as compared with southern land. Consequently, Strotz obtains a net welfare change of $1,700,000. The result is internally consistent with the assumptions and model which he draws. However, Strotz's assumptions do not approximate the normal case, and therefore his solution may not be inferred to the more general problem of how to account

for the effects of land value changes (resulting from a public investment project) outside the project area.

IV. Measurement

The empirical testing of the conceptual model described above
requires measurement of those land value increments which are both
in the project area and are due to the water project. The most difficult
measurement problem is that of isolating project effects on land values
from all other factors that might influence land values. There are two
possible approaches to such empirical measurement. One is a regression model where dummy variables might be used to indicate properties in a project area.

This is represented as a regression of property values in the project
area, $_{proj}PV_t$, on a set of exogenous variables, X_{it}, and a dummy variable, D_t which equals zero before the investment and equals one after
the investment. The subscript t represents time:

$$_{proj}PV_t = a + bD_t + c_iX_{it}. \tag{19}$$

The other approach is a control area analysis where the control
area is expected to be similar to the project area in all respects except the water project itself. If the two areas are similar, they will respond to all other factors in the same way. It should follow that
comparing rates of growth in land values in the control and the project
areas will effectively isolate the increments which are attributable to
the projects. This is done by subtracting control area values, $_{con}PV_t$,
from project area, $_{proj}PV_t$, and explaining them simply with a single
dummy:

$$_{proj}PV_t - _{con}PV_t = a + bD_t. \tag{20}$$

The choice between these models must depend upon: (a) the
randomness of land value determinants between areas, (b) the size
of the variances in these factors, and (c) the availability of data. The
control area method in (20) conserves significantly on data, but will
fail badly when the project and control areas are not strictly comparable. The regression method in (19) can control for nonrandom-
ness between project and control areas, but is very expensive of data.

The two methods could, of course, be combined to yield a system
that utilizes the best advantages of both. That is, a subset, J, of the
exogenous variables X_t used in (19) would be selected for use in a
modified regression-control area method:

$$_{proj}PV_t - _{con}PV_t = a + bD_t + c_j(_{proj}X_{jt} - _{con}X_{jt}). \tag{21}$$

This will reduce the data requirements and maintain a satisfactory reduction of variance in the property values that is due to the non-random occurrences (between areas) of X_{jt}.

These techniques would be applied to a combined cross-section, time series data set. By combining data at least one of the faults of purely cross-sectional studies, criticized above, is eliminated. That is, with time series data it is possible to evaluate the land-improving water investment not as a *ceteris paribus* analysis; rather, the general equilibrium effects of offsetting land values might be isolated. With time series, cross-section data, a property whose values have increased can be compared with unimproved properties in the same time period. It may also be compared with itself before the project was implemented.

The usefulness of combining the control area and regression methods is clearly demonstrated by their abilities to isolate jointly the land value increment due to a project area. The idea is to compare values of a project area property (or project area index[27]) with itself, before and after the investment. This can be done by application of a simple dummy variable analysis model. The coefficient of the dummy will reflect the land value increment due to the project if the dummy takes on the values of 0 for all times before the project and 1 for all time after the project. A problem in identifying the true increment occurs as the values in the project area are inflated or deflated by exogenous forces to different extents over time.

The variance caused by the exogenous forces will reflect itself in secular and cyclical movements in the project area property values. Many of these exogenous variables will have metropolitan wide impact. It is reasonable that these variables will have the same systematic influence on project and control areas. The control can then effectively be used to abstract from these factors by "residualizing" the project area values with some forecasted control area values. That forecast would be made on some mechanical basis such as a best polynomial regression fitting time and the value of time exponentiated, (time),^{2} (time),^{3} . . . to the control area indices. "Best fit" might be defined as that regression having the lowest overall standard error of

---

27. Project area indices may be calculated by using repeat sales data on all properties within an area by weighting all observations into the index. The method is simplified and statistical properties are enhanced by performing the weighting with a least squares regression technique. An example of this is given in Martin J. Bailey, Richard F. Muth, and Hugh O. Nourse, "A Regression Method for Real Estate Price Index Construction," *American Statistical Association Journal* 58 (December 1963) : 933–42.

estimate or highest (corrected for degrees of freedom) $\bar{R}^2$. "Residuali-
zation" would simply subtract from the actual project area values
those forecasted control area values. On the residualized project area
values, a dummy variable analysis would then finally be performed.
This analysis would be similar to splitting the project area values
into two groups—divided at the point in time when the project was
implemented—and running a statistical test for differences in means
for the two groups of data.

Additional refinements may be made to enhance the explanatory
powers of the model. With the methodology that has so far been described, it is necessary that we consider any variance that is local to
either project or control areas as having a purely random character.
It is quite reasonable that the model so far developed will however
have biased effects from local, nonrandom exogenous changes. These
will prevent the model's identification of the true project effects. However, if each data set on the control and project areas is independently
subjected to regression procedures fitting local variables to the property values, we can control for these biasing effects. This specifically
would reduce the variance of the property value indices by controlling
the local variable variance. Indices would be constructed from the
reduced-variance property values and then the control area residualiza-
tion and dummy variable techniques would be applied.

V. Other Problems

The theory and measurement techniques described in the above
sections provide only a broad outline for a research plan that has com-
manded and will continue to command extraordinarily detailed
methodology. In this paper, we have touched only the major areas
of concern. Many behavioral and institutional relationships also will
have an effect on the investment-land value nexus. These include the
diverse considerations of property tax effects, externalities, site improvements, zoning, and migration. We shall only briefly suggest their
role in the general model.

A. Property Taxes

Our theory above provides an analysis whereby property values increase as investment occurs. With most types of property tax systems,
these increasing values will, in practice, raise the property tax base.
That is, the increment in property values will also be subject to a tax.

Oates,[28] Upton,[29] and others have recognized that, because of the existence of a tax, land values are, *ceteris paribus,* lower than they would
be without a tax. A simple extension of this argument on our model
implies that whereas land values would have risen, for example, by $b,
in the absence of a tax, they will rise by somewhat less than $b in
the presence of a tax. The problem, obviously, is how can we standard-
ize benefit measurement across areas subject to varying tax levels. Once
again there exists a need to know the rate of capitalization, this time
of taxes into (reduced) land values.

B. Externalities

Externalities will inevitably occur from an investment in water
supply. These reflect the fact that people living in areas adjacent to a
project area are less likely to be infected by disease as the health of
project area residents improves. Externalities also exist in the form of
a reduced cost for future provision of public water supply to current
nonproject areas.[30] Presumably there would be other factors which
would similarly affect neighboring, nonproject properties. Each exter-
nality may be capitalized into neighboring properties just as direct
project effects are capitalized into project properties. Since we would
like to measure these as a part of the benefits from the project, they
force us to accept a wider, spatial, group of properties to treat as we
have treated project area properties. Aggregate benefits would necessarily be the summation of land value increments not only over project properties, but also over some nonproject, but neighboring, properties that are subject to externalities.

The existence of externalities also implies a danger in selecting a
control area. It must be an area not subject to a project's effects. There
exists, therefore, a conflict in choosing a control. On grounds that the
control and project are desired to be similar, there is a tendency to
select contiguously neighboring areas. However, on grounds that the
control should be free of externalities, there is a desire to choose more
distant properties. The resultant choice of a control area must com-

28. Oates, "Effects of Property Taxes and Local Public Spending on Property
Values," pp. 957–71.

29. Charles Upton, "The Provision of Local Public Goods: The Tiebout Hypothesis," Urban Economics Report No. 44 (Chicago: University of Chicago, November 1970).

30. Alternatively these externalities reflect a higher probability that adjacent
nonproject areas will be given water in the future since the public water mains
have now been extended nearer to the nonproject areas.

promise between the alternatives. Any choice may be criticized that it is not similar enough to project areas and that it is subject to some externalities.

C. Site Improvements

Site improvements may naturally arise in connection with water projects. These, of course, are of central importance when the project and new construction are simultaneously undertaken. However, they will also occur even when housing already exists on project property. An example is given by a property receiving water but needing to build a bathroom or to install other plumbing in order to utilize fully the new public supplies.

The benefits of these improvements will be capitalized and reflected in land values. These are benefits which should be attributed to the project. However, they are overstated if a correction is not made for the costs of the improvements, since associated costs are just as closely related to the project as are the benefits of the improvements. We wish to attribute only net site improvement benefits to the project. Hence, we must find the cost of the improvements and subtract the capitalized value of these costs from the measured land value increment.

D. Zoning

Water projects (and to a larger extent sewer projects) can have an effect of changing the institutional zoning requirements. These changes automatically add another complicating dimension to benefit evaluation. That is, a zoning change implies a shift in the supply curve (as opposed to a move along it). Certainly, zoning regulations are considered as a constant "background" condition against which a supply curve is drawn. A change in zoning or any other background variable suggests a supply shift. Intuitively, it now becomes cheaper at any given time to subdivide and increase the supply of residential properties from a given fixed physical area. Consider the owner of a three-fourths acre plot faced in one situation with one-half acre minimum density zoning and faced in another situation with one-fourth acre zoning. In the first case, he must speculatively buy other properties if he wishes to subdivide. This quite possibly means that he will face a risk premium, raising the cost of subdivision. In the second case, he can readily subdivide the original property into three one-fourth acre plots without any risk.

The resultant change is an outward shift in the supply curve. Without doubt, this represents an increase in welfare to the community since it permits an increase in density (which will only be increased if it is desired) without any changes in the technological capacity to produce other goods. It may be interpreted as an outward shift in the community's production possibility surface. Harberger suggests that evaluation of this benefit is no more difficult than evaluation of other benefits; he suggests using a compensating or equivalent " 'income effects' of changes in resources, technology or trading conditions."[31]

The conceptual problem arises in determining whether these benefits should really be attributed to the project. The real question is whether the decision to reduce zoning requirements simultaneously with investment is purely arbitrary, an institutional decision. If it is, then these benefits are not project related. However, if the zoning reduction creates density increases that are only tolerated because of the project, then the benefits are investment-induced and we should want to count them. The decision on how to handle zoning changes is a difficult one.

E. Mobility

In developing countries, rural to urban migration is common. The existing migratory patterns should adjust to the investment project, increasing rates of migration for project area properties relative to nonproject area properties. In a dynamic and realistic sense these patterns provide at least a portion of the shift in relative demand that is observed. We should need also to know whether the total rate of migration has been affected and whether the investment does distort rates of migration in the control and project areas by more than the relative effect of the investment on control and project areas.

VI. Summary

The model presented here proposes that revenues derived from the sale of water in the urban water market underestimate the true benefits of water supply. In evaluating many different types of projects, the consistently conservative measures used for water projects will put these at a disadvantage relative to other projects that are more correctly evaluated. While in practice it is preferable to underestimate rather than overestimate benefits, this paper attempts to explain the systematic underestimation for water supply project benefits.

31. Arnold Harberger, "Three Basic Postulates for Applied Welfare Economics: An Interpretive Essay," *Journal of Economic Literature* 9, no. 3 (September 1971): 785–97; see especially p. 793.

Two questions are raised by this research. First, what methods can be devised which will totally measure the underestimation of benefits. Second, what methods can be easily applied to improve the measurement process but which will, if in error, still underestimate rather than overestimate benefits.

The solutions for both questions are provided by our hypothesis that any consumers' surplus in the water market will be transferred to the land market. Specifically, for the first question, the econometric estimation of the demand curve for property will yield the desired solution. All benefits not measured by the revenue technique will shift the demand curve for housing outward. The integral value of this shift totally measures the extent of the underestimation. This method, however, may be of more value as a heuristic device than as an applied measurement concept.

Consequently, for applied benefit measurement, it is important to be able to determine the extent to which outward shifts in the demand curve are capitalized by the market. If the effect of water projects on property values can be isolated, then the result can be added to the initial measure of water revenues. The sum of the two measures must be less conservative than water revenues are by themselves. Yet, if the two fail to measure benefits exactly, they will fail in underestimation. This conforms to the criteria that the applied benefit measure must meet.

Finally, although the generalizations have not been made here, we hope that this method will be applicable to other types of investment and not just to water. If these techniques can be used in analyzing other investments, the wide spectrum of methodologies used for benefit analysis can be made smaller. This would facilitate the comparison of benefits measured both across different projects and between time and space. The present limitations of cost-benefit analysis in these respects severely restrict its usefulness. If this paper can be regarded as a step in the direction of providing a standard methodology for benefit measurement, then its own value will have increased tremendously.

10 *Darwin W. Daicoff*

CAPITALIZATION OF THE BENEFITS
OF WATER RESOURCE DEVELOPMENT

Introduction

Capitalization is usually associated with the influence of taxes on capital values. In that context, concern is given to the reduction of income as a result of a tax and to the effect of that reduction on the capitalized value of the income stream—that is, the effect on the value of the taxed object. Just as tax levies reduce an income stream, government expenditures may make a positive contribution to an income stream. By discounting a stream of expenditure benefits and adding them to the discounted stream of private benefits, the present value of the expenditure-benefit augmented income stream may be found. Then, by simple subtraction, the capitalized value of the expenditure benefit may be estimated. This paper presents an analysis of an aspect of the consequences of one type of public expenditure; it considers the capitalization of benefits of water resource development projects.

In the usual discussion of tax capitalization, the capitalization of expenditure benefits is almost completely neglected. For example, although Jens P. Jensen analyzed expenditures financed by the property tax, none of his mathematical examples considers the capitalization of benefits. This omission stems from his contention that the public services of local government are largely of a personal character, not closely related to property values.[1] Herbert Simon reached the same conclusion by arguing that individuals are unlikely to give as much weight to service advantages as is given to tax differentials.[2]

Among the requirements that must be met for a tax to have an effect on property values, for the tax to be capitalized, is one related to the benefits financed by the proceeds of the tax. It is generally argued that,

1. Jens P. Jensen, *Property Taxation in the United States* (Chicago: University of Chicago Press, 1931), pp. 82–83.
2. Herbert A. Simon, *Fiscal Aspects of Metropolitan Consolidation* (Berkeley: Bureau of Public Administration, University of California, 1943), pp. 3–4.

to the extent that some particular types of expenditure benefits result directly from a tax, the value of the taxed object need not decline by the full value of the discounted tax levy; the amount to be capitalized is the net fiscal residue. This conclusion rests on the analysis of a long line of authors writing on public finance and on just a bit of empirical research.

Historically the consideration of the importance of expenditures benefits began with the distinction made between onerous and beneficial "rates," the British term for the levy which corresponds with our property tax. This consideration was introduced into the discussion of tax capitalization by George Murray in 1893.[3] By defining a beneficial local rate as a payment for services which consumers would purchase voluntarily, those who discussed these rates in the early part of the twentieth century concluded that, while onerous rates may decrease the value of taxed property, such a decrease need not occur in the case of beneficial rates.[4]

The Italian public finance authors of the time were greatly concerned with the economics of public expenditures. In a fairly typical presentation, Luigi Einaudi employed rather complicated numerical examples to show that, as more and more of the tax proceeds go to provide benefits accruing to the taxed object, the tax has a less and less detrimental effect on the value of the taxed property.[5] Some American authors considered the benefits financed by the property tax as important determinants of the extent of tax capitalization. In his discussion of tax capitalization, Jensen stated that, if no benefits resulted from a tax, tax capitalization might be complete; if the benefits were generally diffused, the capitalization might be diminished appreciably; and finally, if the tax were wholly beneficial, there would be no tax capitalization.[6] At about the same time Shoup, Blough, and Newcomer concluded that a special tax on property, which provides the funds for expenditures yielding a special benefit to the taxed property, occasions little or no net change in its value.[7]

3. George H. Murray, "Notes on the Growth and Incidence of Local Taxation," *The Economic Journal* 3 (December 1893) : 698–704; see esp. p. 703.

4. C. F. Bickerdike, "Taxation of Site Values," *The Economic Journal* 12 (December 1902) : pp. 472–80; and Edwin Cannan, *The History of Local Rates in England*, 2nd ed. rev. (London: P. S. King & Son, 1912) , pp. 164–80.

5. Luigi Einaudi, *Saggi Sal Rispasmio E L'Imposta* (Turin: Giuilo Eimaudi Editore, 1958) , pp. 221–29.

6. Jens P. Jensen, "Tax Capitalization," *The Bulletin of the National Tax Association* 23 (November 1937) : 45–56; see esp. p. 55.

7. Carl Shoup, Roy Blough, and Mable Newcomer, *Facing the Tax Problem* (New York: Twentieth Century Fund, 1937) , p. 242.

There is at least one fairly old empirical study of the benefit aspects of the property tax. Edwin Spengler attempted to quantify the extent to which that tax is a benefit tax.[8] He concluded that about one half of property tax revenue was used to provide direct service benefits to property and thereby made property more desirable. This conclusion seems to have been strong enough that most subsequent tax capitalization studies begin by assuming that part of the property tax is capitalized and some part is offset by public expenditure benefits. In a more recent empirical study, it has been argued that differential service level changes explain why differential tax rate changes have not produced differential property value consequences when the property is located in different jurisdictions.[9]

Necessary Conditions

The capitalization of water resource development benefits requires conditions that are quite similar to those under which capitalization of taxes may be expected. These conditions relate to the type of object or activity benefited by the public expenditure and to the specific nature of the expenditure benefit.

The object or activity benefited must be salable. For example, a levee providing flood control may make some agricultural land suitable for industrial uses. This potential change in land use would be reflected, at least partially, in the value of the land. The same levee might reduce the probability of a loss of life through floods (some consideration may even have been given to this potential benefit in the justification for the levee), but since this benefit would be personal and thereby bestowed on a nonsalable object, no capitalization would be possible. Any change in property value produced by these benefits would be quite indirect. Moreover, since an estimate of project benefits by the measurement of changes in land values would pick up the secondary consequences of the project, measures of incremental land values are not generally satisfactory estimates of primary benefits.

There are additional requirements for capitalization which relate to the nature of the expenditures benefit. First, some of the benefits must be in the future. A currently available one-time supply of water for

8. Edwin H. Spengler, "Is the Real Estate Tax a Benefit Tax?" Memorandum Number Five, *Report of the New York State Commission for the Revision of the Tax Laws,* Legislative Document (1932) No. 77 (Albany, 1932).

9. Darwin W. Daicoff, "The Capitalization of the Property Tax," *Essays in State and Local Finance,* ed. Harvey E. Brazer (Ann Arbor: Institute of Public Administration, University of Michigan, 1967), pp. 70–71.

electrical power generation would have no effect on the future stream of income to a power company and, thus, the benefits of that supply of water would not be capitalized. Second, there must be some differential to be capitalized. Irrigation water made available everywhere may affect total agricultural production and the price of agricultural products, but this would be equivalent to affecting the capitalization rate—a differential supplement to the income stream would not be created. A partial and localized irrigation project is another matter; in this kind of project the price effect induced by the output change may be expected to be minimal. Because of the availability of water, a differential productivity advantage for some parcels would come to exist; this differential would be capitalized into property values.

This irrigation example can illustrate a third requirement for capitalization. Only a nonshifted benefit will be capitalized. If the consequence of increased agricultural output is a reduction in the price of an agricultural product, a farmer may find his production increased without an accompanying revenue gain. In this case, there would be a full shifting of the benefits to the purchaser of the agricultural products and no possible land value consequence. This example continued yet one step further produces an interesting sort of secondary consequence which may result from the increased agricultural output. It may be that some linked phase of the production process (railroad services, the processing of dairy products or sugar beets, or some types of fruit and vegetable dehydration) may have a monopoly-monopsony characteristic as a result of some resource indivisibility or lack of mobility. As this situation exists, it is quite possible that the benefits of the project will be shifted to the linked production activity and that if any capitalization occurred, it would occur there. Perhaps this result tells us why some of the strongest supporters of water-development projects are who they are.

There is one aspect of the capitalization of water-expenditure benefits that may seem different from tax capitalization. A fee or price is often charged for water. It has already been shown that only the net fiscal residue is capitalized. Only those benefits in excess of the payments for the water, which are similar to a consumer surplus, can influence land values.

Four other aspects of the capitalization of water-expenditure benefits deserve mention. First, note should be taken of the timing of the benefits. Since capitalization involves the current value of an anticipated income stream, the change in the value of property can easily occur long before any benefits are actually received. Land values have been observed to rise rapidly with the announcement of a water project. This speculation seems to peak fairly soon afterwards; a relative decline then occurs; and finally, only after the project has been completed, values begin to rise again. Second, a transfer of the property would be required for the realization of the appreciation in the property value, but a transfer would not be required for the occurrence of the value change capitalization. Third, uncertainty associated with water benefits should add an additional factor to the discounting procedure. For multiple-purpose water projects there often is a hierarchy of claims for the water; in a period of water shortage some low-ranking claimants may be excluded from using the water. This hierarchy sometimes applies to irrigation and recreational uses as opposed to navigation and municipal water supply claims. Fourth, benefits need not result from output increases. It is entirely possible for the benefits to be a result of a cost reduction. For example, in the evaluation of recreational benefits, it is common to refer to land value increases in the vicinity of recreational facilities as the capitalized value of foregone travel expenses—expenses that are avoided with a location near the facility.

Characteristics of Water Projects

With this general background, it is now appropriate to turn to an analysis of the incidence of water resource expenditures and particularly the influence of the expenditure benefits on property values. An analysis of the incidence of water resource development expenditures has two major advantages over an analysis of many other public expenditures categories. First, there has been a long history of cost-benefit studies of water related projects. While these studies cannot be considered incidence studies in seeking to define and quantify benefits, they provide a classification system for these benefits and an estimate of their size. In this way they provide a formulation for an analysis of incidence. Second, water resources research has had the advantage of widely diffused federal funding. In many states water resources institutes have been functioning for a considerable time. Some of the voluminous research that has come from these institutes is of direct relevance to an analysis of the capitalization of expenditure benefits.

Benefit-cost analysis entails calculating the future benefit stream from a specific project, discounting the benefit stream to a current value, and comparing that value to the discounted cost of the project. It is generally recognized that benefits can be estimated by calculating the change in asset values resulting from public expenditures.

Benefit-cost studies typically are restricted to comparing the present values of future income streams which are considered to be augmented by the benefits and costs associated with the project—with little or no use of alternative or supplementary measurement devices such as changes in property values. This restriction does not imply that land-value-enhancing benefits should be omitted from benefit cost analysis, because many categories of public expenditure benefits show up most clearly as changes in property values. Measurement of these changes is often an alternative to income analysis and is a particularly valuable approach to benefit evaluation for goods and services not generally exchanged in the marketplace.

Water resource development projects are often multipurpose. In the analysis of the benefits and costs of such projects, considerable effort is expended on the separate measurement of the benefits for each benefit category. Whether a particular water development project is single purpose or multipurpose is of little significance for the following analysis. What is important is the nature of the expenditure benefits. The following discussion considers the influence of some of the major expenditure categories on the value of property.

Some Water Benefit Categories

Flood Control

An interesting group of studies of agricultural flood control benefits and land values has been conducted by the Economic Research Service (ERS) of the United States Department of Agriculture for the Army Corps of Engineers.[10] These studies involved developing and testing a methodology for using land values to estimate benefits to agricultural land from flood-control projects, and therefore they represent an attempt by the Corps to consider alternative procedures for estimating one type of water resource development benefit.

The analytical procedure adopted was the multiple-regression model to estimate the differential land value effects resulting from the re-

10. U.S. Department of Agriculture, Economic Research Service, *Analysis of Alternative Procedures for the Evaluation of Agricultural Flood Control Benefits*, Report 71–4 (Alexandria, Va.: U.S. Army Corps of Engineers, 1971) ; U.S. Department of Agriculture, Economic Research Service, *The Relationship Between Land Values and Flood Risk in the Wabash River Basin*, Report 69–4 (Alexandria, Va.: U.S. Army Corps of Engineers, 1969) ; Raymond L. Struyk, ed., *Agricultural Flood Control Benefits and Land Values*, Report 71–3 (Alexandria, Va.: U.S. Army Corps of Engineers, 1971) ; and Raymond L. Struyk, "Flood Risk and Agricultural Land Values: A Test," *Water Resources Research* 7 (August 1971) : 789–97.

duced probability of flooding. In one of the ERS studies, the coefficients for a regression equation involving the determinants of value were estimated for land with no flood risk; these coefficients were then used to calculate the fully protected value of land subject to flooding. This estimate of fully protected value permitted the calculation of a difference between the per acre price of land in the floodplain and the price of this land if it were fully protected; this differential was used as the dependent variable in the regression analysis. In another study following the ERS methodology, the dependent variable was the per acre value of the farm without improvements. In both tests of the methodology, a large number of variables that might be expected to influence farm land values (such as size of the tract, acres of cropland, and quality of the soil) were employed as independent variables. To these variables a number of terms reflecting the risk of flooding were added to measure the effect of flooding on land values.

These applications or tests of the ERS methodology were made in different river basins. The first involved three study areas in the Wabash River basin (upper Wabash, lower Wabash, and White River) with a considerable difference in the geographic character of the land. In the upper and lower Wabash areas, after controlling for differences in productivity, topology, location, and date of the sale, a statistically significant differential was found in the value of land per acre associated with flood risk between farms located on the floodplain and the upland area adjacent to the flood plains. In the White River analysis the differential in land values associated with flood risks could not be established. The Wabash study only partially involved an evaluation of the benefits of a particular flood-control project. There was also a quantification of the benefit that might be expected if new flood-control projects were undertaken.

The second application of the ERS methodology was for the Saint Joseph reaches of the Missouri River. This study area contained some levees (both public and private) and thereby the study related land values to an existing water development facility. Again three study areas were employed: an unprotected floodplain area, a protected floodplain area, and an adjacent upland area. The results of the Missouri application generally reinforce those of the Wabash application in that statistically significant differentials were established between differences in land values and flood risks.

While these projects assign a dollar value to flood protection, they do so only with a rather low level of confidence. In the Missouri River study, it was found that the average premium for flood protection was $25 per acre but the interval necessary for a 90 percent level of confidence was $0 to $50. This same sort of wide confidence interval was found in the upper Wabash study, where the value of flood protection was estimated to be $49 per acre, with a $14 to $84 range required for a 90 percent level. In the lower Wabash the flood protection was estimated to be $5.89 per acre per year—with a range of $5.06 to $6.72. While these ranges are quite large and seem to have troubled the Corps, they may not be any greater than the ranges of the estimates of the Corps's benefits if a confidence interval could be calculated for its estimates.

For the Wabash study it is possible to compare the ERS estimates of benefits with independent benefit estimates made by the Corps through its standard estimating procedure. In the upper Wabash the Corps's estimate of benefits was $40 per acre—reasonably close to the $49 ERS estimate and well within the $14 to $84 range. For the lower Wabash estimate the Corps and ERS estimates are somewhat closer ($6.81 vs. $5.89), but the Corps's estimate is slightly above the upper bound of the confidence range of $6.72.

Thus, the ERS procedure seems to produce estimates that (1) have a relatively high standard error but (2) are within 20 percent or so of Corps's estimate.

Navigation

Navigation benefits of a water project are usually considered to be received initially by industrial firms. While these firms undoubtedly receive a considerable portion of the total navigation benefits, farmers can also share in these benefits because of the reduction in transportation costs of farm products. For example, it has been estimated that an extension of the Arkansas River Navigation Project will raise the wheat revenue of Kansas farmers by 10 cents per bushel. It should be obvious why Kansas farm groups have supported the project and its extension.

Navigation projects also create desirable industrial sites along the waterway. The booming industrial development, and booming land values, along the Arkansas River Navigation Project, particularly at the Port of Catoosa in Oklahoma, gives evidence of the strong positive effect of such a development.[11] In contrast, when waterway sites are

11. Adrian Williamson, Jr., "Economic Development Related to the Arkansas River Navigation Project" (Speech delivered at the seventy-fifth meeting of the Arkansas-White-Red Basins Inter-Agency Committee, Little Rock, Ark., April 21, 1971).

no longer desirable, substantially depressed land values come to exist, as is the case along the Chicago Sanitary and Ship Canal.[12]

Recreation

A fairly large number of empirical case studies of the impact of reservoirs have been made, particularly of the impact of their recreational aspects on land values or of the reservoir's more general economic consequences, land-value changes being one aspect. Almost all of these studies employ a comparative analytical method. A large number observe land values or land-value trends in an area (usually a county or a small group of counties) that has had reservoir development and compare their land values or trends to a control area that is similar in all other important aspects. An even simpler approach is involved in studies which entail a before and after analysis of the reservoir area, with or without a comparison to a control region. In some cases the mathematical technique involves the calculation of simple averages for property values, on a per acre or a per county basis; at the other end of the scale of mathematical sophistication, covariance, linear programming, and multiple regression have sometimes been used.

Three aspects of property values are dealt with in this group of studies. The first relates to the determinants of the value of property.[13] Water quality, topological, and other physical characteristics of the parcel, as well as characteristics of the particular geographic region, have been identified as having significant influences on the value of property located near a reservoir. To a considerable extent these parcel characteristics determine the ability of the users to enjoy the benefits of the reservoir. In addition, it has been found that proximity to the facility is an important determinant of land values.

A second property aspect of value in these studies is an analysis of the consequence of the reservoir development on the fiscal operation of the political jurisdiction in which the reservoir is located. In an early study, Bates found some declines in the total value of taxable real property in the area when land was purchased for the reservoirs.

12. David M. Solzaman, "The Value of Inland Waterfront Industrial Sites," *Land Economics* 45 (May 1969) : 456–62.

13. Elizabeth L. David, "The Exploding Demand for Recreational Property," *Land Economics* 45 (May 1969) : 206–17; Jack L. Knetsch, "The Influence of Reservoir Projects in Land Values," *Journal of Farm Economics* 43 (February 1964) : 231–43; and W. A. Schutjer and M. C. Hallberg, "Impact of Water Recreational Development on Rural Property Values," *American Journal of Agricultural Economics* 50 (August 1968) : 572–83

This fall in value was related to the fact that the three reservoirs he studied were quite large, with as much as 20 percent of the county's property being removed from the tax roll.[14] In an analysis of fifteen facilities, Epp also found some immediate total value declines as the land was acquired.[15] But both Bates and Epp observed that this total value decline did not persist and as a result there was no necessity for the property tax rate to rise. The Bates study is unique in that it also attempts to consider the expenditures of local governments; he concluded that, even considering both sides of the budget, the local governments gained as a result of the reservoir.

The third aspect of property value considerations relates to the timing of property value changes. Bates found a one-year drop in value of taxable real property and recovery within two years; similar rapid recovery was observed by Epp. The data presented by Downing and Jansma and by Williams and Daniel show that the period of most rapid property value increases can be near the announcement date of the project and that significant value increases need not wait until water-related benefits are actually received.[16]

All of the studies mentioned above, and others as well, show that per-acre land values rise in the vicinity of a newly constructed reservoir. The studies also show that this rise is more rapid than the property value increases in other comparable areas without a reservoir and more rapid than the area had been experiencing before the announcement of the facility. The studies show that there has been a capitalization of expenditure benefits. Unfortunately, these studies do not show how much of these benefits is capitalized and how much is not. Only one of the studies, that by Knetsch in 1964, is speculative; he employs the estimates of the determinants of property values that he developed to estimate the land-value-embodied benefits of a proposed reservoir.

14. Clyde T. Bates, *The Effect of a Large Reservoir on Local Government Revenue and Expenditures* (Lexington: University of Kentucky, Water Research Resources Institute, 1969).

15. Donald J. Epp, "The Effect of Public Land Acquisition for Outdoor Recreation on the Real Estate Base," *Journal of Leisure Research* 3 (Winter 1971) : 17–27.

16. Roger H. Downing and J. Dean Jansma, *The Economic Impact of Public Investment on Property Value in York County, 1950–1965,* (University Park: Pennsylvania State University, Institute for Research on Land and Water Research, 1970), pp. 43–44; and D. C. Williams, Jr., and Donnie L. Daniel, *The Impact of Reservoirs on Land Values: A Case Study,* (State College: Mississippi State University, Water Resources Research Institute, 1969), pp. 20–23.

Conclusion

From the analysis presented above, it should be clear that the capitalization requirements are met for most water resource development projects. While all the expenditures should not be expected to be reflected in property values, some public spending on water projects should show up in changes in the value of real property. The empirical studies of certain water projects show that a considerable portion of the benefits from such projects are observable in property values. Although some question remains as to the degree of capitalization and the extent to which it can be accurately measured, the presence of the capitalization of the benefits of water resource development projects cannot be denied.

Part IV. Urban Renewal: A Seminar

11 *Arthur P. Becker*

THE DISTRIBUTION OF BENEFITS AND COSTS OF THE FEDERALLY SUBSIDIZED URBAN RENEWAL PROGRAMS

In attempting to understand the distributional effects of the federal urban renewal program, it is first necessary to identify and measure, if possible, its direct and indirect benefits and costs. This chapter will examine the possible vs. the actual benefits and costs, because the magnitude and the extent to which they materialize vary with each project. It is a mistake to lump all projects, whether federally or locally subsidized, into one category to characterize them all in one way. It is far better to recognize that, in terms of net benefits or costs, there are all kinds of urban renewal projects, and each must be treated individually rather than uniformly for general praise or criticism.

A major reason for the deviation of actual from possible benefits and costs is the fact that so many "unintended" benefits and costs arise. Some of these appear because of the way in which the program is administered and carried out. We shall examine some of them, because they often hold the key to an accurate evaluation of a project's net benefit or cost.

Possible Benefits of Urban Renewal

Elimination of Substandard Housing and Replacement with Standard Housing

Two possible benefits of urban renewal are (1) the elimination of substandard housing and (2) its replacement with standard and above-standard housing. Housing that is dilapidated, unsafe, and unsound can be thought of as the result of an unsatisfactory market response. We would like to eliminate such housing and replace it with standard and above-standard housing. If we do, the benefits could be substantial enough to motivate and justify the costs of an urban renewal project.

The renewal program was born of the federal government's experience, beginning in 1937, in providing public housing. During the first dozen years it became evident that public housing could not raise substandard housing to a standard level.[1] So the United States began its urban renewal program in 1949.[2] Subsequently, the program went through several basic changes.

Raising the Level of Land Use

A third possible benefit of urban renewal is the conversion of urban land from low-use to a higher use. There are two reasons for this change. One is the plottage factor, namely, the assemblage of land by the power of eminent domain, thus making possible an increase in land productivity over that possible with numerous smaller plots. The plottage factor often prevails for multifamily residential land use, as well as for nonresidential land use. The assemblage of land provides benefits because it achieves the unification of ownership which is necessary before redevelopment plans can proceed. Only then is it possible in many cases to take advantage of neighborhood effects from surrounding areas, and this advantage cannot result so long as fractionated ownership prevails.

While urban renewal thus facilitates the assembly of land for the possibility of putting it to a higher use, it also makes land available to redevelopers at a price lower than they would have to pay to private owners. For site purposes redevelopers shy away from paying the full cost of real estate (including the razing of improvements) that they otherwise would need to pay for land without urban renewal subsidy.

The extent of the land acquisition subsidy (or cost) in the urban renewal program has been estimated by some as involving an average

1. Scott Greer, *Urban Renewal and American Cities* (Indianapolis, Ind.: Bobbs-Merrill Company, Inc., 1965), p. 17.
2. Housing Act of 1949, Public Law 171, 81st Congress, approved July 15, 1949.
3. Milwaukee's first two projects resulted in a write-down of 52 percent to 69 percent, depending upon the method of calculation:

Project	a Cost of land purchase	b Total land cost (incl. admin. cost)	c Resale proceeds	c/a	c/b	Write-down
UR WIS 1–1	$3,205,988	$3,927,754	$1,530,077	48%	39%	52%–61%
UR WIS 1–2	2,700,000	3,513,142	1,099,318	41%	31%	59%–69%

Source: Records of the Department of City Development, Milwaukee, Wisconsin.

write-down of 60 percent in the price of land.[3] So by making land available at a lower price and by assembling land in larger plots, urban renewal can take advantage of spill-in benefits and increase internal benefits (to the owners of the combined plot.) In addition, the urban renewal project may have positive external effects.

One of the hopes of urban renewal is that it will improve the neighborhood and nearby property as well, thereby raising the property value. Of course this is not always the case, and we can have an unexpected cost instead of the hoped-for benefits. But this should not be surprising. The slow process in redevelopment and the illogical sequence of projects often create a bombed-out effect during the interval of demolition and redevelopment. Obviously this has a negative effect on neighborhoods. However, an inspection of the area after the project is completed will often show positive external effects.

In contrast to earlier examples, public housing today usually does not involve the large clearance of slum land and the destruction of an entire neighborhood in order to erect a grandiose set of buildings. Instead, we now have "scattered sites" housing projects that involve some spot clearance and the immediate construction of small-scale public housing. The latter is usually one building in one place so as to provide the benefit of externalities immediately and avoid the long-term depressing effect of large and languishing urban renewal projects.

The large-scale urban renewal project is generally a thing of the past, and it is doubtful that many such projects will be begun in the foreseeable future. Of course, many cities with uncompleted large-scale urban renewal projects will want to complete them. However, new projects, under what HUD (Housing and Urban Development) calls the Neighborhood Development Program (NDP), are scaled-down projects that can be completed in a year or two at the most. This new program should prevent, or at least minimize, the damaging effect that large-scale public urban renewal projects have had on neighboring areas.

The Decrease in Social Costs

A fourth possible benefit of urban renewal is the decrease in social costs, one of the important goals of urban renewal. Social costs include such items as those caused by crime, sickness, and unemployment and are connected, both in terms of cause and effect, with fear, anger, anxiety, misery, uncertainty, hate, and hopelessness. The philosophy of urban renewal assumes that the provision of standard housing in an improved neighborhood will mitigate the personal problems that lead to crime, sickness, and unemployment. However, while there

seems to be a high inverse correlation between the quality of housing and environment and social costs, no conclusive causal relationship has as yet been demonstrated.

Because reducing social costs is an important goal of urban renewal, we would like to be able to quantify these benefits. This quantification may help to resolve the question of what proportion of
public and private funds should be spent on raising the quality of
life of low-income and welfare families. Since we know that social
costs are not solely attributable to poor housing, it is highly desirable
to quantify social costs and determine what portion may result from
substandard housing. Until we can answer this question, it will not
be possible to spend public funds in the most efficient manner to reduce social costs.

Greater Efficiency in Public Decision-Making

A fifth important possible benefit of urban renewal is increased
efficiency of public decision-making. Citizen cooperation and the responsive implementation of public policy in slums and blighted areas
is notoriously difficult. It is hoped that the elimination of slums and
blight will be accompanied by an increase in the understanding and
cooperation of citizens in response to urban policy.

The advantages and benefits that have been mentioned manifest
themselves in several ways. For example, we have stated that urban
renewal can increase both productive capacity and the actual productivity of a project area once the renewal project is successfully
completed. Second, greater efficiency in resource allocation occurs as
resources are diverted into improvements of all kinds, private as well
as public. Public improvements will occur that would otherwise not
have appeared in certain areas for a long time, and private developers
also will allocate resources for renewal much sooner where essential
public improvement investments have already been made.

The Distribution of Income and Wealth

A sixth important possible benefit of urban renewal, and one which
some persons regard as the most important of all, is the redistributional effect of urban renewal. The beneficiaries of the redistributional effects are many and include low-income-family owners and
renters of renewal housing, creditors, savers, the building industry and
businesses with which they deal, developers, and some owners of
property sold to the Local Public Agency (LPA).

There is little doubt that in many declining neighborhoods the
property owner is simply waiting for somebody to come along and

bail him out, and this has happened in many urban renewal projects. But a satisfactory bail-out would occur generally if a neighborhood did not collapse suddenly (with panic flight and sales) upon the announcement that the neighborhood may or will be subject to urban renewal. It must be a neighborhood where a sound economic foundation obtains. Some owners can sell at a high price if their property is strategically located and necessary to get a plottage effect. Moreover, most property is acquired by negotiation in the very real and large effort to maintain good public relations and avoid the adverse aspects of condemnation procedures. As a consequence the renewal agency may pay a "market price" that is estimated slightly high.

A study was made about ten years ago in New York City of ten of the city's first urban renewal projects during the first ten years of operation. It was found that the average condemnation award to owners was about 55 percent above the full market value of the property, as determined by the property tax assessor, indicating that the owners of the property sold benefitted substantially from their awards.[4] Next we shall look at the effect on landowners after redevelopment. The developers paid $25,000,000 for land whose full market value after renewal (according to the assessor) rose to about $82,000,000.[5] So the developers who bought land from the LPA enjoyed a considerable benefit in land value appreciation from their urban renewal participation.

We might broaden our horizons and think of redistribution in terms of local governmental jurisdictions. One view here is that the federal government, through its urban renewal program, provides a subsidy or special benefit to the central city's economy and government, as compared to suburbs in a metropolitan area.[6] This may represent a redistribution of income within the metro area from the suburbs to the central city. On the other hand, one might hold the view that what is good for the central city is good for the metro area, and that urban renewal redistributes income from rural areas and small community (that is, nonmetropolitan) areas to the metropolitan areas. Still another view which has gained considerable support and

4. On the other hand, it is more likely that the condemnation awards, which are supposed to be determined at full market value, revealed that the property had been grossly underassessed.

5. Tax Policies Committee, *Tax Policies and Urban Renewal in New York City* (New York: Citizen's Housing and Planning Council of New York, Inc., 1960), Appendix A, Table I.

6. Jerome Rothenberg, *Economic Evaluation of Urban Renewal* (Washington, D.C.: The Brookings Institution, 1967), pp. 16, 92.

which we will explore in some detail is that urban renewal assists the
flight of the middle-income groups to the suburbs, thereby literally
redistributing higher income to the suburbs *vis à vis* the central city.

Thus there is a long list of possible redistributional effects of urban
renewal. These different views raise all kinds of interesting possibilities and challenges in any exercise attempting to quantify these effects as they appear in various renewal projects.

The Costs of Urban Renewal

With respect to the direct costs of urban renewal, it is important
to know that the burden is essentially on the federal and local governments. State expenditures for urban renewal are possible, although
quite rare.

Higher Income and Property Tax Burdens

One way of looking at the costs of urban renewal is in terms of the
effect on the rates and bases of the taxes that are utilized to finance
federally assisted urban renewal projects. Direct project costs are usually two-thirds federally funded, presumably from the income tax,
and one-third locally funded, probably from the property tax. Thus,
the funds expended for federally assisted urban renewal programs
must be raised by increasing the rates of the federal individual income tax and the local property tax. But this tax burden view is
vastly oversimplified. The picture must be rounded out by considering the effect of urban renewal on the bases of both of these taxes in
the short and long runs.

The clearance of land involves the direct destruction of capital and
the income streams which such properties help to support. Property,
income, and sales tax revenues derived from a project area usually
decline between the time of acquisition of property and the resale of
all the land in the project, or the completion of the project. Moreover, in terms of the long run, in some of the older projects and in
most of those after 1967 only a portion of this loss in tax base is re-
generated after completion of the project. The costs of urban renewal
are, however, usually identified and analyzed in terms of expenditures,
especially those necessary to carry out the project, and not in terms of
total costs.

Project Expenditures

Project expenditures involve two categories of input costs: direct
project costs and those costs related to increasing the incentive of de-

velopers to participate in the project. Direct project costs include capital transfer costs, or the cost of real estate acquisitions. Of course one might regard these as not being real costs, if one takes an aggregate view of the economy, and as constituting simply a transfer of capital from one group to another. In any event, demolition costs and the loss of sound structures that are razed constitute real and direct costs. In addition, there are the considerable administrative expenses.

Interest and Rent Subsidies

Incentive costs include various kinds of interest subsidies, to public and private redevelopers as well as homeowners, that are provided by the federal government to increase the supply of housing or other improvements. There are also government outlays providing rent supplements. Both costs are a necessary part of the federal urban renewal program. Unless they are incurred, the program will not succeed because of languishing redevelopment of cleared land, especially for lower-income housing.

An original hope of urban renewal, as compared with public housing, was that the production of housing would be much more efficient and effective by allowing private developers to participate. However, unless there is some kind of subsidy, developers will have to go to upper-income markets, business enterprise, and luxury apartments. These kinds of land redevelopment have provided the basis for some of the most successful urban renewal projects throughout the land. Some people still carry around the notion that urban renewal is for the purpose of providing housing for middle, upper-middle, and higher-income people and not for low-income people. Since the riots of 1967, the Department of Housing and Urban Development has generally refused approval for development except for low-income housing. The only exceptions to the rule are unfinished projects that are so far along that a change of goal is not feasible. Some other land use might occasionally be allowed, but only where the project is already in the execution stage and had been properly planned and approved before federal guidelines channeled almost exclusive attention to low-income people and minorities. In general, practically all housing initiated today in urban renewal project areas is primarily Section 235, 236, and public housing.

A Temporary, if not Permanent, Reduction in Housing Stock

Another often-mentioned cost is the regressive income redistribution that may occur in renewal because of the effect on the structure of the housing stock. This possibility is based on the assumption that the stock of low-income housing is reduced with land clearance. This has occurred, at least temporarily, because of the long-time interval between demolition and completion of new low-cost housing. However, at present HUD does not allow any project to proceed unless low-cost housing has been provided to relocate the people who would be moved out of project areas. This requirement has stopped any number of projects all over the country.

In terms of total expenditures between 1949 and 1970, about $9 billion in federal grants were approved for urban renewal projects. However, approximately only $4 billion were actually paid out, which shows how slowly these projects have been proceeding over the past twenty-one years.[7]

If a project replaces fewer dwelling units than it removes, a permanent reduction in the housing stock occurs in the project area. While this was true for a number of earlier projects whose primary objectives were central business district or downtown renewal, this has not been true during the last three or four years for new projects. The earlier projects provided a more diversified land reuse than low-income housing only. During this period urban renewal received a lot of support. However, since renewal objectives have been changed again to low-income housing, it is running into a lot of "flack," as it did in its early years between 1949 and 1954, when it was looked upon simply as an alternative to public housing.[8]

A reduction in the stock of low-income housing occurs also if codes are enforced and rehabilitation is carried out or if, as mentioned above, the new replacement housing is provided for higher-income groups. All of these programs will reduce the stock of housing for low-income people and increase the price of such housing, whether it is ownership or rental housing, and cause a redistribution of income that is regressive for low-income groups. However, these results will not necessarily obtain if proper relocation provisions are made and more low-income dwelling units are built, inside or outside a given project area, than are razed. Thus, it is not necessary to reduce the stock of dwelling units occupied by low-income families.

7. United States Bureau of the Census, *Statistical Abstract of the United States: 1971*, 92d ed. (Washington, D.C., 1971). From 1949 to 1968 in Wisconsin, $68 million was authorized, while $19 million (or 28 percent) was actually disbursed during that period for renewal projects.

8. See Greer, *Urban Renewal and American Cities*, p. 18. As originally enacted, Title I authorized federal aid for the clearance and redevelopment of slums. Project areas had to be predominantly residential before or after renewal. The Housing Act of 1954 authorized federal aid for rehabilitation and conservation of blighted and deteriorating areas.

Transitional Costs Produced by the Announcement Effect

Next we must allow for transitional costs that are seldom considered, and then inadequately. The first of these is the cost arising from urban renewal announcements. The latter costs are important and yet they have never received sufficient attention. When it is announced that a given area is recommended or should be considered for urban renewal, there is a loss in productivity and value in the area almost immediately. A good illustration of announcement costs was experienced in an urban renewal project in Milwaukee, known as Kilbourn-town No. 3. The announcement (a newspaper report) stated that a given area was slated for renewal, but that the Redevelopment Authority would not begin to acquire the property for several years, after numerous administrative and planning stages had been completed. However, even before the planning work was finished, a great many of the houses in the area had been vacated and were subjected to vandalism and arson.[9]

The Redevelopment Authority was blamed for the lag in redevelopment, yet the Authority had not even received approval to redevelop the project area nor had it received funds whereby it might have acquired any of the property. However, many people react vigorously to the least publicity on a possible project and assume that authority to go ahead with the project has been, or assuredly will be, granted along with the necessary money. This case shows that the announcement effect can sometimes be as devastating as an enemy army.

One cannot predict the magnitude or direction that the announcement effect will take. The first renewal project in Milwaukee, the Lower Third Ward Project, had a minor announcement effect on property values in the project area. Total cost of real estate purchases almost coincided with total appraisal estimates.[10] Such a coincidence is a happy situation because it avoids various complaints of inequity.

However, in the Kilbourntown No. 3 Redevelopment Project mentioned above in connection with the announcement effects, when the

---

9. Project Wis. R–11 (Kilbourntown No. 3) was initiated in December 1960. In May 1964, an application for federal funds was authorized. In January 1965, a contract for planning funds was executed, and planning contracts were executed. In October 1965, plans were sent to HUD. In July 1966, plans were approved locally. In June 1967, federal funds were assured by contract. In July 1967, the first acquisition took place, on a forty-five month schedule. Twelve months later, 86 percent of the 687 properties had been acquired.

10. Total cost of real estate purchases reached $3,205,988, or $4.40 per square foot. Sales outside the project, upon which appraisals were based, varied from $4.17 to $6.25 per square foot.

Redevelopment Authority was ready to acquire the parcels of property as planned, their market value had dropped substantially, and in some cases nothing but the land value was left.[11] Of course, many people thought that that was unfair; however, federal regulations allow the Redevelopment Authority to pay an acquisition price, and federal funds are provided for such acquisitions, only if based upon market value *at the time of acquisition* and not at the time of announcement. It is clear enough that in some renewal projects many property owners really suffer, financially and otherwise, and some suffer grievously.

The time-of-acquisition basis for condemnation awards has been challenged by aggrieved property owners in the courts. However, many legal and practical problems would arise if any attempt were made to shift the basis for the acquisition price to the time of announcement. For example, what in fact is the time of announcement?

1. When a renewal project is initially discussed as a possible project by some local officials? (1960 for Kilbourntown No. 3.)

2. When the Redevelopment Authority authorizes the study of a possible project? (1961 for Kilbourntown No. 3.)

3. When the Redevelopment Authority decides it wants the project and files for planning funds from the federal Department of Housing and Urban Development? (1964 for Kilbourntown No. 3.)

4. When the federal Department of Housing and Urban Development approves of planning the project and agrees to release funds for planning only? (1965 for Kilbourntown No. 3.)

5. When the local governing body approves the project plan? (1966 for Kilbourntown No. 3.)

6. When HUD approves of the project and plan and agrees to fund its implementation? (1967 for Kilbourntown No. 3.)

Thus, time of announcement is not really a single time but the times of several announcements, beginning with one that is vague and informal to the last of several required official announcements. Moreover, to complicate matters, any of the first four announcements may or may not receive publicity in the local communication media, and this raises the question of the degree of responsibility for the announcement effect which might justifiably be attributed to the mass-communication media.

Even if the final official announcement could be legally considered as the time basis for acquisition cost, only a part of the adverse effect of the announcement might be alleviated. Several months to several

---

11. The original estimate of total real estate purchases was $6,244,108. Actual purchases reached $4,768,794.

years may elapse before various properties could be acquired. During this time the neighborhood could deteriorate and values decline significantly. It would be extremely difficult to establish the previous condition of improvements after vandalism and arson have occurred, and to appraise the improvements in retrospect. Such a presumed market value based on assessments at the time of an announcement is not always reliable and may not be admissible legally by the courts, even if it would be to HUD.

The circumstances that attend the particular project area will determine whether land acquired for urban renewal will be above market value, at market value, or below it. If the project area is in turmoil or unsafe, property in the area will probably go down in value, whereas if the area is adjacent to a sound area, it may hold its value until the Redevelopment Authority is ready to acquire it, and thereafter may even increase. Despite this valuable lesson, one that was learned during the early period of the renewal program, in recent years HUD, under state and federal law, has resisted the redevelopment of project areas adjacent to sound neighborhoods and has favored projects in the worst areas and where the probability of success is lowest. The announcement effect is thus more likely to result in a loss.

Just what effect the announcement will have on acquisition costs depends entirely on where the projects are situated, what external neighborhood effects there are, and other factors that will determine the real chances for replacing urban decay in a particular area in the near future. These are the determinants that are really important, and redevelopment authorities increasingly applied them between 1961 and 1967. But since the riots of 1967 and the Housing Act of 1968, the new HUD guidelines include criteria that redevelopment should be primarily an instrument to provide housing and employment opportunities for low- and moderate-income people, with neighborhood citizens "participation." These restrictions limit land use in much the same way as zoning. All of this means that local authorities have had to proceed with urban renewal in areas and with projects that did not provide much hope of strengthening the economic base of central cities.

There are many questionable features in the Housing Act of 1968, as amended to date,[12] and local authorities have objected to them and

12. The Housing Act of 1968 provided: Sec. 235 and Sec. 236 housing, more funds for rent supplements and public housing, new communities, the neighborhood development program (NDP), increased rehabilitation loans and grants, interim assistance, more model-cities funds, and so on.

have tried in vain to get the Johnson and Nixon Administrations to change their policies. Politics these days seems to require of our presidents and Congress that they offer direct assistance to low-income and disadvantaged people rather than indirect assistance by revitalization of our central cities, which was the policy for the ten-year period before 1968. Ironically, unless our central cities are strengthened economically by retaining their middle- and higher-income residents, the future of the low-income person in the central city is bleak. The current federal policy is worsening conditions by keeping and attracting more low-income families and, in effect, driving out higher-income families.

Political and Administrative Costs

The longer the time span between announcement and acquisition, the greater the probability and magnitude of the loss. Consequently, in the interest of minimizing this risk, it is highly desirable to reduce the time span between announcement and acquisition. However, most efforts along these lines have failed because of political and administrative delays.[13]

Milwaukee was ready to proceed on one of its biggest projects and had sent its plans to Washington for approval just after President Nixon was first elected.[14] The administrative changeover was followed by a one year reorganization of HUD during which all project requests were held up. Then, after reorganizing HUD, Secretary Romney initiated Operation Breakthrough. It took about a year to familiarize all concerned with what it was about, another six months to solicit plans, several more months to a year to review the submitted plans and select the winners, and then six months to a year to build the Breakthrough projects. All this took place while regular renewal projects were in abeyance. Now, after President Nixon's reelection, HUD is once more going through reorganization. The Department of Housing and Urban Development has been reorganized at least

---

13. The timetable for Milwaukee's first two redevelopment projects was as follows:

Project	Boundaries adopted	First land disposition	Last land disposition	Certificate of completion
UR WIS 1–1	1952	1960	1965	1971
UR WIS 1–2	1953	1962	1971	1973

14. On April 29, 1968, the Midtown Project's contract was executed, but with contingencies.

once during every administration since the department was established.

These delays occur not only at the federal level but also at the local level because of the additional steps required by federal law for "project selection," to safeguard property and human and social rights of minorities, as well as majorities. Federally funded programs have been virtually paralyzed by these requirements.

The Loss of Business Enterprise and Productivity: Economic and Social Costs

Any reduction in the economic productivity of the project area must be included, from the time of announcement to the completion of the project, or longer if lost productivity is not restored. Both the loss of the physical capital in terms of sound structures (or values of the capital) and the loss of the flow of service (or income) production, even in run-down structures, and the higher tax rates on the shrunken tax base must be accounted for in determining total costs of urban renewal. Moreover, these losses involve profound social and psychological, as well as economic, costs.

The destruction of business enterprise has been dramatized by Jane Jacobs. It is a sad fact that a majority of the businesses wiped out in urban renewal are never reopened, and those that are reestablished are seldom relocated within the central city.[15] It requires too much effort, and there is not that much "instant initiative" left in entrepreneurs, most of whom are "small entrepreneurs," to start over again. The loss of small business can really be serious in some areas.

In the Marquette Urban Renewal Area in Milwaukee, the Redevelopment Authority acquired some property for clearance and sale to Marquette University so that it can develop a campus that looks like a campus. One parcel of property is occupied by a National Food store and is the only food store of moderate size within a sixteen-square-block area where about 3,000 people live. This store is to be demolished under the renewal plan, and Marquette University intends to extend its open space or to make a parking lot of the store site for some twenty cars. How is it possible that either of these suggested new uses should be given priority over food shopping convenience for 3,000 persons?

It is clear that the destruction of business enterprise can be crucial to customers and perhaps cruel to the proprietors. It is not just a matter of getting rid of little shoeshine parlors or their equivalent whose

15. Jane Jacobs, *The Death and Life of Great American Cities* (New York: Vintage Books, 1963) , pp. 73, 191 ff.

elimination may improve the neighborhood aesthetically. Some businesses are absolutely essential to residents or workers. In fact, one area of Milwaukee consists of a complex of new public and private housing projects without a single place to shop for food within walking distance. Many of the occupants have no cars and cannot walk except to a corner grocer because they are elderly and infirm. Since private enterprise is so vulnerable, the preservation of essential business should be included in renewal plans.

Relocation Costs

In response to the hardships inflicted on owners and renters who do not want to have their ownership and/or occupancy disturbed, a variety of relocation benefits (and costs to the taxpayer) are offered. We can begin with moving expenses. Some businesses are compensated handsomely for moving expenses, maybe more than is necessary, and they have become better off than they were before, although this is not usually the case. However, compensation for moving expenses is allowed not only for business but also for individuals, homeowners and renters. The extent to which relocation expenses are provided is well illustrated by the relocation expenses paid to Marquette University students for moving from one rooming house into another.[16] Although the students may have little to move besides a suitcase of clothing and a box of books, they are paid enough to hire professional movers, if they want to do so. The big expense of relocation is not the cost of moving, however, but those expenses of acquiring another business property or house, which may cost more than the total benefits allowed for relocation.

More persons are uprooted and more buildings leveled for public purposes, such as schools, parks, and expressways, than for urban renewal. Yet, everybody blames renewal, in spite of the fact that the renewal program was the first that tried to do anything about these hardships. HUD requires that local authorities provide relocation

---

16. In fact relocation payments will now be greatly increased under the federal Uniform Relocation Assistance and Real Property Acquisition Policies Act of 1970 (the Muskie bill), and by the recently enacted Wisconsin State legislation (the Conta bill). It has been said that the relocation benefits under the new Uniform Relocation Act are so generous as to be self-defeating. For the fiscal year ending June 30, 1972, one-half billion dollars in relocation payments were made out of a total of $1.45 billion dollars budgeted for renewal, sorely depleting funds needed to carry forward existing projects. See Emanuel Gorland's "Relocation Inequities and Problems are Emerging as Result of 1970 Uniform Relocation Act," *Journal of Housing* 29 (April 1972) : 137–38.

housing for all displacees, no matter which agencies are causing the displacement. This requirement has caused many projects and programs undue hardship. Federal funds have been withheld for the continued execution of several of Milwaukee's projects for a year and a half because HUD claims that not enough replacement housing is provided for all displacees, including those of expressways and other nonrenewal public projects. On the other hand, the expressway authority actually does little to discharge its responsibility for the displacement it causes. Moreover, it accentuates the unequal distribution of income of the central city and its suburbs. The city of Milwaukee is required to help subsidize those living in the suburbs who use the expressways, and it has to suffer the "no-man's land effect," the vacuum caused by people moving to the suburbs because of expressways, which destroys parts of the city for years, all to help commuters.

Besides the economic costs of relocation, there are social costs. These include the destruction of neighborhood patterns and the psychological costs of relocation for the person who cannot fit into or find another neighborhood in which he feels comfortable, because he cannot reconstruct or bring back what once was. While these social and psychological costs cannot be quantified, they are nevertheless serious.

A Widening of Economic, Social, and Financial Disparities among Local Jurisdictions

The final urban renewal cost that must be recognized is the negative effects that occur on nearby property. These include all of the negative effects that would be suffered by the central city as an economic, social, and political entity, as well as any possible adverse effects on the metropolitan area. The latter have been brought to light by Jay Forrester.[17] If a central city continues providing more hospitality to the unfortunates, the poor, and minorities and creates a magnet which attracts even more of the same persons, it may ultimately find itself without any economic and financial viability. If the attraction of the poor and old to the central city is at a faster rate than they can be "modernized," or faster than the city's capacity to absorb them and bring them up to the level at which people in the city must operate, then central cities will continue to deteriorate.

Cities are becoming increasingly the haven of the poor, while the affluent and middle class are more often to be found in suburbs; this economic, social, and geographic polarization is encouraged by the federal programs of urban renewal and expressways. While some peo-

17. Jay Forrester, *Urban Dynamics* (Cambridge, Mass.: M.I.T. Press, 1969), p. 117.

ple claim that this internal metropolitan maldistribution should not be a matter for concern because we are interested in the overall national effect, since federal funds are involved, this provides no comfort to our deteriorating cities as they find themselves ever poorer and more miserable because they are not equal to the task that is being imposed upon them. Considering all of the costs of urban renewal, particularly those which are stressed here, I am not at all sure, as one writer claims, that the suburbs are subsidizing our central cities.[18] It may very well be the reverse.

Measuring Net Benefit or Cost

The most important costs may be those that we have the least ability to quantify—the social costs and the negative effects of rearranging our population structure. While they are elusive, it is possible to conduct valuable studies of urban renewal projects which would quantify whatever costs and benefits lend themselves to such treatment. Even if there are some remaining costs and benefits that cannot be quantified, enough may be measurable to provide a clearer picture of the overall value of urban renewal than is now available.

One measure of urban renewal benefits is the total increment in land values inside the project area and those values outside that can be attributed to the project. But there is no guarantee that a renewal project will actually increase land values, especially those projects since 1968 which stress low-income housing for minorities. In fact, it is not unusual for a renewal project to depress land values, at least up to the time that the project is completed, and even for some time thereafter. This depressing effect of low-income housing on land values has been clearly demonstrated in a Milwaukee core area where an urban renewal project is sandwiched between two public housing projects. All three were completed except for a one-square-block commercial development site to serve consumers in the area.

The Redevelopment Authority made repeated efforts to sell the land to any redeveloper with reasonable plans for commercial land use. However, with the first effort, the only redeveloper that showed any interest in the land was a group of black entrepreneurs who wanted to receive the land as a gift, which federal regulations forbid. At HUD's request, the Redevelopment Authority readvertised for bids several times. Each time the same group, and only the same

---

18. Rothenburg, *Economic Evaluation of Urban Renewal*, p. 75.

group, submitted a bid at a slightly higher, but still very low, price. The Redevelopment Authority was under pressure from HUD to close out the project, yet HUD did not want to authorize the sale of the land at a "give away" price when its fair market value prior to redevelopment had been appraised at $1.00 per square foot. However, since no other redevelopers had shown a serious interest in the land, the Authority requested permission to sell the land at $0.17 per square foot, to which HUD reluctantly agreed.[19] Here we have an example of the depressing effect of urban renewal on land value. The value of cleared and assembled land dropped drastically, even after the projects were completed, despite the general increase in land values in the City and Standard Metropolitan Statistical Areas (SMSA) of Milwaukee due to inflation and growth (in the SMSA at least).

Perhaps the most harmful trend is the relocation of middle- and upper-income families from central cities to the suburbs and other outlying jurisdictions and the resulting concentration of the poor in the central cities. This is the major problem that urban renewal must and can do something about. Projects can be encouraged that provide middle- and upper-income families the facilities that they want so that central city living will be as interesting as suburban living.[20] Before 1968 renewal objectives were designed to do just that, and to save our central cities from becoming the poorhouses of the nation. Since 1968 the major federal objective of land use in urban renewal in central cities has been to provide direct help to low-income families.

Now, despite the difficulties that arise in attempts to quantify benefits and costs, it should not be difficult to show that projects begun prior to 1968 have produced higher benefit-cost ratios than have projects since 1968. I suggest this as a hypothesis that can be proved quantitatively, despite difficulties in measurement. For example, the Golden Triangle in Pittsburgh is an outstanding example of a highly successful project which probably would produce a high benefit-cost ratio.[21] On the other hand, some well publicized low-income housing projects in Saint Louis and Chicago would probably show a very low ratio.

19. In December 1964, with the application for federal funds, the land price was appraised at $1.00 per square foot. In April 1966 (at the time acquisition began), HUD concurred in a price of $0.75 per square foot, based on updated appraisals. In May 1967, upon invitation for proposals, one was received at $0.09 per square foot. In September 1968, after more invitations and hearings, a proposal at $0.17 per square foot was accepted.

20. Milwaukee has only one such project, the Eastside A Project.

21. Pittsburgh's Allegheny Center project, which went into execution in 1961, cost $26 million in federal grants.

Maximizing Benefits and Minimizing Costs

The Difficulties of Establishing a Balanced Federal Urban Renewal Program

If urban renewal has as one of its primary objectives the raising of land to a higher potential use, and if it is carried out with the benefits of past experience to minimize the announcement effect, then urban renewal projects can maximize benefits and minimize costs. Although it may appear to some that the federal government is maximizing benefits in its direct advocacy of housing for poor only in project areas, this drives middle-income persons out of the neighborhood and city. Success in renewal requires the right kind of projects and conditions. Political, social, and administrative considerations make it more difficult than ever to assemble these right circumstances.

A balanced urban renewal project must include such economic objectives as using land more efficiently, putting land that has a higher potential to its best use, improving the allocation of resources, and improving the economic and tax bases of the city. The Administration's policy is contradictory because, despite HUD's present policy, Secretary Romney also has been urging expansion of low-income housing in the suburbs. This policy is sound in terms of preventing the central city from acquiring a disproportionate share of the poor, and it should be combined with one that would permit land in the central city to be put to a higher potential use. It obviously will not always be low-income housing which is too often located in the choicest areas. But the federal government has policies which prohibit or make it impractical to have low-income housing in the suburbs. The suburbs themselves refuse to accept low-income housing because they do not want the unfortunate, the poor, and the minorities, and suburbs in some cases adopt policies that are prejudicial to such people. That is why many suburbs are sound economically and financially.

Now there is no one single, simple reason to explain the rural-urban migration. Job opportunities are probably the primary attraction. But one would think that housing opportunities also would be important, because earnings can be supplemented or diminished by the rent one has to pay for housing. The two are looked at almost simultaneously. The level of welfare benefits is another factor influencing the attraction of an urban area.[22]

22. William R. MacDougall, "Fiscal Centralization and Federalism," *Proceedings of the Sixty-fourth Annual Conference of the National Tax Association* (Harrisburg, Pa., 1971), p. 75.

A Return to pre-1968 Guidelines

It may be the two-thirds subsidy that encourages local governments, through their redevelopment authorities, to go along more readily with federal project criteria that produce lower benefit-cost ratios than they would otherwise. If guidelines for the new use of land cannot be changed to pre-1968 standards, a reduction in the federal subsidy ratio might be considered as an alternative. This probably would result in fewer renewal projects, and they would also have to produce greater benefits relative to the costs to local governments to get the approval of the latter.

The ironic and even tragic thing about the 1968 guidelines is that, while they intend to help the poor and black by direct means, in reality the guidelines constitute a policy for turning a renewal project into a haven for the poor. The influx of the poor into the central city and the flight of the middle class to the suburbs are accelerated. This may foreshadow a long-run disadvantage to the poor in the central city as economic and tax bases melt away. The quality and quantity of business and industry remaining in the city diminish as commercial and industrial firms move out to the suburbs, thereby reducing job and shopping opportunities. This has already happened in the core areas of central cities. Not far behind follows the reduction in quality and quantity of public services for the poor, just when their increasing numbers demand an even greater supply of public services. The direct approach of helping the poor and minorities in urban renewal may very well harm them over the long run because of the patterns of residential migration that it encourages.

It is a mistake to utilize an urban renewal program to achieve income redistribution, at least directly. The difficulty is that a central city is not a closed system in terms of population and economic base and tax base. The new uses to which urban renewal land is put have a profound effect on the movement of people and business enterprises within a metropolitan area, as well as between a central city and the rest of the country (for example, other central cities, smaller cities, and rural areas) .

The Time-Lag Problem

It was not unusual for the time span of a conventional urban renewal project to stretch over ten years or more from the first announcement of the project to its completion. An equitable price to the owner in the sale of his property to the renewal agency depends not only upon reducing the time span between announcement and the execution of the beginning of the project but also upon its completion.

Conventional urban renewal projects have been large enough to be divided into a number of take-down stages, that are begun and phased into, in a staggered fashion, thus providing an opportunity for a great variety of obstacles to arise fortuitously and to be raised deliberately. For example, HUD often raises new requirements annually that a city must meet if it is to receive approval of its Workable Program and the release of funds necessary to continue the project. The annual recertification of Milwaukee's program was held up recently for more than a year because HUD felt that the city's Housing Authority should first provide 1,200 more public housing units to relocate families displaced by all public programs, including expressways.

The new requirements for greater citizen involvement have increased the time lag in urban renewal. One such requirement was the need for approval by a resident council of the local Model Cities Agency. This may involve months or years of wrangling over the composition of the council, the manner of selection of members, and the struggle by factions for publicity, power, and jobs. The Model Cities program does not contribute directly to renewal efforts but subjects renewal to a possible veto by the Model Cities resident council if its requirements are not met. Yet Model Cities requirements are not essentially different from those of HUD. The renewal involvement of Model Cities is to encourage citizen participation in the effort to maintain support for renewal. I do not mean to suggest that the Model Cities program has no useful function at all. Its primary purpose of marshalling and coordinating all governmental and community resources to fight urban problems is basically sound, at least in theory.

HUD has also increased the time span for renewal, with the new requirements that the renewal agency provide the coordination of social services to families displaced in project areas. The Redevelopment Authority is obliged to contract with some social services agency or firm to provide the coordination of services, for a fee ranging from $1,000 to $3,000 per family to be relocated. Services are relatively simple and of the type that the family can determine and secure with its own initiative and effort in most instances, such as finding another house or apartment in which to live or where employment or welfare agencies can be found. Coordination is an extremely costly service, and I suspect that most families would find out these things on their own initiative. The social service subsidy now is made primarily to the many new agencies that have suddenly been organized for their own financial gain.

The Workable Program was instituted to increase the responsibility of local government and the participation of private citizens in the neighborhoods to be renewed, something that urban renewal, as begun in 1949, had lacked. However, the Workable Program inevitably raised delays in compliance by cities and in administration by HUD and gave the latter a powerful tool with which to push cities into reluctant compliance if they wanted continued funds to complete their projects. In effect, it meant that the local agency had to get its renewal program reapproved each year, and this reapproval was conditioned upon the meeting of new and additionally imposed requirements by HUD administrators. The Workable Program is, in fact, a one-sided contract in which only one party, HUD, can reopen the contract on a given project annually and make additional demands.

Efforts to Minimize the Time-Lag Problem

The essential inequity of the Workable Program from the viewpoint of local governments and their renewal agencies has set both against the use of the device. The National Association of Housing and Redevelopment Officials, on the recommendation of its Renewal Committee, of which I was a member, recommended to Congress that HUD not be allowed to change the Workable Program requirements for a given urban renewal project beyond those requirements met by the local government and renewal agency in originally gaining official approval of the project. The request was modest but got nowhere with HUD, which yielded only by requiring a biennial rather than an annual Workable Program review and approval.

Another suggestion offered for reducing federal red tape is the block grant or special federal revenue sharing. One version of this idea suggests that the local renewal agency be given money annually to complete projects which HUD has approved. Thereafter the entire responsibility for executing projects would be in the hands of the local renewal agency. It would then no longer be necessary for the latter to receive approval for such things as property acquisition, contracts for hard and soft-ware goods, revenues, financing, land dispositions, and so on. Local agency efficiency and speed of performance could improve markedly. Funds for future projects would depend upon reasonable adherence to federal guidelines. However, HUD and Congress seem unable to yield control, even if such control threatens to destroy the program and its objectives.

The most significant plan brought forth by HUD in answer to many of urban renewal's problems, and the time-lag in particular, is the replacement of the conventional large-scale renewal program with the Neighborhood Development Program. The latter encourages the renewal of far smaller project areas with the intention of completing the project within one year, although it may be extended another year, or possibly two if necessary. By scaling down the size of the redevelopment project, it is hoped that the renewal process itself will not be a depressant to the surrounding area. The neighborhood will not be disrupted, destroyed, or radically changed. Instead, it can evolve into a better neighborhood by being improved in modest-sized stages.[23]

The program provides funds which can first be used for the purchase of vacant land, parking lots, and land holding unoccupied and irreparable buildings. New housing can be constructed on this land to provide homes for residents who will be displaced in the remainder of the project area and who want to remain in the neighborhood. The relocation of these residents would be eased by the provision of a variety of generous, now-existing benefits. Homeowners would be encouraged to remain and to rehabilitate and improve their properties through grants and loans on favorable terms. Lastly, residents of each project area must select from among themselves the members of a Project Area Committee to assist in planning the redevelopment of the neighborhood, and the PAC receives some funding from the program to carry out its function.

It is yet too soon to evaluate the NDP approach. The program has barely started in many cities and is still overshadowed by unfinished and deteriorating conventional renewal programs. The NDP approach was to be an improved concept in theory; however, it is still shackled by bureaucratic requirements that are socially and politically oriented. Although these requirements are based on good intentions, they hinder the urban renewal process and decrease the scope of its accomplishments.

Market Demand for Land and the Cost of Land

Analyzing the federal urban renewal program may be considered an exercise in futility or trivia by some persons interested in the improvement of the environment of urban areas, and the central cities in particular, where the decay is greatest. They may well be convinced that the federal urban renewal program is based on certain faulty premises and works at cross-purposes with itself, and therefore cannot possibly achieve many of its objectives. One of these is a greater in-

23. The Roosevelt Redevelopment Project in Milwaukee had many of the characteristics of an NDP.

volvement of private enterprise in urban redevelopment and an acceleration in the production of housing.

The failure of private enterprise to renew our cities without government assistance has been laid in large measure to the high cost of land to would-be developers. There can be little doubt that this is a major cause of the stagnation of land-use succession in central cities. The congressional authors of the federal urban renewal program accepted this diagnosis and came up with a prescription which they believed would provide the cure, namely, a system of federal subsidies to permit the write-down of land costs to private developers. In practice the slow and insufficient production of new housing by means of the federal program has left much to be desired. Now the very rationale of the program is in question. This should not be surprising at all because it conforms to the classic characteristics of subsidies.

The federal subsidy tends in and of itself to raise the price of project land and also of adjacent land. The demand for project land by the renewal agency is made effective with federal and local funds. The normal, relatively weak demand for slum land is thus augmented with the force of the federal government. The price of real estate which was rapidly declining can be now sustained, and perhaps even raised, if the program does not languish or if there is no lack of interest and confidence in the future of the area. In many pre-1968 projects that were carefully conceived and planned to bring renewal land to its highest use, the price of project and adjacent land increased. The demand for renewal land by the local agency was added to a firm, if not strong, private demand; and the rise in project and adjacent land was strong and inevitable.

However, as we have noted, in recent years the normal private demand for urban renewal land has fallen drastically, often more than enough to offset the increase in the demand for the land by the government, with the result being a declining price of land. The complete or near collapse of the demand for urban renewal land by other than subsidized users and developers has forced private enterprise in project areas into a parasitic role.

An Alternative Program for Urban Renewal

The federal urban renewal program is based on the philosophy that renewing our cities and increasing housing requires maximum private redevelopment activity. Furthermore, the program is designed to remove the two greatest obstacles to renewal by private entrepreneurs, namely, (1) the high price of land and (2) the multiple and complex patterns of landownership which make it difficult and costly to assemble land into parcels large enough to meet the redevelopment needs and standards of today. No fault can be found with this basic assessment of the needs of successful renewal and the obstacles it faces.

The fault lies in the federal government's particular program for removing these obstacles by means of a subsidy and the use of a single local renewal agency in each city. The concentration of all renewal activities of a city in one or two public agencies has led to a disorganization of land markets, disparate land values (some higher, which inhibit further redevelopment where hope of success continues, and some lower where hope of success wanes), limited private participation by developers, endless government requirements and inordinate delays, and encouragement of unbalanced projects (such as undue emphasis on and preference for low-income housing projects) that weaken the economic base and widen the social and racial spectrum of large central cities.

Thus, while the few developers who succeeded in bidding for project land were subsidized most generously, the concomitant rise in cost of nonproject land in some projects has produced windfall real estate gains and tended to inhibit private redevelopment. This tendency has occasionally been obscured by the still larger increase in demand by potential users of project and adjacent land. However, it is sufficiently clear that the federally guided urban renewal program today contributes too often to the weakening or destruction of the demand for land, within and adjacent to the project, by users and private developers. A superior program for stimulating renewal by private activity is desperately needed.

An alternative program for urban renewal and increasing the quantity and quality of housing merits consideration. It also attempts to remove the handicaps for private enterprise that take the form of high land acquisition costs and inadequate plottage of land. The program consists of a property tax reform, the establishment of quasi-public urban land cooperatives, and direct rental housing allowances.

Land Value Taxation

In place of the present subsidy for the purpose of providing lower costs and increased economic incentives to private redevelopers, a far more effective incentive is that of property tax reform along the lines of land value taxation. Whereas the subsidization of urban renewal tends to increase the cost of land and makes the obstacle even more formidable to all private developers except the successful bidder, the untaxing of improvements and higher taxation of land will lower the price of land and the annual cost of the improvements. Revenue lost by the untaxing of improvements is made up by taxing land more heavily. Many primary and secondary advantages of this kind of property tax reform have been identified.[24]

The theory underlying land value taxation, including its effect on development, has been presented often in recent years[25] and it would not be appropriate to expand on the subject here. Of course, some persons maintain that this reform of the property tax would create many unfair burdens and that it is fraught with great practical difficulties. However, one wonders whether the burdens could possibly be as unfair, and the practical difficulties as great, as those in the federal urban renewal program.

Urban Land Cooperatives

The second part of our alternative program for urban renewal addresses itself to the plottage problem. Whereas the present federal program centralizes the responsibility of assembling land and other renewal functions in a single renewal agency in each local political jurisdiction, it is suggested here that this function be carried out by urban land cooperatives instead.

Enabling legislation would have to be enacted by state governments (with or without federal encouragement) to authorize the formation of the cooperatives, generally one for each square block of the city. If the owners of a majority of the landholdings (parcels) on any square block request the formation of a cooperative, its charter would be granted and landowners would receive shares of stock in exchange for their land (according to the appraised values). The cooperative must be given the power of eminent domain, which can be used if necessary, in order to acquire any parcels whose owners refuse to join the cooperative. Funds for financing such purchases might be made available from a Federal Urban Land Bank that could be created for that purpose.

An urban land cooperative's first task would be to consolidate landownership in the name of the cooperative. This would enable the board of directors to take the initiative and assume effective responsibility for the conservation, rehabilitation, and redevelopment of

24. Arthur P. Becker, "Arguments for Changing the Real Estate Tax to a Land Value Tax," *Land Value Taxation: Pro and Con, Tax Policy* 37 (September–December 1970) : 15–31.

25. Arthur P. Becker, ed., *Land and Building Taxes: Their Effect on Economic Development* (Madison: University of Wisconsin Press, 1969).

all of the land in a one block area. This kind of organization for
renewal could overcome the sometimes insuperable difficulty of consolidating multiple, fragmented, complex, apathetic, and absentee
ownership interests which often prevail today. Furthermore, the owners of any block may organize themselves to renew as they wish without interference by HUD or the local urban land renewal agency.
Land reuse would be subject, nevertheless, to local zoning regulations.

The cooperative could be a vehicle for maintaining the interest of
shareholders in the conservation and renewal of their block and the
surrounding area. The ownership of land would be stabilized in the
cooperative, thereby eliminating panic sales of land. Lastly, it is highly
probable that the time period to achieve redevelopment would be
drastically reduced. The demolition of existing buildings would not
occur until the cooperative is ready to redevelop.

Urban land cooperatives provide maximum flexibility by encouraging renewal wherever interest and feasibility are the greatest. Redevelopment need not be restricted to present project areas and may be
actively engaged in by urban land cooperatives set up for any block
in any city. In fact, an urban land cooperative may have as its initial
objective, after consolidating block-land holdings, a more efficient use
of its land to serve the present land uses. Of course, once the concept of the urban land cooperative is accepted in principle, many
details would need to be worked out. In fact, as with other institutions, they are started in a rather rudimentary form and evolve as
experience requires.

*Direct Rent Allowances and Responsibility for Finding One's Own
Housing*

Instead of providing subsidies to developers, public housing, and
renewal agencies, a far better approach to income distribution via
housing for the poor is that of providing direct cash rent allowances
to each eligible family (or vouchers for those who cannot be trusted to
use the cash for housing) .[26] Each family would be allowed to find its
own housing if it wishes to do so. This procedure would help to
scatter the poor throughout most of a metropolitan area, as well as to
avoid their overconcentration in one area as now occurs in public
housing and redevelopment project areas. Moreover, the stock of
housing would be privately supplied and owned, and the renters and
taxpayers would enjoy the benefits of competition among the sup-

26. Henry J. Aaron, *Shelter and Subsidies* (Washington, D.C.: The Brookings
Institution, 1972) , pp. 167 ff.

pliers of housing. This has been attempted recently in Pittsburgh with considerable success.

The alternative program presented here requires little administration and will not increase the federal or local bureaucracy much, if at all. It can be established to operate outside, but perhaps some times within, the project areas of the present federal program. The latter probably would be strengthened and its positive benefits enhanced. The challenge of urban renewal grows with the passage of time and as older cities decay faster than they are renewed. We must utilize all of the tools we can muster to meet this challenge.

ACKNOWLEDGMENTS

The author would like to acknowledge the assistance of Martin Bachhuber of the Department of City Development of Milwaukee in providing greater specificity to a number of points, as well as in tracking down some footnote references.

INDEX

MANUFACTURED BY
KINGSPORT PRESS, INC., KINGSPORT, TENNESSEE
TEXT LINES ARE SET IN BASKERVILLE, DISPLAY LINES IN HELVETICA

Library of Congress Cataloging in Publication Data
Main entry under title:
Government spending & land values.
(Publications of the Committee on Taxation,
Resources and Economic Development, 6)
"Proceedings of a symposium sponsored by the Committee
on Taxation, Resources, and Economic Development (TRED)
at the University of Wisconsin—Madison, 1971."
Includes bibliographical references.
1. Government spending policy—United States—
Congresses. 2. Subsidies—United States—Congresses.
3. Real property—United States—Congresses.
I. Harriss, Clement Lowell, 1912–   ed. II. Committee
on Taxation, Resources and Economic Development.
III. Series: Committee on Taxation, Resources and
Economic Development. Publication, 6.
HJ7539.G68   338.1'873   72–7988
ISBN 0–299–06320–8